The Secret History
of the
South Sea Bubble

The Secret History
of the
South Sea Bubble

*The World's First Great
Financial Scandal*

Malcolm Balen

FOURTH ESTATE · *London* and *New York*

FIRST EDITION
Printed on acid-free paper
Library of Congress Cataloging-in-Publication Data available on request
ISBN 0-00-716177-8

Karen, Mischa and Katya

Contents

The value of money, now and then

Money was a confusing business in eighteenth-century America and the British were, in part, to blame.

When the first colonists arrived, they stuck to the currency they knew best – pounds, shillings and pence. But British silver coins were scarce, so, confusingly, they also adopted foreign coins, especially Spanish American silver from Mexico and Peru. The most widely used coin was the eight *reales*, which was the highest unit of Spanish silver in the New World; but then there were the *thalers* of the various German colonies, the Portuguese *cruzado*, and the *ducatoon* of Holland. In the French colonies, John Law's marvellous project saw him issue *livre* bank-notes in 1718.

In short, there was no single currency as there is today, though the colonists planted the seeds of financial history by calling the eight *reales* coin a 'dollar' (from the Dutch *daalder*). But, alas, even the value of the 'dollar' varied from colony to colony. Still more confusingly, as demand exceeded supply, silver coins traded at a premium, so that the value of exactly the same unit of silver coin in Massachusetts and London could differ widely. In 1704, Queen Anne issued a royal proclamation to try to clear up the mess. Even so, the colonists were still allowed to trade silver coins at up to a third more than the British rate.

This must have made life difficult for everyone at the time, and it certainly does for an author three centuries later. In the end, I have taken the coward's way out by using the pounds of eighteenth century London, and the livres of Paris, without trying to convert them into present-day dollars.

I can, however, provide a rough guide to the sums of money won and lost in the stock-market boom of the day, though the cost and standard of living was very different then. If today's multi-millionaire had been living in the early eighteenth century he might have had around £100,000 or $150,000 to his name, at a time when anyone with an income of a few hundred dollars a year was comfortably off. Further down the social scale, a domestic servant could earn about £10 (or $15) a year, while it would take the stone-carvers of St Paul's Cathedral a whole week to earn just £1.

We should probably think of an eighteenth century investor who won a quarter of a million pounds on the stock-market with more than a touch of envy, as if he was the sole winner of a lottery jackpot, the sudden recipient of wealth beyond our dreams.

It's also important to remember that countries had only puny economies then compared with the muscular enterprises of today. For example, the British national debt, in 1720, was held to be a disastrous £30 million, while today it has grown, without fuss, to more than £400 billion. So, measered against the nation's modest wealth, the stock-market gamblers of 1720 were winning, and losing, sums of money which were simply staggering. Not even if Bill Gates were to lose his entire fortune overnight could America match the scale of the stock-market melt-down of three hundred years ago.

CHAPTER I

The Dome

It could be fair to describe what happened at the turn of the
millennium as the Great Silicon Valley Swindle, a popular
delusion that will take its place in economics textbooks alongside
the Dutch Tulip Mania of the seventeenth century and the South
Sea Bubble of the eighteenth. Investors appeared convinced that
venture capitalists were capable of generating extraordinary returns
on technology and consumer Internet companies. The effect was to
drive up prices to ridiculous levels for companies that scarcely had
business plans, let alone revenues or profits.
The scale of subsequent value destruction is colossal. Most of
the money that was invested in those twenty-four months is likely
to be lost. When apportioning blame, it would be tempting to
single out the venture capitalists. They, after all, are the ones
who invested the money in business plans for ideas as ridiculous
as online dog food.
Financial Times, 20 August 2001

London, 1710.

The city is reaching for the heavens.

More than fifty steeples point towards the sky, raised arms above
the dark, narrow streets whose dwellings are so low they appear to
be at prayer. From the Thames-side terrace at Somerset House, there
is a breath-taking sight – the architectural clutter of later centuries
is not yet upon us. Lead and stone, cupolas and towers, crosses and
columns stand exuberant against the sky. There is, perhaps, a gentle
breeze, carrying with it the smell of sea-coal from the north of
England which the bargemen are unloading on the river.

Downriver lie the two domes of Greenwich Hospital, identical
twins along the water's edge, each with a supporting army of
columns. To the east, in Cheapside, more than two hundred and
twenty feet up, a bronze weathervane in the form of a dragon swings
gently in the wind. Below it stands the pencil-slim elegance of
St Mary-le-Bow. As the church rises beyond its square tower it
narrows sharply: a temple of simple columns yields to a balustrade,
above which, tapering together like fingers, a dozen stone bows are
gathered. The church soars skyward, ever slimmer, until the steeple
touches the dragon's feet. For the elegance of its buildings, and above

all for this, the most beautiful of his creations, the city gives thanks to the genius of Christopher Wren, whose brilliance has led him down a path of magnificent architectural variety in the rebuilding programme he has inspired since the Great Fire. He is a mathematician first and foremost, but over the years he has trained himself as an architect, absorbing style and simplicity from France, Italy and Holland, but showing a uniform adherence to the influence of no one but himself.

No sooner has he completed St Bride's in Fleet Street with an octagonal stairway, four steps high, than he tops Christ Church in Newgate with a square one; to St Magnus Martyr he gives an octagonal tower, and to St Vedast in Foster Lane a concave crown; most dramatically, he allows St Martin to rise above Ludgate with an octagonal tower topped by the longest, slimmest steeple of them all: a black lance to pierce the sky.

But its sharpness on the eye is blunted by the great grey shield of St Paul's Cathedral which curves towards the clouds. As yet unfinished, its incompleteness serves only to emphasise human frailty and humility which its eventual perfection will deny, sealing off the worshippers, separating them from direct contact with God. The church roof is open to the elements and inside workmen are still perched on scaffolding in the chancel, making mouldings above the vaulting. In a large hut, sculptors are at work on statues which will stand in the space before the church – Queen Anne in white marble on a black pedestal, and round her the kingdoms of her domain. Sir Christopher himself can be seen, clambering into a basket to be hauled skywards to inspect the progress of this monument to his brilliance, an ascent he makes three or four times a week. It is his lifetime's work. From start to finish, he has overseen his cathedral's rise from the ashes of the city.

The dome to which he is travelling has an inner and an outer part, constructed like two layers of an onion skin so that if Wren was somehow able to peel away the outer covering, a cupola would still remain, resting on eight piers whose arches form the Whispering Gallery where the dropping of the lightest coin of the realm can be heard more than a hundred feet away. And it might be appropriate on this day, as Big Tom strikes the hour in the cathedral tower, if a coin *was* dropped in this temple, if the outer skin of the roof was peeled away, to reveal the true object of England's worship. Not St Paul, carved above the central pediment and the great oak doors, nor God himself, but money.

For below Wren's feet, among the busy maze of streets where some of the capital's thousand hackney carriages and chairs jolt past, the early signs of financial madness can be detected. This is the kingdom of the 'moneyed-men', the stockjobbers who buy and sell their shares in the coffee houses, which are the heart of London's new financial district, where not just coffee but tea, chocolate, sherbert, sherry and pale ale are consumed and where news spreads as quickly as the Great Fire itself.

Coffee houses are the most popular public places in London: there are more than two thousand of them, the preserve of men who wish to while away the hours free of the opposite sex. Inside, there are long tables and benches, a roaring fire in the hearth, lines of clay pipes and newspapers spread out to read. There is a warm, secure fug of smoke, and drink, and chatter. It is a male club, where the species can protect its own and ignore the world outside, especially the despairing women who once campaigned 'against coffee and The Grand Inconveniences to their Sex from the Excessive Use of that enfeebling Liquor'.

The terrain of the moneyed-men, marked out by the coffee houses, is small but profitable, a series of narrow passageways called Exchange Alley, which lie within the maze of narrow streets captured at the intersection of Cornhill and Lombard Street. A minute and a half is all it takes to walk through this lively, noisy financial centre, hemmed in on each side by tradesmen and barbers, lawyers and insurance clerks. On the second floor of Wren's favourite coffee house, Garraway's, there is a sale room where the jobbers ply their trade from a rostrum between the hours of eleven and three. Nearby, just down the street, is an upstart bank, grown lean and sharp from the days when it was an import company bringing in the Huguenot steel, which was favoured by swordsmen over its English rival. The bank has expanded through land speculation in Ireland and stands on the brink of power, aiming now to cut down its two rivals, the young Bank of England and the East India Company. In this respect, its name does not disguise its intentions. It is the Sword Blade Bank.

The buying of stocks and shares in Exchange Alley is, as yet, in its infancy. The trade was carried out previously in the Royal Exchange, a stockjobber's shout away on the other side of Cornhill, but this discomfited the traders in the country's more conventional merchandise, such as their largest export, wool. So the brokers moved to 'Change Alley, as it is known, taking with them their ceaseless noise. Here, the practitioners are already versed in the notion of buying and selling more than they can afford. It is the fashionable new form of gambling. There is a growing sense that shares will go ever upward, like one of Wren's perfectly balanced spires.

The dealers are raucous and seedy, unscrupulous and rough. Their aim, in the saying of the day, is 'to sell the bear's skin before they have caught the bear': they are selling stock before they have paid for it in the hope that they will be able to meet the cost from the profit – or 'bubble' – on the deal. One anonymous observer on a journey through England in the year 1710 watches the moneyed-men of 'Change Alley at work, and reports on the scene to a friend abroad in a series of letters; in one, he comments: 'You will see fellows, in shabby clothes, selling ten or twelve thousand pounds in stock, though perhaps he mayn't be worth at the same time ten shillings, and with as much zeal as if he were a director, which they call selling a *Bear's-Skin*; and these men find Bubble enough to get bread by it, as the others do by gaming; and some few of them manage it so as to get pretty large estates.'

So the city-dwellers go about their money-making schemes, heads down and voices loud, and ignore Wren's masterpiece as if it has no connection with their lives. And the truth is that it has little: the cathedral belongs to a world which they do not inhabit; it is a beautiful object of refinement and contemplation in the midst of the daily dirty struggle to survive: to earn enough to eat, drink and keep clean. As they walk, London's citizens keep close to the walls of buildings, fearful of the water which cascades out of crude spouts from each roof; more fearful still of the sewage pumped into the gutters of the street when the houses' wells are full.

The pavements are crammed with stalls, sheds and signposts; where they end and the road begins is hard to tell: there are no kerbstones to separate the path from the carriageway, although on the wider streets there is a line of posts and chains or wooden palings. The wide expanse of Tottenham Court Road, stretching north, has been paved for only a few years. London is not all that Wren would wish. 'Natural beauty is from geometry,' he has declared, 'consisting in Uniformity and Proportion. Always the true Test is natural or geometrical Beauty.' But the city is untidy, disorganised, unsymmetrical, full of chaotic winding streets that snake round and disappear. It is a jumble, a jungle, a teeming maze where the people live cheek by jowl – half a million of them, nearly a tenth of England's population, crammed together in a city that has not yet spread. Piccadilly, to the west, marks its furthermost boundary.

But the capital is not just a commercial and trading centre. It is a gambler's paradise. In the inns, bets are taken on brutal, bloody sports: bull-baiting, bear-baiting and cock-fighting, the vicious pastimes of a nation frequently at war. One German visitor to London in 1710 notes, with surprise, the aggressive nature of the English crowds:

> In the afternoon we went to see the cockfighting. This is a sport peculiar to the English . . . a special building has been made for it near 'Gras Inn'. The people, gentle and simple, act like madmen, and go on raising the odds to twenty guineas and more. It is amazing to see how the cocks hack with their spurs. Their combs bleed terribly and they often slit each other's crop and abdomen with the spurs . . . they belong to great Lords who have brought them from Kent and other places and win a great deal of money by their wagers. Towards evening we drove to see the bull-baiting. First a young ox or bull was led in and fastened by a long rope to an iron ring in the middle of the yard; then about thirty dogs, two or three at a time, were let loose on him. Then they brought out a small bear and tied him up in the same fashion. As soon as the dogs had at him, he stood up on his hind legs and gave some terrific buffets. But the worst of all was a common little ass who was brought out saddled with an ape on his back. The ape began to scream most terribly for fear of falling off.

Later the same traveller watches two men fighting for money at the Bear Garden at Hockley in the Hole, on the outskirts of town by Clerkenwell Green, cheered on by spectators who crowd into the galleries of raised seats.

They went for each other with sword and dagger and the Moor got a nasty wound in his hand, which bled freely. When they had attacked each other with broadsword and shield, the good Moor received such a dreadful blow that he could not fight any longer. He was slashed from the left eye right down to his cheek to his chin and jaw with such force that one could hear the sword grating against his teeth. Straightaway not only the whole of his shirt front but the platform too was covered with blood. The onlookers began to cheer and threw down vast quantities of shillings and crowns.

London is a brutal, dirty, lively, joyous place. Plague and fire, and civil war, have done their worst and departed; fear of God is subsiding. Life is rushing back.

But there are warning signs that the established order can still be threatened, that England may not yet be built on firm foundations. Behind the remains of the Palace of Whitehall, torched by a recent fire, lie the marks made by the scaffold where Charles I was beheaded. And despite the splendour of Wren's church-building, the view from Somerset House is deceptive: a thin layer of dirt has gathered upon his stonework. Already his masterpiece is tarnished, blackened by the smoke from the sea-coal, shipped from the northern mines. The coal, named from its journey rather than its origins, is taxed when it is unloaded at the Port of London in order to raise money to rebuild the city. But it is slowly eating into it instead, discolouring its buildings, clogging the nostrils of its people, coating their tongues and clouding their eyes.

Wren's professed aim was to defy the corrosive elements and stretch across the centuries, ignoring fashion to appeal to an ideal, immutable form of design. He insisted: 'Architecture aims at Eternity; and is therefore the only Thing uncapable of Modes and Fashions.' His great vision was of a cathedral dome that would be grander than any other, capping not only St Paul's, but his career. It would signify, architecturally, the might of the capital and the grandeur of England. It would lift spirits. And it would celebrate the stability of the country, its monarchy and people, after the trials of the Civil War and then the Glorious Revolution of the previous century.

For all his splendid dreams, however, it was as hard for Wren to raise money for his great project as it was to quarry the blocks of stone for the cathedral's construction. The Act of 1670 which allotted St Paul's four and a half pennies in tax for every chaldron, or twenty-five hundred-weight of coal, brought it only some £4,000 a year, and in 1677 the cathedral's commissioners were forced to mount an appeal to the nation. Even the monarch was enlisted to the cause. Sermons were preached around the country, collections taken, and gradually the ordinary people sent in their pennies and their pounds to the rebuilding fund. Still, the greatest building the country had seen was in danger of being left uncompleted – until the workmen themselves came up with the solution: they suggested that their wages should be considered as a loan to the building project, and they would work instead for the interest on the money they were due. By the end of 1697, more than £24,000 was owed to them, including £1,500 to the master carver Grinling Gibbons. The cathedral slowly rose.

Thirty years after he first started, Wren's task is nearly done. Above the Derbyshire lead and Kentish timber of his dome, a ball and lantern top out his mighty work, three hundred and fifty-five feet above the streets. His is the largest, most beautiful cathedral in England, a fitting homage to the patron saint of the City of London whose wealth has helped make the country one of the grandest on the globe. Out of a total of three-quarters of a million pounds, it has cost Sir Christopher Wren £2,000 of his own money, a small fortune for the times.

Soon, however, such a sum will appear to be a trifle. The financial world is about to be turned upside-down in the streets below.

Ten years after Wren completed his cathedral, to mark his vision of eternity, a city which had survived plague and fire to prosper as a mercantile centre – a city which, to the untrained eye, had risen gloriously from its ashes – was beginning to live only for the moment, chasing financial liberation by buying shares in extraordinary new projects that had no foundation. The Age of Reason, which held that science could explain all, was giving way, indeed was being unceremoniously elbowed aside, by the Age of Insanity. The country was rushing headlong into enterprises founded on little more than an understanding of human greed and corruptibility. By speculating on the stock market, a humble bookseller trading near the cathedral churchyard would win *a third* of the total cost of building St Paul's.

An age inspired by the genuine achievement of men like Christopher Wren and Isaac Newton had the misfortune to collide at full speed with the age of the moneyed-men. Hundreds of projects were launched in these vertiginous times. Here was invention, inspiration and downright fraud, all merging in a pot-pourri of frenzied activity. Schemes arose thick and fast with just enough scientific credibility to fool the layman. 'Projectors' – as such speculators were known – were held to want money

For a wheel for perpetual motion
For extracting silver from lead
For carrying on a trade in the river Oronooko
For trading in hair
For paving the streets of London
For furnishing funerals to any part of Great Britain
For insuring and increasing children's fortunes

The country appeared to have discovered a new industry with new rules of credit which held out the prospect of immense riches, removing traditional class barriers to wealth. It was an exciting, vibrant era in which huge fortunes could be created overnight by a simple share launch.

One of the most famous projects was launched by James Puckle, who designed a flintlock machine-gun for making a 'total revolution in the art of war'. The Puckle gun was mounted on a tripod and fired nine shots a minute, one after the other and three times faster than a soldier's musket. Puckle had two versions of his design. One weapon, intended for use against Christian enemies, fired conventional round bullets. The second, designed to be used against the Muslim Turks, fired square bullets, which were believed to cause more painful wounds.

But some of the schemes were not half as sensible as this. There was even said to be a 'Company for carrying on an undertaking of

Great Advantage but no-one to know what it is'. Crowds of investors were reported to have surrounded the company's office in Cornhill, snapping up shares at £2 each. Some of the schemes were swindles, others were hoaxes – not with a view to making money but simply to illustrate the country's madness. Spread by greed and by the newspapers' zeal in reporting daily on the changing prices of shares, the new way to make money without having to do an honest day's toil appeared to be obsessing the whole country.

Speculators scrambled to invest in the thousands of new projects, launched in the wake of the grandest scheme of them all, a scheme which would grow to such a size it seemed as if there was not enough money in the kingdom to support it. Some would make or lose up to a quarter of a million pounds in the madness of 1720, when shares in some ventures rose as high as the cathedral itself. Few investors kept their feet firmly on the ground; many felt under pressure to join in as they watched their neighbours climbing a new social ladder through the sudden acquisition of riches. Politicians, the clergy, landowners and the poor all joined in the scramble. Social mobility appeared to race out of control, with barriers between the classes seemingly removed by the chance of easy money. Women, defying convention, invested too – to claim, albeit briefly, an equal place in society. A mere porter in Exchange Alley was said to have made £2,000 – ten times the annual income of an entire well-to-do family and *a hundred times* his own likely yearly earnings. Investors flocked to Britain from Holland and France. The canton of Bern in Switzerland made a corporate decision to invest. The streets of Exchange Alley heaved with desperate souls seeking to place their money in the mushrooming schemes. Fortunes, it appeared, could be made overnight.

The story of the events of 1720 holds more than just the elements of greed and pathos. It was, to those on the edges of the affair, so ridiculous that it inspired a generation of satirists to make fun of the human condition. And it was cruel, causing suffering among many families across the land. Ultimately, it showed England at its most corrupt, exposing the poisonous underbelly of the monarchy, of the ruling classes and of the elected politicians.

The three actors in the drama would be John Blunt, the aspiring son of a Kent shoemaker; John Law, a Scottish gambler; and Robert Walpole, a scheming Whig politician from Norfolk with an ambition as large as his girth. Blunt and Law would, in very different ways, lead the search for the alchemy that would overturn the vast debts of two nations and fill ordinary people's pockets to overflowing. From 1710 to 1720 their careers would collide, and the impact would change the political and economic direction of two great countries, England and France. One was a shallow schemer, who conned a nation; the other a brilliant economist, far ahead of his times, whose intellectual theories blinded him to reality; but both would be condemned as charlatans when their inventions failed. On the backs of their triumphs and disasters, Walpole would, through cunning and ability, rise to unparalleled political power.

When reality returned, as inevitably it would, the old industries of shipping, farming and land-ownership, too dull for the exciting times of the stock-market ride, would once more be seen to be the places to put hard cash. The same would be true of the trade of which Wren was the architectural master: bricks and mortar would come back into favour. Those who had transferred their allegiance to the share market would be left to bemoan their fate and mourn their thumping losses. The Duke of Portland quietly applied for, and was granted, the governorship of Jamaica. A more ignominious position for a member of the eighteenth-century aristocracy can scarcely be imagined. But he needed to draw a salary.

CHAPTER II

A National Lottery, and a Rake's Progress

A National Lottery, and a Rake's Progress

Edwin Thrasher was stony-broke before he won, and one day he touched the ring that his father left him when he died, and said, 'Dad, please send me some money.' That afternoon he won £50,000 on an Instants scratch card.
'Fun Facts About Winners', the UK National Lottery website

With hindsight, it was five shillings' worth of metal that changed the course of history.

In April 1694, in the London suburb of Bloomsbury, two men walked purposefully out of a tavern, glancing around in case there were any bystanders. Within a few paces, they had drawn their swords to settle their differences over a woman they both loved. It was over as quickly and silently as it began. The younger man made a single quick thrust; his rival fell to the ground, and was left dying, alone in Bloomsbury Square.

Within a day the survivor was arrested and thrown into Newgate jail. Within a fortnight he was in court to hear the charge against him: that 'of his malice aforethought and assault premeditated he made an assault upon Edward Wilson with a certain sword made of iron and steel of the value of five shillings with which he inflicted one mortal wound of the breadth of two inches and depth of five inches, of which said wound the said Edward Wilson then and there instantly died'.

John Law, 'Beau' Law, scion of the Laws of Lauriston, gambler and ladies' man, was sentenced to hang. There was little time to lose if his life was to be saved. According to the official version of events, Law was handed the means of escape by friends: they managed to supply him with a file with which he cut through the bars of his cell; also, drugs which he somehow managed to slip into his guards' food or drink, to put them to sleep; and, for when he had achieved both these tasks, Law's friends had a carriage waiting outside the prison, ready to whisk him away. Shortly after New Year's Day, 1695, Law jumped thirty feet from his prison wall, and, although he apparently sprained his ankle on landing, he made it to the carriage and was promptly driven to the coast and smuggled aboard a boat to Holland. It appeared, in every detail, to be a daring escape, and one which became more and more colourful in the telling.

Soon afterwards, the newspapers were supplied with this description of the man on the run: 'Captain John Lawe, a Scotchman, lately a prisoner in the King's Bench for Murther, aged 26, a very tall black lean Man, well-shaped, about Six foot high, large Pockholes in his Face, big High-Nosed, speaks broad and low, made his Escape from the said Prison. Whoever secures him so he may be delivered at the said prison shall have £50 paid immediately by the Marshal of the King's Bench.' Descriptions can be misleading: Law had a clear complexion, and his nose was not large. Nor was his voice broad and low, and neither, for that matter, was he a captain. It appeared that influential friends had persuaded the newspapers to run a misleading description. Escape routes from justice, in the seventeenth century, could be arranged for the influential.

For the best part of two decades, John Law would wheel around Europe in exile. A quarter of a century would pass before he returned to London to receive a royal pardon. A quarter of a century in which he became the most important politician in Europe, a millionaire who invented a financial system that would capture the shattered economy of England's greatest enemy and transform it into the most powerful in the Western world.

In 1710, after much manoeuvring behind the scenes, the Tories wrested power from the Whigs. The new Chancellor of the Exchequer, Robert Harley, had become Queen Anne's favourite, not least because he had befriended her chambermaid and through her had insinuated his way into his monarch's affections. But he had also managed to overturn the government because, unlike the Whigs, he was pledged to peace. The task facing Harley was enormous and could be measured by the debts he had inherited. In total the government owed more than £8 million, of which the Navy alone owed half. Yet Harley could find only £5,000 in the Exchequer's kitty.

One problem was that the size of the nation's debt had outpaced the development of any centralised machinery to process taxes. The Treasury, for example, relied on sticks made out of hazel to account for its loans. These 'tallies', as they were called, were split in the middle and notched according to the amount of money that had been loaned, with the depositor retaining one half and the Treasury the other. Such was the country landowners' belief in the financial incompetence of the outgoing Whig government that they were convinced the Treasury must have mislaid their money. Robert Walpole wrote that 'in every coffee-house and ale-House I may hear it with confidence asserted that thirty-five millions were lost to the public during the late administration'. Though the rumour was false, it seemed too plausible not to be true – why else were taxes so high and still more money needed to feed the great maw of the military machine?

When he took office, Harley knew he needed a plan to bail out the country and keep himself in power. But to find the money he so desperately needed there were few places to which he could turn. Poor Harley found it was virtually impossible to borrow money from the Bank of England or the East India Company, because of establishment opposition to the newcomer in power.

Two men were to offer very different solutions: John Blunt and John Law.

John Law was well brought up and should have known better than to get himself into the trouble that had seen him exiled. His father, William, was a goldsmith who had made so much money from banking that he had bought two large estates, Lauriston and Randlestone, on the outskirts of Edinburgh. With Lauriston came a family castle, which William Law bequeathed to John along with most of his estate when he died in 1683. When John left school he took a keen interest in the business his father had left behind. At the same time, perhaps in the absence of paternal control, he began to develop a taste for women and gambling – becoming, as one contemporary put it, 'nicely expert in all manner of debaucheries'. Luckily for him, women found him fairly irresistible: tall and dark, he was so good-looking they called him 'Beau Law' or 'Jessamy John', to indicate he was a fop or a dandy.

Law decided, while still a teenager, to try his luck in London, no doubt influenced by the stories he had heard of its racy social life. He moved into rooms in St Giles-in-the-Fields, a mixed area which included Bloomsbury and Covent Garden. In many ways, St Giles matched Law's changeable personality: it could not quite decide whether it was respectable, including as it did many members of the fashionable set, or rough, with its narrow, dirty alleys which were home to Irish immigrants and French refugees. Here, Law lost no time in conducting himself in a way that reflected both sides of his character: he took a mistress, a certain Mrs Lawrence, but also made sure he made the acquaintance of Thomas Neale, the Master of the Mint and one of the leading 'projectors' of the day – the name given to men who promoted the cause of the new ideas and businesses that abounded in the capital. Neale was also Groom Porter to the King, which meant he was responsible for providing cards and dice at court. It was not hard to see why Law was keen to meet him.

Law spent most of his nights in the clubs and gaming houses of London. But he was no idle gambler. He began to investigate the odds of throwing a sequence of numbers with the dice, and studied the patterns of games like 'hazard' – a form of craps – which were very popular. His early calculations were not successful. He was forced to sell his castle, and his mother bailed him out by buying the estates from him. At the same time, Law kept up his interest in banking and in particular addressed the issue of whether a national bank should be established to take over from the goldsmiths, like his father, who generally held money for the merchants of the day.

The two sides of Law's engaging personality were to collide – and in spectacular fashion. All his plans, and hopes for the future, were ended by the duel that he came to fight in Bloomsbury in April 1694.

His rival in love, Edward Wilson, was a man whose taste for high living exceeded even that of Law, and in the wake of his death his lifestyle became the subject of much comment in the newspapers, the *London Journal* declaring that 'Mr Wilson was the wonder of the time he lived in; from low circumstances he was on a sudden exalted to a very high pitch for in a gay dress, a splendid equipage and vast expense, he exceeded all the Court. How he was supported, few (very few indeed) truly know; and those who have undertaken to account for it, have only done it from the darkness and uncertainty of conjecture. But in the midst of gaiety, he fell by the hand of the then private Mr Law, and not fairly neither.'

One theory for Wilson's giddy lifestyle, which was based on no discernible income, is that he was the lover of Elizabeth Villiers, the mistress of the King, and that she was subsidising his standard of living. It may also explain why the King apparently took an interest in Law's trial. However, the reports of the proceedings make no mention of Miss Villiers: 'The matter of fact was thus. There was some difference happened to arise between Mr Lawe and the deceased concerning a woman, one Mrs Lawrence, who was acquainted with Mr Lawe; upon which on 9th of April instant, they met at Bloomsbury Square, and there fought a duel in which Mr Wilson was killed.'

Whatever the cause of the fight, the consequence was clear. Wilson lay dead, and Law had to flee for his life.

Law's departure, though enforced, was not without its consolations. Exile proved profitable: within a few years he had made a fortune by gambling. He was not just making money – he was making his *own* money: so high were the stakes he placed that he even arranged for special gold counters to be minted. He was frequently to be seen arriving at the gaming tables carrying £6,000 worth of coins. Nonetheless he built up his wealth carefully, playing to a system and using his mathematical skills to calculate the odds. In Italy he won £20,000, and by the time he reached France in 1714, four years after Harley came to power in England, he had £90,000 to his name. He was seriously, independently, wealthy – the equivalent of a multimillionaire today.

But Law was not the dilettante his background suggested. While he was in Amsterdam, rather than simply trying to make money, though he did that too, he began to think seriously about it as a theory. The Dutch, too, had suffered from the financial problems with which Harley was wrestling in London. But they were far ahead of the English in their economic thinking. The Bank of Amsterdam, a government bank owned by the city, had been established specifically to help oil the wheels of commerce. Most countries faced the same problem, which was how best to guarantee the value of their currency. To try to secure a basis for international trade, a handbook was published listing the 500 gold and 340 silver coins which were circulating in the world. But traders complained that coins were frequently 'clipped' to reduce their metallic content, so their values fluctuated. England had been forced to call in all its silver coinage in 1696 and remint it, but paper money had been issued at an alarming rate to finance the war effort, out of all proportion to the coins in circulation.

The Bank of Amsterdam tackled the problem simply but effectively. It put the coins on the scales and allowed credit according to their real value, their weight, by replacing them with promissory notes. Such pieces of paper were, to all intents and purposes, early banknotes and they became a popular form of currency because their value was guaranteed: they could not be debased. Indeed, they sometimes changed hands at a premium because their value was always honoured. It made Law think: 'This Bank is a secure place where merchants may give in money and have credit to trade with. Besides the convenience of easier and quicker payments, the banks save the expense of bags and carriage and losses by bad money.'

Law's eyes were opened to the possibilities such a bank would bring. Why else, he considered, was Holland more prosperous than England or Scotland, even though it had fewer natural resources? Why else did its ships dominate both the North Sea and the South Seas? The reason, surely, was that the Bank of Amsterdam had loaned money to the Dutch East India Company, not in return for coins, duly weighed and bagged, but against its own assessment of the Company's trading prospects and reputation. Indeed, the Bank actually owned half of the Company; it was effectively *creating* money by buying ships to carry out trade to bring back goods to make more money. It was a virtuous circle, and one which would not exist without the Bank.

Law began to work out his own theories concerning money, theories he would eventually get a chance to put into practice on a national scale. Holland was Europe's largest printing centre and books were readily available, so during his exile he had read widely. For the moment, his thoughts were practical ones and confined to his writings. He set out to make his case for a paper currency, for a form of credit that could not be clipped, debased or altered in any form. His great revelation was that money was not intrinsically valuable. It was simply a means to an end, and one which ultimately reflected the strength, or weakness, of a country's economy. 'Money,' he declared, 'is not the value for which goods are exchanged, but the value by which they are exchanged.' But Law did not want to remain an idle theoretician. He wanted to put his ideas into practice; and he wanted to return home.

Scotland was still, in 1705, constitutionally separate from England though it was moving towards union; the two countries shared the same crown, but had a separate government and parliament. So Law set his mind on persuading the Scottish Parliament, and by extension Queen Anne and her government, of his intellectual credentials to try to win his pardon. It was a back route out of exile and into London's thinking.

Law applied his mind to economic problems generally, and to Scotland's in particular, in a forty-thousand-word document called *Money and Trade Considered with a Proposal for Supplying the Nation with Money*. It was an overview, written anonymously by a 'Scots gentleman' and printed and published in Edinburgh, of the role money played in trade, and the benefits that could accrue from a credit-based economy. But it was also, Law hoped, his ticket home.

Money and Trade is the work of a great thinker, but one who could express himself in everyday language. It is a treatise of startling clarity and economic insight, written by a man who was still just thirty-four. First, John Law established the historical background to the development of money: the use of barter, and the use of silver. Both depended for their basis on an analysis of supply and demand: 'Water is of great use, yet of little value; because the quantity of water is much greater than the demand for it. Diamonds are of little use, yet of great value, because the demand for diamonds is much greater than the quantity of them. Goods change their value, from any change in their quantity, and in the demand for them. If oats be in greater quantity than last year, and the demand the same, or lesser, oats will be less valuable.'

Law may have been the first economic writer to use the concept of demand – he was certainly one of the first. He wanted to show how economies had outgrown the concept of bartering and even the use of silver. He pointed his readers towards what he considered to be the essential quality that money should have: stability. In contrast, he showed how the value of silver could change if supply outstripped demand, or if its quality was diminished. Sometimes there was too much of it, so its value fell, and sometimes it was debased by European governments. Instead, land was, in Law's view, a more stable instrument of economic prosperity. Land was, he opined, more valuable than silver because it produced everything, and silver was only a product.

Law then moved on to the lessons he had learned first-hand in

Amsterdam. Banks, he declared, offered the best method of improving trade and increasing the supply of money, because of the way they could facilitate credit. To move away from corrupted, debased coinage, he proposed the replacement of metal coins by banknotes: 'The paper money proposed being always equal in quantity to the demand, the people will be employed, the country improved, manufacture advanced, trade domestic and foreign will be carried on, and wealth and power attained.'

Initially, Law proposed a land bank, where paper money would be backed by the value of land. Notes were to be issued by the bank to the value of land that was sold. As he developed his argument, the colonial ambitions of the trading companies, whose financial aspirations became so entangled with the economies of European countries at that time, were implicitly blown away: their search for foreign booty was effectively deemed by Law to be absurd. France and Spain were 'masters of the mines', leaving other nations to buy their silver at high prices even though they had 'a more valuable money' of their own – paper, backed by land. Truly, declared Law, 'the nature of money has not been rightly understood'.

Inauspiciously, it was on Friday 13 July 1705 that the Scottish Parliament, riven by factional fighting, agreed to hear Law's proposals for a land bank and paper money. But its main business that day, to Law's misfortune, was to debate the possibilities of the union with England, and here Parliament's hand was being forced both by the economic straits it found itself in and by the terms of the bill which had been placed before it. The proposed Alien Act was designed to allow the Queen to appoint commissioners to work for the union. But if the Parliament voted to reject the move, the Scots would be deemed to be aliens, and their exports to England banned. With the economy destroyed by the Darien venture, the bill was deliberately framed to concentrate minds. Law's proposals would inevitably be seen, at best, as a radical alternative to union, and at worst as an irrelevant sideshow. Moreover, it was unlikely that any discussion in the Scottish Parliament could ever be straightforward.

Passions ran high. Two members became so exercised by the issue of paper money that they challenged each other to a duel. Finally, Law's proposals were rejected: the forcing of paper money upon the country was deemed to be 'unfit for this nation'. Instead of striking out on a radical solution to its economic difficulties, which arguably might have delivered the financial stability the country needed and with it independence, the Scottish Parliament chose the path of least resistance, concentrating instead on joining the country to England in the Act of Union. Under its terms, one Parliament of Great Britain would replace the two of Scotland and England. Self-rule would be ceded by a piece of paper; it could, just perhaps, have been established by paper banknotes.

For Law, this was a bitter blow. His theories remained academic and his future once more lay in exile. Without a royal pardon, he could not even return to Scotland if it was to be formally united to the English nation. Once more he appealed to the Queen; once more, on her government's advice, she turned him down. Within weeks of the Scottish Parliament rejecting his scheme, it voted to appoint commissioners to arrange the union with England. Law was at heart a patriot who wanted to use his intellect to benefit his homeland. Thwarted, he could only turn his thoughts abroad, destined to circulate his economic theories among more accommodating heads of state who admired his genius and were content to ignore the youthful duel which had forced him into exile.

Within a few years, Harley's new government in England, faced with the burden of its ever-growing war debt, turned to a man with no intellectual convictions whatsoever, but a burning desire to make money for himself.

CHAPTER III

Blunt Advice

Ladies some Rich and Old some Young and Fair, —
Are Raffling in a Shop for China Ware ;
Their Brokers waiting at their Elbows cry,
What Stock, my Ladies, will you Sell or Buy.

George Soros became frustrated because his huge wealth seemed to give him no political influence in the West. He realized he needed to become a public personality. In the late summer of 1992, a time of great pressure on European institutions, he did so with a vengeance.

He shorted, betting that the pound would not be able to hold its value against other currencies traded within the Exchange Rate Mechanism.

On Sept. 16, with Soros and others selling pounds, the British government responded by raising interest rates 2 percentage points to attract buyers. By evening sterling had been forced from the ERM. Soros scooped up $1 billion from that escapade and became known all over the world as the Man Who Broke the Bank of England.

'I had no platform,' he says today. 'So I deliberately [did] the sterling thing to create a platform. Obviously people care about the man who made a lot of money.'

Time.com, 1 September 1997

John Blunt was not a handsome man. He was fat and pompous, and a very different character from John Law. Unlike with Law, there would be no madcap chase for the wilder things in life, nor any occasion when, through gambling, he would have to sell his family home or be bailed out by his mother. He had one aim in life, which was to better himself through business. His would be a focused search for wealth and power. Unlike Law, he had no intellectual backbone – he simply had a desire to get rich quick.

But John Blunt did have one redeeming quality. Whilst he was loud and overbearing, he possessed great self-confidence, even charisma; he was on the make but charming – a man bursting with ideas and energy, who dominated any group. His gift was for making money, and he would prove himself to be an inspired promoter of companies. Within a decade he would become rich from backing a project to bring water into London, despite the rivalry of the New River Company, and another for the manufacture of linen. Within a decade, too, he would move closer to the political world, winning election in the City as a councillor in the Cornhill ward, which included Exchange Alley. Blunt was religious, a Baptist by faith, and as the years went by the three worlds of business, politics and religion would merge seamlessly to his advantage.

Blunt was the son of a reasonably well-off shoemaker in Rochester; but he had come up, if not the hard way, then via a route that was tougher than Law's relatively privileged upbringing in Scotland. He had started his working life as a humble member of the Worshipful Company of Scriveners, serving his apprenticeship in Holborn, London. Fittingly, for someone who wanted to aim high, his company's coat of arms was an eagle, coloured gold, standing on a red book, its wings raised, poised to soar. Blunt's choice of profession may have been a deliberate step in his planned path to power and influence. The scriveners were originally a kind of legal assistant, calligraphers with a monopoly on the paperwork for buying and selling houses. Gradually this gave them inside knowledge of the business affairs of merchants and landowners, and they became brokers who negotiated loans, an early type of merchant banker or land speculator. Such was the range of their financial activities that they seemed to occupy no firm place in society; one scrivener might tidy up the legal affairs of large estates, to the chagrin of the lawyers, while another might make his living by acting as a moneylender.

It was, in all, a fitting profession for a man on the make. During his long apprenticeship to Daniel Richards in Birchin Lane, on the perimeter of Exchange Alley, where he wrote letters for a groat (or sixpence), Blunt built up a view of English society, steeping himself in the knowledge of who was rich and who was poor, and those who seemed well-to-do but were just keeping up appearances. But few scriveners became as rich as the goldsmith-bankers like John Law's father, who could lend large sums on credit, and make much more in return. The motto of the scriveners through the years was *Scribite scientes* – 'Write, learned men.' For Blunt, this was just a means to an end. He wanted to be the exception to the rule that few scriveners rose to great wealth or eminence in the City. In 1689, at the age of twenty-five, he left his apprenticeship to seek out new opportunities. Within four months of leaving his apprenticeship, he was married, a first step on the ladder towards social respectability – the string of affairs which John Law had enjoyed was not for Blunt. His choice of bride was Elizabeth Court, who came from a solid

Warwickshire family. Blunt had married above himself, but not indecently so. A second marriage further up the social scale, to the daughter of a former Governor of Bengal, would come later.

Blunt was seeking his fortune in an England humming with new ideas. In the 1690s, the moneyed-men, grown rich on lending to the government, had begun to promote an extraordinary range of companies. The catalyst had been the success of a sea captain, one Captain Phipps, who had salvaged Spanish silver by the ton and precious jewels by the sackful from the bottom of the sea off the island of Hispaniola in the West Indies. He returned to England in triumph and to an instant knighthood: his backers had made an extraordinary 10,000 per cent profit on the adventure, a sum close to £200,000 – many millions of pounds today. Inspired by the captain's success, copycat diving companies had arisen by the dozen, many of which came to London to show off their new deep-sea devices in a public demonstration on the Thames. The novelist and pamphleteer Daniel Defoe invested, and lost, £200 in one diving firm; he also owned a brick and tile factory on marshland near Tilbury, and, more quixotically, seventy civet cats – a leading scientist had once advocated breeding them for the secretion of their glands, which was a basic essence in the manufacture of perfume. The many other projects calling for investors to back them ranged from the Night Engine Company, which patented a burglar alarm, to the 'Company for the Sucking-Worm Engines' which had invented a machine to put out fire. Until 1697 when the impecunious government debased the coinage, puncturing investor confidence and putting many firms out of business, the stock market thrived. One coffee trader, John Houghton, published a twice-weekly paper listing share prices, taking care to explain to his readers the mysteries of the new profession: 'The manner of the trade is this: the monied-man goes among the brokers and asks how stocks go? And upon information, bids the broker buy or sell so many shares of such and such stocks if he can, at such and such prices. Then he tries what he can do among those that have stocks, or the power to sell them, and if he can, makes a bargain.'

In such a speculative age, Blunt, with his glib personality and gift of the gab, was a man of his time, just as Law was far ahead of it. His initial route to power was through a company whose original business matched the bellicose nature of the times: the Sword Blade Company.

At the turn of the century, the Sword Blade Company had spotted a gap in the arms market. The English rapier, heavy and flat, was considered both by combatants and by those who wished, more peaceably, merely to make a fashion statement, to be less effective and less pleasing on the eye than the French equivalent, which had a grooved blade. From 1691 the Sword Blade Company, helped by some imported Huguenot craftsmen, was granted a charter to make French blades in England. But the company was soon to widen its horizons and change direction. It moved to Birchin Lane, and John Blunt became its company secretary. Working with him were three men who would play leading roles in the development of the South Sea Company: the goldsmith Elias Turner would become the Governor of the Company; Jacob Sawbridge, the Deputy Governor; and the third was George Caswall, whose family had held the Leominster seat in Parliament for more than a hundred years.

The Sword Blade Company was a child of its aggressive times, an exploiter of the government's financial difficulties, and the progenitor of the most corrupt financial institution the country was ever to spawn. The company's first step was to buy up large tracts of Ireland, at the bottom of the market, acquiring for about £200,000 land worth £20,000 a year in rents. To bankroll its purchase, it decided to issue stock in the company. It did so in a complicated but highly profitable manner, announcing that it would exchange its stock not for money but for government debts called 'army debentures'. Debentures were slips of paper given to people who had lent money to the government, a type of IOU issued by the Paymaster of the Forces to raise money for the constant state of war. The debts were unsecured, however, and had fallen in value since they first came on the market.

The Sword Blade's idea was to call in as many debentures as it could from the people who had lent the government money, by offering them what looked like a profitable exchange deal. The debentures stood at 85 on the stock market, and their holders were offered, in return, Sword Blade shares worth 100. How then could the company make a profit? The answer was that it had, effectively, rigged the market through what today would be called 'insider trading'. It simply bought up as many debentures as cheaply as it could before announcing its plans, knowing that the scale of its share-swap scheme would cause their price to rise. By this method, the company made an estimated profit of around £25,000. The government, too, was satisfied. As well as buying land from it, the company lent it some £20,000 at a low level of interest as a 'sweetener' to facilitate the business between them. Through its financial adventures it became the Sword Blade Bank. It was a key moment in its history, the turning point in what became a growing, and corrupt, entanglement with affairs of state.

The Bank of England looked on unamused. Its banking monopoly had been enshrined in an Act of 1697, and now it seemed the Sword Blade Company was acting as a land bank, not just as a land corporation. Treasury lawyers pored over the case, and pronounced in favour of the Bank, but no action was ever taken. The deal had been too profitable for the government. But there was worse to come for the Bank of England. A mysterious syndicate, its backers unknown but almost certainly including partners from the Sword Blade Company, offered to lend the government £1.5 million. The Bank could clearly see the danger of such a manoeuvre by its unknown rival. Its charter had only three more years to run, and only by offering to match the size of the loan, and by cutting interest rates to 4.5 per cent, did it see off the threat to its position. Its reward was the extension of its charter to 1732.

This early skirmish between the two rivals presaged what would be in 1720 their all-out hostility, and the government seemed to be the beneficiary, paying less for its money than before. But the charter's extension still proved to be a problem for the Chancellor, Robert Harley. The government had, by confirming the Bank's monopoly, tied itself to a single banking institution to raise money for its conflicts and, over the next three years, the Bank increasingly struggled to deliver. What else could Harley do?

In 1710, battling with the nation's finances, he was impressed by the acumen of John Blunt, and the profit he was making. Harley began to discuss the issue of the national debt with Blunt in the hope of finding a radical solution. The first proposal that his new ally put forward, however, was distinctly traditional. Just five years after John Law had produced what would turn out to be one of the greatest analyses of the eighteenth century as a possible cure for Scotland's economic ills, Blunt persuaded Harley to resurrect the old Whig solution of the lottery. It would capitalise on the general fever for gambling and have the delightful side-effect, if it succeeded, of wresting some financial control from the Whig-dominated Bank of England. On 3 March 1711, the new lottery was launched.

Ostensibly, it was the traditional way of raising loans, to be paid back through yearly payments, or annuities, at a guaranteed rate of interest. One hundred and fifty thousand numbered tickets, costing £10 each, were to be sold, inscribed with the legend: 'This ticket entitles the bearer to ten Pounds to be paid in due course with Interest to commence from the Nine and twenty Day of September One thousand seven hundred and eleven or a better chance' – that is, a prize. Interest was to be paid at 6 per cent. But Blunt had made big changes to the scale of the prize money. There were 25,000 prizes to be won, with the smallest at £20 and the largest at a staggering £12,000. The first and last tickets drawn out of the box would win an extra £500. In total, more than £678,000 – nearly as much as it cost to build St Paul's Cathedral – was to be given away in prize money. Not surprisingly, the lottery was a tremendous success. One knight of the realm complained to a friend who asked him to buy tickets: 'You may assure yourself that I used my endeavours to have put your money in the Lottery, but it was impossible to do it though I was very early that morning in the City, and a vast number of persons was disappointed as well as myself . . . As for buying up tickets, I cannot tell how to advise you, such advantage is made of them by the stock-jobbers.'

John Blunt was on his way to the top, but at a price. The lottery was the first to raise huge sums for the state, triggering a succession of similar enterprises over the next decade, while weighing down the government with the annuities it was obliged to pay to the subscribers. By raising the stakes with such large prize money, the lottery also prepared the ground for the grand speculation of 1720. Eventually, there was to be an explosion of investment which made Wren's continual pleas for cash to fund his dome seem like requests for loose change, rather than the serious financial commitment that Parliament invariably resisted.

After the triumph of his first lottery, Blunt immediately marketed his second, known as 'the Adventure of Two Millions' or 'the Classis'. Never before had the state attempted to hold a lottery on this scale; the tickets cost £100, the equivalent of a day's wages to the average American worker today, but half a year's income to a well-off English family then. The top prize was £20,000, the equivalent of the multi-million-pound jackpot today. The tickets were within the reach of only the very rich, except when the stockjobbers sold shares in them. But Blunt's revolutionary idea was to divide the draw into five ranks, or classes, each with a different level of prizes. In the First Classis (or section), 1,330 tickets would win prizes ranging from £110 to £1,000. Then the prize money was stepped up: in the Second Classis, 2,670 tickets would win between £115 and £3,000; in the Third Classis there were 4,000 prizes, from £120 to £4,000; in the Fourth Classis, 5,340 tickets would win £125 to £5,000; and in the final draw, the Fifth Classis, there were 6,660 winning tickets with prizes ranging from £130 to the top prize, again, of £20,000. In effect, there were five different lotteries, draw succeeding draw so as to build the excitement to fever pitch. If their number did not come up, investors would not know whether to be pleased or disappointed until the last ticket of the fifth and final draw was produced from the box to win the biggest prize of all.

The Sword Blade Company was in charge of marketing the game, and all the tickets were sold within nine days. In this short space of time, Blunt's two lotteries raised £3.5 million. Some investors were either very lucky, or bought heavily: the Duchess of Newcastle won eleven times, the Dukes of Rutland and Buckingham eight times. In the Second Classis an apothecary from Reading, Robert Dean, won the top prize of £3,000; in the Third, a gentleman from Westminster, Thomas Layton, the £4,000 jackpot. In the Fourth, Thomas Scawen, an alderman from London, won the £3,000 prize; another London merchant, John Upton, £4,000; and a gentleman from Northamptonshire, John Hunt, the top prize of £5,000. In the Fifth Classis, 'The Hon. Thomas Cornwallis of St Martins in ye Fields, esquire' won £3,000; a London scrivener, James Colebrook, £4,000, and Samuel Strode, a London surgeon, £5,000. The final ticket to be drawn belonged to Thomas Weddell, a merchant of Gray's Inn, who scooped the £20,000 jackpot.

Encouraged by their success, Blunt and Harley now set to work on their most ambitious scheme of all: to try to find a way to reduce the national debt. The government owed money everywhere, in a confusing tangle of loans. There were the goldsmiths and moneyed-men who had lent it money; there were the holders of lottery tickets, and the holders of the Treasury's notched hazel tallies; then there was money raised by the Army, the Navy, the customs, the Commissioners of Victualling – the government's obligations seemed endless.

Harley's idea was to found a trading company. It was a move that appeared conventional enough. Trade and war were the unholy twins of commerce. It suited both the financial nostrums and the bellicosity of England to develop a new company which would trade abroad and, if necessary, kill natives in order to repatriate the proceeds. Daniel Defoe, who was a lifelong admirer of Sir Walter Raleigh, had long been captivated by the spirit of Elizabethan adventurism and impressed by the vast profits that Spain was still coining from its colonies. Galleons from Mexico and South America were held to carry dazzling cargoes of gold, silver and jewels, but Defoe had consistently argued that there was an even greater profit to be made if the trade was better managed. There is no evidence that Blunt and Harley were swayed by Defoe's arguments, but he reflected the spirit of the times. There was, the pair agreed, a huge commercial prize to be won in South America, offering a ready market for English cloth, with an endless supply of gold and silver in payment.

But Harley was also taking a politically radical step: he intended the proposed trading company to become a new financial institution to rival the Bank of England and the East India Company. On 2 May 1711, when he announced the new company's formation, he declared that not only would it trade in the South Seas but it also aimed to take over the 'floating' portion of the national debt, put at £9 million: this was the debt that could be paid off if the government had enough money, rather than the fixed sums it had agreed to pay to annuitants for many years ahead at generous rates of interest. The company would ask the government's creditors to exchange the money they were owed, directly, for shares in the new trading venture. To help service the interest on the debt, the company itself would be paid more than half a million pounds a year by the government.

Harley's spirits were high, and found a ready outlet in symbolism.

The company was awarded a coat of arms, designed by the College of Heralds and emblazoned with the motto *A Gadibus usque Auroram* – 'From Cadiz [still held to be the empire's last outpost] to the Dawn'. And, in keeping with its heraldry, it was given a suitably grandiose, if overly optimistic, monopoly on trade. It was granted the right to the 'sole trade and traffick, from 1 August 1711, into unto and from the Kingdoms, lands etc. of America, on the east side from the river Aranoca, to the southernmost part of the Terra del Fuego, on the west side thereof, from the said southernmost part through the South Seas to the northernmost part of America, and unto, into and from all countries in the same limits, reputed to belong to the Crown of Spain, or which shall hereafter be discovered'.

Ominously, however, there would have to be a peace deal with Spain and France if the lands which were 'reputed to belong to the Crown of Spain' were to yield their supposed riches to the company's trading vessels. There were therefore two big catches: peace had to be struck on advantageous terms; and the conceded territories had to yield the fabulous wealth which it was so fondly imagined they possessed. The government's propaganda machine, ably spearheaded by Daniel Defoe and Jonathan Swift, went into action. They printed lists of exports which might prove suitable on the markets of South America, from silk handkerchiefs to Cheshire cheese, and they spun stories of South American wealth, the ready market for exports and the generous profits to be made from the slave trade. Portugal had been actively engaged in the traffic in African slaves for more than two centuries; Spain had built a lucrative sugar empire by importing slave labour to the New World. Harley was right to think the profits could be immense: between 1698 and 1708 a stake in the Portuguese slave trade to Jamaica had earned the English government £200,000 a year in bullion. Within half a century, Britain would be shipping a third of a million slaves to the New World and the national economy would depend on the trade.

Aided by his propagandists, Harley's plan succeeded in capturing the imagination of investors. Some of them were political opponents who saw a chance to make money. Some were Dutch or Italian financiers, some were merchants, some were goldsmiths. Blunt and his team of directors also bought thousands of pounds' worth of shares, believing they would make their fortune from the enterprise. Intellectuals such as Swift and Isaac Newton held stock, as did a large number of women. So too, curiously, did government departments.

But if Harley was genuinely attracted by the bold adventurism of the project, by the prospect of faraway riches which would replenish the war-weary coffers of the Exchequer, there were to be other consequences far closer to home. Blunt had won for himself a political and financial lever, a place in society and a position in the City. The Bank of England, officially, might have managed to protect its position, but a rival had been born and – whether it considered it or not – the Bank could not predict what sort of creature it might become. A company which had begun life by making sword blades had turned to land speculation. From land, it was now venturing out to sea. Where next?

On 10 September 1711 the South Sea Company was formally created, with Harley as its Governor. Nine of the thirty appointments were political, and five came from the Sword Blade Bank itself.

Not one of them had any experience of trading with South America.

For now, the political and financial path which had led to the formation of the company appeared to be one and the same. Harley genuinely wanted peace with Spain and France, and believed he could extract, as its price, the right to trade in the southern seas. But first he had to negotiate a deal. Peace, if it was to be struck, had to be struck quickly, so as to enable the South Sea Company to trade successfully and pay off the portion of the national debt it had shouldered. Harley had already begun the process, but he had failed to inform Parliament, and he did not yet have its consent.

Harley had the support of his party and of the country: both thought the war had to end. But the Whig-dominated House of Lords was in a rage, and mobilised for attack. Their aim was to bring down the Tory ministry in a political contest that ranged the old aristocratic Whig order against the upstart who was running the country. In some desperation, Harley tried to delay the return of Parliament, which was in recess. But confrontation at some point was inevitable, a sure sign of which was the propaganda war unleashed by Harley and his pet pamphleteer, Daniel Defoe.

For polemical persuasiveness Defoe had few equals. In his pamphlets on *The Balance of Europe*, an *Essay upon the National Credit of England*, and in *Reasons why this Nation ought to put a Speedy END to this Expensive WAR*, where Defoe argued his most trenchant case of all, the ink flowed as thick and fast as the imagery:

> How have we above twenty years groaned under a long and a bloody war? How often has our most remote view of peace gladdened our souls and cheered up our spirits. Our stocks have always risen and fallen, as the prospects we had of that amiable object were near or remote.
>
> Now we see our treasure lost, our funds exhausted, all our public revenues sold, mortgaged, and anticipated, vast and endless interests entailed upon our posterity, the whole kingdom sold to usury, and an immense treasure turned into an immense debt to pay; we went out full, but we are returned empty.

But even with Defoe on his side, Harley faced a struggle to get his policy accepted. When he could avoid a vote on his peace moves no longer, he found himself defeated by a majority of one. His policy lay in tatters. But Harley was adamant that he would not be forced from office, and circumvented the Lords' hostility by creating a dozen peers to back his peace policy, and with it secure the future of the fledgling South Sea Company. Emboldened, he moved against his Whig enemies by charging the Duke of Marlborough and Robert Walpole with corruption over the Army's accounts, sending Walpole to the Tower.

For Harley it was now imperative to circumvent Parliament and strike a peace deal, whatever the cost. Despite the peace negotiations led by the poet and diplomat Matthew Prior the spring campaign against the French was about to start, with the Duke of Ormonde leading British, German and Dutch forces in Flanders. So the British politicians decided to sabotage their own battle plan. The allied forces were ordered by the leading Tory minister Henry St John, Viscount Bolingbroke, to avoid fighting. Worse still, and with official sanction, via a go-between he revealed the battle plan to the French foreign minister. Then he sent the infamous 'Restraining Orders' to the Duke of Ormonde: 'It is the Queen's positive command to your Grace that you must avoid engaging in any siege, or hazarding a battle, till you have further orders from Her Majesty.' Ormonde was in an impossible position: he was the leader of an army which had been forced to keep the peace by not fighting at all. He was not even allowed to tell his allies, but was ordered to make excuses for the attack's delay, until finally – to the amazement of the allies – the French and British announced their truce.

But the French now advanced on the allied army, capturing town after town, inflicting defeat after defeat on a force which, until the British treachery, had confidently expected to win the war. It was one of the most discreditable episodes in British history. It was peace, but not with honour. In the light of future events it was appropriate that it was on the back of this disgrace that the South Sea Company was launched. Bonfires were lit around the country to celebrate its foundation.

But political and financial interests now started, unnoticed, to spin apart. They were two halves of a lottery ticket which at first sight appeared to join but whose flourishes failed to match. In September 1711, Harley addressed the South Sea directors but, significantly, failed to admit he had abandoned his peace demands for trading settlements in South America. In January 1712, the South Sea directors, secure in their ignorance, informed Harley, now Earl of Oxford, that they wanted to raise an expeditionary force of four thousand soldiers, forty transport ships, twenty men-of-war, plus store ships and hospital ships. Harley, keeping his secret to himself, began to stay away from the directors' meetings. By September, twelve hundred tons of merchandise lay rotting in London warehouses, awaiting dispatch to the South Seas.

In March 1713, eighteen months after he had conceived the South Sea Company, a peace deal was finally signed at Utrecht. Harley had triumphed over the old generation, steeped in war. But in return for the decades of fighting, Britain had won a comparatively trifling prize: a thirty-year slaving contract, and a licence to send a single merchant ship a year on a direct mission to one of the seven ports where the Company was allowed to set up trading stations, but not to establish settlements: Buenos Aires, Caracas, Cartagena, Havana, Panama, Portobello and Vera Cruz. Britain had won no territorial guarantees near the South Seas as a result of the peace treaty. The war was over, though, and Harley stood at last unchallenged on the political stage.

But the child of Harley's peace project, the South Sea Company, was in fact becalmed. The next year, seven ships, including the *Hope* and the *Liberty*, carried more than 2,500 slaves – voyages financed by the Company raising £200,000 in bonds. But it never made a profit in its cargo of human flesh, not least because the Spanish charged such heavy taxes. Then Queen Anne declared that she had the right to keep a quarter of any profits. But the Company must take its share of the blame for its failure to make money: in 1714 it took woollens to Cartagena, where there was no market for them, rather than to Vera Cruz, where there was, so they were left behind to be eaten by the moths and rats. By default, if not intention, the Company had become nothing more than a financial corporation, a ship to float the national debt. As a trading enterprise, it effectively lay at anchor.

By 1713, Harley, too, was going nowhere. The political combination of middle-ground Tories he had put together had proved to be a temporary structure without firm foundations. Harley was hemmed in, too, on the other side, by the Tory hardliners in the October Club, whose members drank together in Westminster and proudly took their name from the month in which the strongest beer was brewed. Their constant harassment of the government to try to shake it out of its moderation on occasions ground the Commons' business to a halt. With the war over, and with credit seemingly restored, Harley could not give his party what it most wanted: clear and decisive Tory leadership. He had not even managed to rid himself of the national debt: by the end of his rule, the government owed another £9 million from the lotteries which Harley had continued to run. Ironically, this sum exactly matched the amount of government debt the South Sea Company had taken over.

The pressure told. Like many a politician, he had found solace in drink. On 25 July 1714 Anne was finally forced to sack Harley from his post. She told the Lords he 'neglected all business; that he was seldom to be understood; that when he did explain himself she could not depend upon the truth of what he said; that he never came to her at the time she appointed; that he often came drunk; that lastly, to crown all, he behaved himself toward her with ill manner, indecency and disrespect'. She would not reign long without him: she was dead within the week.

The Hanoverian era was upon the country and with it a change in political power. George I had a distaste for the Tories matched only by the contempt he held for a foreign kingdom which could never match his beloved homeland. Harley was to be impeached for 'high treason and other crimes and misdemeanours'. In contrast, his Whig rival, Robert Walpole, who had been sent to the Tower for corruption, had been handed a route back to office. Before he left his prison, he penned a note to his sister Dorothy:

Dear Dolly,
I am sure it will be a satisfaction to you to know that this barbarous injustice being only the effect of party malice, does not concern me at all and I heartily despise what I shall one day revenge, my innocence was so evident that I am confident that those who voted me guilty did not believe me so.

His enemies should have taken note. Robert Walpole would prove to have a long memory.

CHAPTER IV

Walpole and the Maypole

The most fundamental overhaul ever carried out on the rules governing the way members of the royal family run their business lives was announced by Buckingham Palace last night. In an attempt to ensure that family members do not exploit their position for financial gain, the palace said new safeguards would ensure a 'complete separation' between official engagements and commercial projects.

'It is entirely in tune with today's world that members of the royal family should be allowed to pursue careers, including in business, if that is what they wish to do,' a Palace statement said last night.

Observer, 8 July, 2001

King George I exhibited his eagerness to take over his new throne by dawdling all the way from Hanover to London. Weeks went by before his pernickety nature was satisfied with the detailed preparations for his forthcoming ordeal. When he finally set out, he made sure he stopped all the way along his route to receive the congratulations which befitted his new status and which put off the point at which he could no longer avoid stepping on to the timber-clad deck of the royal yacht for the sea journey to the grey, cold, inhospitable island which it was now his fate to rule. So disagreeable was this prospect that he clung to Holland as if it was home, meandering through its cities and basking in the receptions he was accorded, so that he did not embark for England until 27 September 1714, nearly two full months after Anne's death.

Political stability was absent at the start of George's reign. He was a contingent king, an interloper who had taken the throne after a political battle of wills, not through divine right or the hereditary principle. His presence assured the Protestant succession, but not the warm embrace of his new countrymen. Both sides in this convenient compact eyed each other warily, not knowing quite what to expect; neither felt an emotional pull towards the other. George was an administrative convenience, a fruit grafted on to Anne's barren reign, a foreigner who would have to win the respect of his citizens, but who possessed neither the charm nor the intellect to do so. Cruelly, the traveller and letter-writer Lady Mary Wortley Montagu noted:

'The King's character may be comprised in a very few words. In private life he would have been called an honest block-head.'

This was an exaggeration. George was a complicated man, not clever but not entirely stupid either; idle, but energetic enough to want to rule in his own way without interference, and short-tempered enough to cast out those who did not fall into line. At fifty-four, he was not in the full flush of youth; nor was he handsome, but he more than made up for this with an extraordinary appetite for women which was to make him an object of ridicule in his kingdom – less for his sexual charge per se, more for the way he chose to express it: the objects of his desire were, by common consent, downright ugly. Added to which, there was something positively *medieval* about his family background. His wife Sophia had once taken a lover, perhaps in retaliation for her husband's considerable dedication to his extramarital activities. George's revenge was terrible to behold. The lover, the Swedish Count von Königsmark, disappeared after he was lured to a false rendezvous with his lady. George probably ordered the murder, though he was away in Berlin when it happened. Sophia was divorced and incarcerated in the Castle of Ahlden, near Hanover, forbidden to see her children again. For her, there was no fairy-tale rescue by a handsome prince. For thirty-two years she languished there until her death, while George frolicked with his mistresses.

The two mistresses he brought with him to England were both, in their own ways, improbable recipients of their monarch's favours. Baroness Eremengarda Melusina von der Schulenburg was tall and bony. She was called 'the Maypole' by the King's subjects; Madame Carlotte Sophia Kielmansegge, fifty and fat, was known as 'the Elephant'. As a child, the writer Horace Walpole was scared witless by her: 'I remember being terrified at her enormous figure . . . [she] was as corpulent and ample as the Duchess was long and emaciated. Two fierce black eyes, large and rolling beneath two lofty arched eyebrows, two acres of cheeks spread with crimson, an ocean of neck that overflowed and was not distinguished from the lower parts of her body, and no part restrained by stays – no wonder that a child dreaded such an ogress!'

John Blunt, surveying the new political landscape, had wasted no time in pressing his cause with George I. He was keen to make the

South Sea Company part of the new establishment, and with it secure his own place in society. In order to do this, he wanted to bring some famous names into the Company's orbit. In place of Harley, he persuaded the Prince of Wales himself to become its Governor in 1715. It was a recognition both of the changed political times and of Blunt's desire for the royal imprimatur. For the Prince, it was a useful way of making money, given the high running costs of being royal.

George I, too, was amenable to Blunt's overtures and acquired a large shareholding in the South Sea Company for himself. It did not take long for the Company to change its composition: in the first year of the reign, leading Tory politicians were voted out as directors by the shareholders, to be replaced by Whig businessmen. Even the Duke of Argyll, a Whig and a loyal Hanoverian, became a director of the South Sea Company – an extraordinary step for a man of such social standing and a sign of Blunt's ability to capture the upper echelons of society with his schemes. But there was another sign, too, of the Company's future direction: half a dozen of its directors, including Blunt, had begun their careers with the original Sword Blade Bank, and had an eye on manipulation of the markets rather than any genuine interest in trade. The deaths, three months apart in 1718, of two great men among the directors, the sub-Governor Bateman and the Deputy Governor Shepheard, tipped the balance of the Court of Directors firmly towards the Sword Blade men, and away from the experienced financiers.

In 1715, to cement its place in the Hanoverian order, the Company had declined the interest payments which were due from the government for servicing the national debt. This had saved the Treasury more than £1 million, and in return the Company was allowed to increase its capital size by the same amount, so that it now had several thousand shareholders, more than either the Bank of England or the East India Company. In the same year, for the first time, its share price reached par, the value at which the stock had been launched under Harley. Four years later, in 1719, the Company was also allowed, through an Act of Parliament, to convert a further part of the government's debt into shares. Unlike Harley, who had merely converted the floating debt (the debt that could be paid off if the Treasury could afford it), the government proposed to sell off that part of the debt to which it was committed for years ahead: this was called the funded, or 'irredeemable', debt. By transferring its subscribers to a stock-market holding in the Company, this new small-scale conversion scheme aimed to remove the burden on the Treasury created by the lottery of 1710. Two-thirds of the annuitants eventually took up the offer, and under the terms of the deal the Company agreed to lend the government more than half a million pounds. As a reward, the Company was allowed to sell extra stock for itself, on a rising market, to increase its reserves of cash.

By 1719, therefore, the Company's capital size had risen past the £12 million mark – and this was financially absurd. In the previous two years, forty-five ships had carried a total of thirteen thousand slaves for the Company under the slaving contract, but it had still not made a profit. Nor had it made any money on its direct trade with South America. Yet, paradoxically, the financial health of the Company, as the dispenser of half the entire joint-stock capital in the country, was vital to the economic security of the nation. And it readily embraced this nonsensical reality: its desire to develop the Sword Blade Bank, from which it had emerged, grew stronger than its attempts to sell its goods abroad. Robert Knight, the general manager of the bank, was appointed as the Company's cashier and became the main conduit between the two sides of the operation, his advancement a tangible sign that the Company was more eager to pursue its role as the holder of the national debt than as a trading concern.

Even as its trading base shrank to nothing overseas, the Company's political horizons grew wider. Its domestic ambitions were reflected in its plan to move into a magnificent flat-fronted building on the north-east corner of Threadneedle Street. More than thirty windows, on three levels, enabled the directors in South Sea House to look down on to the financial district at its feet; there was a dark basement below the iron railings at the front, while a colonnaded entrance made a grand statement of its claim to be an accepted part of the establishment. Appropriately, its rival, the Bank of England, stood at the other end of the street.

To the Bank's chagrin, the connection between the Company and the government was close, and becoming closer. John Aislabie, as Chancellor of the Exchequer, appointed Francis Hawes, one of the

Company directors, to be Receiver-General of Customs; four directors were also MPs, and another six had posts that had connections with the public purse. These men provided a key link between the Company and the institutions which controlled public money. The South Sea Company had become a fully fledged member of Britain's political, financial and social order, and, in recognition, the Company's newly launched ship was called *The Royal Prince*. The Prince himself, and his courtiers, were treated to a lavish party on board, to celebrate the ship's impending departure for the South Seas in search of the bottomless riches on which the Company's foundation was supposedly predicated.

It should have been a big moment in the Company's history. But the royal establishment which Blunt was courting was far from united. The King's frequent absences in Hanover had made him ever more intolerant of his son, suspicious as he was that the Prince had been manoeuvring against him, and resentful of having to return to the foreign land he had inherited against his better judgement. All the signals pointed towards there being a familial explosion, and, given the curious nature of George's family history, it duly came in the happiest of circumstances.

In November 1717, the Prince's beautiful wife Caroline of Anspach had given birth to a baby boy, her fifth child. Instead of celebrating, however, the King and his son fell out in spectacular fashion. It was, strictly speaking, the King's right as ruler to name the boy's godparents; but the Prince wished to do so himself, and chose the Queen of Prussia and the Duke of York. The ensuing fall-out was dramatic. The King banished the Prince and his wife from the palace without their children. A few weeks later, the baby boy died. The Hanover family seemed genetically programmed for disaster.

The political impact of the schism was immediate: George had, through his intemperate actions, forced his son into internal exile. A rival court was established, with the Prince choosing Leicester House at St Martin's in London as his base, barely a mile from St James's Palace. No longer was the King in total command of all he surveyed. This time, dissent had a focus, a rival power base in which the thwarted ambitions of the powerless and the embittered could find expression. The political tensions were reflected most obviously in the South Sea Company's make-up, with the rivalry between the King and his son reflected in the efforts made by their respective candidates, in 1718, to be elected to the Court of Directors. Walpole and Townshend's candidates stood against the government, and by implication the King, with some success. Harley's brother Edward wrote: 'the King's people . . . have lost it for sub- and deputy-governors of the South Sea, and those who are reckoned of the Prince's party have carried it'.

Crucially, the row between the King and his son led directly to George I, as an act of revenge, assuming the role of Governor of the South Sea Company. It was the highest accolade the ambitious directors could have sought for their upstart venture, but it was dangerous territory for the monarchy. It signified not just royal approval of the enterprise, but royal entanglement too. By his presence at the head of the company, the King had signalled that the business was to be trusted. But the obverse might be proved, too. If for any reason the Company failed, where did this leave a monarch unloved by his people, assailed by Jacobite incursions, and viewed with intense suspicion, if not animosity, by members of a dispossessed Tory party? The Company, launched by the Tories, had effectively been reinvented as a Whig project, with the King as its guarantor.

The omens were not good. War with Spain broke out again at the end of 1718, and with it the South Sea Company's last hopes that it would live up to its motto and travel 'from Cadiz to the dawn', that it would trade with faraway lands and bring home booty to compare with the Elizabethan adventurers'. Instead, its seven overseas trading posts were seized by Spain. *The Royal Prince*, its hold crammed with cargo, lay at anchor and could not sail for Spanish America. A full two years were to pass before she made her maiden voyage, to Vera Cruz, at which point the Spanish fleet attacked her: so she gave up and languished in port for half a dozen years more. A second ship, named *The Royal George* in honour of the King, was launched in 1718 but war prevented her, too, from setting sail. The Company now looked not to a faraway dawn for inspiration, nor to Cadiz, though that was nearer the mark.

Instead, it was the ambitious economic theories of the Scottish outcast John Law that helped to change the destiny of the South Sea Company. Under his leadership, France was transforming its fortunes with a speed and skill that George's indebted government, and the South Sea Company of which he was now head, could only admire and fear. 'I wish to God,' complained a despairing British diplomat in France to an under-secretary back home, 'there may be something done quickly to put our affairs in order before it is too late; and that the great men of Britain would think of something else than merely of tripping up one another's heels.'

The unthinkable had happened – France was winning the peace. War had been replaced by something which proved to be far more dangerous for Britain: economic rivalry.

CHAPTER V

Who Wants to Be a Millionaire?

*Britain's financial markets are in the grip of an unprecedented
stock-buying fever as punters rush to buy almost any share with a
whiff of the Internet about it. The City has been caught on the
hop and cannot cope with the surge in demand. People report
spending up to a day waiting for a free line to some stockbrokers
and then having to wait up to an hour more before it is
answered. The City regulator is right to warn people of the risks,
but that won't be enough to stem this get-rich-quick boom as
punters everywhere stake their claims to some of the instant
fortunes made by Internet start-up companies.*
Guardian, 11 December 1999

After the Scottish Parliament's rejection of his dream of introducing
paper money, John Law had escaped once more across the Channel,
only pausing in his flight, or so it is recounted, to win an estate
worth more than £1,000 a year by gambling. True or not, it would
have been of little comfort to him, for there is no doubting the
severity of the setback Law had suffered. He was clearly condemned
to a life of permanent exile unless the union of England and Scotland
failed or the Act of Settlement, which excluded the exiled Catholic
James II from the throne, was overturned, for only a political sea-
change, it seemed, could now grant him passage home. This was
painful enough, but equally hurtful was the knowledge that his cogent
analysis of the benefit paper money could bring to a country might
not now be put into practice. Law was not only physically in exile,
he was in intellectual exile too, fated to be a perpetual academic rather
than a participant, forever denied the chance to put his certitude into
practice.

So sure was Law that his intellectual vision was accurate, however,
that he determined to succeed despite the hand he had been dealt.
Just as he had developed a system at the gaming tables that had made
him personally wealthy, so he was certain that his system for a whole
country would bring it riches too. Neither activity, in his own mind,
was a gamble: in both cases his system was a certainty. An enlightened
ruler, he was sure, would share his vision, and accordingly he had
set out across Europe to try to find a country more amenable to his
project. If his homeland could not see the merits of his proposals

then he would show what it was missing: as a patriot, he had done his best to convince his own people to take up his ideas.

For nine years, from 1706 to 1715, Law had trudged across Europe, vainly trying to convince a succession of monarchs and ministers to back him with their money. Until 1713, the closest he came to success was in Turin, where he suggested to the Duke of Savoy, Victor Amadeus that he should be allowed to establish a state bank in Savoy-Piedmont. He designed a bank that would issue paper notes and also act as a trading corporation to buy and sell property. It would lend money at a fixed rate of interest and the gold and silver in the ducal treasury would act as its reserves, backing, in tangible form, the authority of Law's paper currency, which would bear the royal coat of arms. To guard against inflation, Law ruled that there must be a strict ratio between the notes in circulation and the reserves. While the bank would have the power to print notes, he declared that the vaults must never hold less than three-quarters of the value of the paper money it had released into the world beyond.

Victor Amadeus was easily swayed by Law and took little convincing, but the project ran into immediate political difficulties. The powerful finance minister objected, and when the Duke was forced to back down Law once more packed his bags and took off in search of a country that would adopt his system: first, it is said, to Vienna to try to convince the Emperor of his plans; then to The Hague, where he applied his mind, successfully, to making as much money as possible from the state lotteries; finally, in the summer of 1713, he reached France with a fortune put at more than 1.5 million *livres*. (There were about 14 livres to the £.)

France would be the making, and the breaking, of John Law and his project. The country's economy was, if anything, in a worse state than England's. Two wars lasting more than a quarter of a century had left it crippled. In 1715, after the War of the Spanish Succession had ended, the national debt was as high as three billion *livres*, and the budget rejected all attempts to persuade it to balance. The failure added another eighty or ninety million *livres* a year in interest payments to the runaway overspend, and the government was living hand to mouth. It could keep going only by anticipating its revenue, begging for advances on future taxes it would levy – and already taxes had been committed three or four years in advance. Louis XIV was forced into the humiliation of borrowing eight million *livres* from one of the country's leading financiers, Samuel Bernard, for thirty-two million *livres*' worth of credit notes. So dire was its predicament that a full two-thirds of the nation's running costs were met either by the time-honoured practice of selling offices or by borrowing money. But the King could not pay his creditors and they, in turn, could not pay anyone else. One contemporary commentator wrote that 'the shortage of credit was universal, trade was destroyed, consumption was cut by half, the cultivation of lands neglected, the people unhappy, the peasant badly dressed and nourished'. Some of the country's representatives abroad had not been paid regularly for years, nor had they much prospect of ever seeing their money: the finance minister suggested it would take eleven years to balance the books. Indeed, so parlous was the state of the nation's finances that the Council of Regency, presided over by the Duke of Orleans, which ran the country on the death of Louis XIV, had even considered declaring the state bankrupt.

Before Louis XIV died Law had presented him with plans for a state bank to issue paper money along the lines of the bank he had so nearly established for Victor Amadeus in Turin. He would pay off the national debt by issuing stock, with the shares to be redeemed after twenty-five years, and he promised to cut interest rates from 7 per cent to 5 per cent. Few gamblers, if any, can break a bank; fewer still can create one with wealth gained from the tables. But Law offered to pay for the cost of establishing the bank himself, from his gambling riches, and to give half a million *livres* to the poor if the project failed. Perhaps with his rejection by the Scottish Parliament in mind, he also declared he would restore French credit to a higher level than that of Great Britain. So hopeful was he of a positive outcome to his proposals that he had even drafted the letters patent authorising the bank's creation for the King to sign. But Louis had turned him down.

On Louis's death, power passed to the Duke of Orleans, who, as Regent, held the throne on behalf of the child-king, Louis XV. The Duke was more amenable to Law's project than the late King had been, and perhaps more realistic too about the condition of the country and the stark choices it now faced. His finance minister opined that 'we have found matters in a more terrible state than can be described; both the King and his subjects ruined, nothing paid for several years past and confidence entirely gone'. Desperate times needed desperate measures. On 1 May 1716, Law was finally offered the chance he had been seeking for most of his adult life. A decade after his rejection in Edinburgh, he was given the opportunity to put his ideas into practice. Now in his forties, he was no longer a young gambler, but well on the way to statesmanship.

The Banque Générale was based in Law's own home, a sign both that it was his fiefdom and of its modest beginnings. It had a narrow capital base of only just over 4 million *livres*, or £300,000, and less than a tenth of this was held in cash, but it was a start. Law finally issued his much vaunted paper money, on the understanding that at any time it could be exchanged for 'coin of the weight and denomination of that day'. It was the first time in France's history that banknotes had been in circulation, and it was one of only six states in the world that had paper money, joining the club of which Sweden, Genoa, Venice, Holland and Great Britain were members. It was the first time, however, that paper money was being used in a systematic and disciplined way – not just as a means of *representing* money, but as money itself. Law wanted to move to an economy where coins were no longer in circulation, to a metalless financial system where banknotes were the *only* form of currency. His System – and it was always given a capital S – was potentially harsh. The penalty for forging or altering the paper currency that bore John Law's signature was death. By this signal Law, and implicitly the Regent, declared that the project would work only if the rules were stringently obeyed. Break the link between the paper currency and the financial integrity and solidity of the bank which it represented, and the System was corrupted, and doomed to failure. Fail to honour the banknotes by being unable to pay in metal, should anyone demand it, and the paper was fit only for the bonfire.

The newspapers condemned Law as a charlatan, but gradually he won over the public's confidence. Two factors helped him: his sharpness of purpose, which meant he could accurately anticipate what would appeal to his customers, and, crucially, the Regent's support. By offering to pay bills through his bank, free of charge and in any part of the country, Law showed his customers that his System could work, and that his experiment could apply to the whole country and not just to Paris. The Regent's support was public and to the point: in broad daylight he deposited a pile of coins at the bank worth a million *livres*.

At first, the public was suspicious of the new paper banknotes, but gradually the project began to catch hold, not least because of the financial backing offered at the highest level. The Regent's confidence bred confidence among his people: the initial scepticism of the French citizens was finally overcome when they saw that the banknotes were the one type of currency that could not be randomly diminished by clipping or devaluation. Law's bank soon reduced its discount rate and began to lend money to businesses. Trade picked up; industry gathered pace; and so did Law's career. At Law's request, the Regent ruled that his tax collectors in the provinces were to send their money to Paris in the form of the bank's notes, and to accept the notes for any coins they had in their own treasuries. At a stroke, the Regent helped Law see off the vested interests of the revenue collectors, who had formed a joint-stock company which became known as the Anti-System, to oppose him. Soon, taxpayers were *forced* to pay their dues in paper. Thus the currency spread throughout the nation.

But Law wanted more. He knew that a bank did not have to be the passive recipient of other people's money. It could be instead a driving force of the economy, a motor which could create wealth by granting credit. Gold and silver, *fool's* gold and silver, would no longer be needed. The ultimate prize was worth the inevitable political and economic battles that lay ahead. His project could end the depression and deflation which had so addled Europe in the new century.

England could only look on with alarm.

When Queen Anne died, so did the Tory party as an immediate fighting force. As the remnants of Harley's supporters made their way to the opposition benches, or even, in Henry St John, Viscount Bolingbroke's case, into Jacobite exile, so too there was a changing of the guard amongst His Majesty's representatives and diplomats abroad. Matthew Prior, the peace negotiator, had stayed on in Paris after successfully completing the negotiations which led to the peace deal of the Treaty of Utrecht, the diplomatic 'triumph' built on military ignominy, which had provided the dishonourable foundations of the South Sea Company's rise to prominence. But on George I's accession, Prior was dispatched to spend more time on his poetry, and in his place came John Dalrymple, the Earl of Stair. With Law in Paris too, in the city there were now two Edinburgh men of similar mien: perhaps, to Law's eventual discomfort, too similar.

Stair, like Law, was a mixture of the cavalier and the puritan. It was said that he had forced his wife to marry him by hiding in her bedroom, so that only a wedding ceremony could save her reputation. But he was, as if in contrast, a stern defender of his country's honour and almost from the start he took a watching brief over Law's activities. Stair was the first person Law had sought out on his arrival in Paris, pressing him to intercede with the government in London: brimming with ideas and with the accumulated wealth of a thousand gaming tables, Law had informed the Earl that he still wished to serve his own country, that he wanted to put his talents at the disposal of the King, but not for personal gain. Stair had agreed to help, writing to the Secretary of State, James Stanhope, who was the most powerful figure in Sunderland's government: 'there is a countryman of mine named Law of whom you have no doubt often heard. He is a man of very good sense, and who has a head fit for calculations of all kinds beyond anybody. Could not such a man be useful in devising some plan for paying off the national debts? He is a man of very solid good sense, and in the matters he takes himself up with, certainly the cleverest man that is.'

The government in London declined the offer. Despite the weight of the national debt, England's banking system was more advanced, its trading companies more established and credit more readily available than in poor beleaguered France. Why go to extraordinary lengths to bring back home a convicted killer? Apart from the intellectual leap of faith demanded of King George and his ministers, it would have been a blatant admission of failure. Law's future, if he had one over and above dry theorising, clearly lay in France.

But from the outset, as Law struggled to build his career, Stair's presence was important. Every action he took was observed by the Earl, weighed in the balance and reported back to his masters in London. Though the accession of the Regent had softened the relationship with France, England, having forged a peace, feared a revival in the economic fortunes of its old enemy. It took a close but wary interest in the land that had not just given sanctuary to the Jacobite pretender to the throne but had recognised James Edward Stuart officially as king. Peace meant England had to satisfy itself that its relations with France were conducted from a position of relative economic strength: Europe's power balance must not tilt again. With a regent in charge, and an emasculated economy, France had emerged from its wars sufficiently enfeebled to allow England to be confident of its position in the nearby world. The English government wanted to keep it that way.

There were other reasons, too, why England could not avoid noticing developments in Paris. Led by its Hanoverian king who took such delight in returning to his roots, the country was international in its outlook. London sensed, too, that it was in effect closer to Europe than it was to some English cities. It was said to be easier to travel to Paris from London than it was to struggle to the west or north of England. News from abroad travelled quickly and freely, carried by merchants by land and sea as they plied their trade. So when Law's bank began to take root in France, it began too to take root in the minds of the political establishment in London, its initial success perhaps magnified and certainly feared. If Law proved too successful with his radical ideas, the balance of power would change again; and if Law could not be stopped, then he could at least be matched and even beaten by an English version of his scheme, and the country's relative superiority maintained. Finance was the fashionable new battlefield; the creation of money, the new war. On a personal level, too, for the creators of the new wealth, a quick fortune and social advancement were the prize. John Blunt saw Law's rapid and staggering success and refused to be outdone. If an outcast could rise to the top of French society, then an upwardly mobile scrivener could do the same in England.

Until 1720, however, it was John Law who would be inspired by developments in England rather than the other way round. Law reflected that France's difficulties were more complex than those he had encountered in Scotland or England. The whole system was gripped by a financial crisis, he considered, for France had none of the new financial institutions which its rival across the Channel had established. There was no state bank, and no large trading company like the East India Company, nor indeed a South Sea Company, which the Treasury could use to manage its debt. So, ironically in the light of later developments, the Bank of England was a model for Law's bank in Paris; and the South Sea Company too played an important role in his initial thoughts. Law was struck by the way both it, and the East India Company, had effectively circumvented the need for *any* money at all. Balancing the amount of gold and silver against banknotes, as he had decreed, was fine up to a point; but they were, in Law's mind, two different systems. With the paper-money system as he had conceived it, credit could not expand beyond the artificial limits imposed by the size of a bank's deposits of mere metal.

In Law's mind, the trading companies provided a third way, massaging the government's debt by lending money at low rates of interest in return for exclusive trading rights. The shares of such companies in turn could, he considered, become another form of paper currency, and indeed were frequently traded in Exchange Alley in return for cash. The trading companies could grow or shrink according to the judgement of investors. In place of money, credit had been created, a far more substantial form of credit than anything that was limited by the valuable materials the earth might choose to yield to prospectors or miners across the world. After all, coins were simply an artificial, manmade creation which, as Law had put it in *Money and Trade Considered*, might just as well have been named 'Number 1, Number 2, and so on'. But goods were different. Even oats might be valuable if they were scarce and demand was high. So what price a company with a profitable business? What credit that would create within a country's economy!

In June 1719, Law put into place the next stage of his glittering project, one which saw his System become, briefly, the wonder of the Western world. The move which brought Law such fame and riches, and which drove the English to distraction, was his decision to merge his bank with a great French trading company that had been brought to its knees by the failure of its foreign ventures. He determined to revive it, and in the process pump credit into the economy, by selling shares in its activities. The consequent race for shares in the Mississippi Company was as fierce as any in history. In Paris, the share explosion turned the narrow rue Quincampoix into a crowded, noisy, barrow market, the equivalent of London's Exchange Alley.

For England, it was a staggering development. Law had managed to turn the tables.

Unlike the South Sea Company, with its ships still moored at port with little prospect of a voyage, the Mississippi Company had at least tried to trade with and colonise faraway lands, even if with no conspicuous success. France had first claimed Louisiana as her own in 1682 when the explorer René-Robert Cavelier discovered a part of the great river's yawning mouth. A colony was established two decades later, more to prevent the perfidious English from claiming territory than as a realistic commercial enterprise. But rumours spread as wildly as disease in these overheated lands, and the grandest rumour of them all, that Louisiana was rich in minerals, provided Law with his strongest selling-point. Louisiana underwent a masterful rebranding exercise: poor, swamp-ridden, pestilential Louisiana was declared to be the land of plenty, where a fortune in precious jade, or silver, or emeralds, lay waiting, begging, to be harvested. New Orleans, named after Law's patron the Duke, was pronounced to be the thriving, humming centre of the New World. The reality was a town with ramshackle huts prey to Native American attack. But the citizens of Paris were bewitched.

Law's bank had established its paper-money foundations, and its reputation, on the physical reality of coins held in its vaults; his next enterprise established its reputation for delivering the prospect of fabulous wealth on the chance that there was treasure hidden in the ground. Helped by racy accounts of Louisiana's riches written by unreliable travellers who had seen less and invented more than their readers realised, Law depended upon and exploited hearsay to attract investors to his scheme. The vast territory of Louisiana was held to be the richest area in the world, wrote one traveller in his memoirs: 'pearls could be fished there in abundance; the streams which watered it rolled on sands of gold, and precious metal was found on the surface of the earth without any need of profaning its bosom'.

The reality was very different. During the first winter of Louisiana's settlement at the beginning of the eighteenth century, the first few hundred men and women had been reduced to half their number by the torments to which they were subjected; the scorching heat and a lack of fresh water put paid to many, while their means of arrival and escape, their two frigates, were eaten by worms. The colony never recovered from these terrible beginnings; never more than seven-hundred strong, it merely marked time over the succeeding years while its political masters in Paris alternately reviewed or ignored its fate. Now, under Law's vision, two long-running sores, the French economy and the province of Louisiana, could combine to produce a healthy and profitable cure for each other. The French government wanted to run its economy efficiently, and to stem its foreign losses. In this way, under the leadership of Law, the financial recovery of France and the future of the Mississippi Company were destined to become entangled. The territory he came to run was vast: nearly half the United States of today, comprising Louisiana, Mississippi, Arkansas, Missouri, Illinois, Kansas, Oklahoma, Nebraska, North and South Dakota, Iowa, Wisconsin and Minnesota.

Law was taking over the New World by raiding the capital of the Old. The founder of a bank once run from his own home now determined to raise a hundred million *livres* for the reborn Mississippi Company. It was a staggering sum to try to extract from the public, the more so as there was no evidence whatsoever that his trading empire would succeed in producing a profit. It was, like the launch of his bank, an intellectual exercise, but this time his project was based on speculation rather than on empirical fact. Much travelled though Law was, his adventures had led him no further than Europe, his sea-travels no further than the Channel. The tales on which he based his view of Louisiana's prospects had travelled far further round the world than the exiled Scotsman.

To meet the economic demands and the expected growth of the promised land, Law undertook to settle six thousand colonists and three thousand slaves in Louisiana. In charge of the settlement, directing its economy and applying his own financial System, Law was king of the Americas in all but name, the ruler of the Company of the West, as it first became known, and then of the Company of the Indies, as it was renamed when it absorbed two great trading corporations, the East India Company and the China Company. That it never shook off its older, more established title, the Mississippi Company, was appropriate; it could not shake off, either, the deep-rooted failure of the rotten settlement Law had fought so hard to command.

His first challenge was to entice enough citizens to uproot and cross the oceans to the land of plenty. The French, perhaps sensibly, were far more keen on travelling to Paris to buy stock in the company than on experiencing at first hand the supposed riches that were to be the foundation of its growth. So Law cast his net wider and started, successfully, to recruit in Germany for the new town he was founding in Arkansas. But still the French remained obdurate, and there simply weren't enough willing volunteers to start the colony.

Law had come a long way since his relaxed, bohemian days in London. Just as he was now running the economy with planned central control, so he decided that if people could not see for themselves the right course of action, he would seize social, as well as economic, control of their lives. He decided to force some of his adopted countrymen to follow the path he knew was right. Louisiana would be a convict colony. The Duke of Saint-Simon noted that 'in order to people these colonies, persons without means of livelihood, sturdy beggars, female and male, and a quantity of public creatures were carried off . . . not the slightest care had been taken to provide for the subsistence of so many unfortunate people . . . they uttered cries which excited pity and indignation, but the alms collected for them not being sufficient . . . they everywhere died in frightful numbers'. So it was that Louisiana, that paradise abroad, received the outcasts of French society, in an exercise in mass deportation which rounded up a wide range of misfits. There were the madmen, and the fraudsters; prison inmates who had been sentenced according to the due process of law, and those who were still awaiting judgement. Families were even held to have volunteered troublesome children for the faraway life.

In France, under an absolute monarchy and with the continuing support of the Regent, Law could act with absolute authority. In his quest for success, in his rigid application of the brilliant economic dogma which he held so dear, he showed no spirit of toleration. The *Journal of the Regency*, which chronicles Law's rule, recorded that on 14 August 1719 the police 'took 500 boys and girls from the hospitals of Bicêtre and de la Salpêtrière to be embarked at La Rochelle and transported to Mississippi. The girls were in wagons and the boys on foot, escorted by 32 guards.' More comically, a butcher came home to hear a noise upstairs, and called for help. It turned out that he had disturbed his wife and her lover, but the couple persuaded the police that he was a burglar and only his friends saved him from deportation. It gave rise to a popular refrain:

Now all you husbands hear, if your wife should have a dear,
When you find him in your bed, do not hit him in the head,
For they'll ship you out to sea, straight to Mississippi.

Law's career now entered its final phase, where his bank and his company worked as one, and the economy gorged itself on their paper profits. He realised that the key to his success lay in captivating the ordinary man and woman; he needed them to invest in his scheme. If his System was a popular success, what a transformation that would make to the country's finances!

For the first eighteen months of his stewardship, the price of shares in the new Mississippi Company had barely moved. It was time, Law considered, for a dramatic gesture to capture the imagination of investors. Not for the first time, he put his money on the line, and gained wide publicity for his actions. Law underwrote investors in the Mississippi Company by guaranteeing that in six months' time he would buy back the shares for the par value, the amount they had cost when the company had first been launched. This was an incredible offer because the shares had fallen by half since then – so Law was offering twice the current rate. As the investors could plainly see, he was prepared to double their money. It was a gamble with human nature, doubtless financed by his own activities at the gaming tables; he publicly deposited, and promised to forfeit if he broke his word, 40,000 *livres*. As guarantees go, it was unique. France had never dealt in 'futures' before and it found the concept irresistible. How could an investor lose? Buy now, and there was a guaranteed profit! A combination of his extraordinary money-back guarantee, and the rising tide of banknotes in circulation, led investors to believe that the Mississippi Company was the opportunity of a lifetime, their belief confirmed by the continuing rumours of Louisiana's mineral riches.

Law's aim was to ensure that investors began to speculate in the company's shares, in the hope that more and more people would be attracted to the prospect of owning them. He succeeded perhaps even beyond his dreams. The shares inched upwards, at first slowly and then gathering pace; rose to their par value, and were still moving upwards long before the deadline Law had set himself to buy them back. So, too, his reputation as a financial genius soared, and he began to expound his dream of a single great trading corporation that plied the seas and controlled the markets of the world.

To raise the necessary capital, the French government allowed Law to issue fifty thousand shares in this global venture, pitched very cheaply at the par value of 500 *livres*. Crucially, however, an investor had only to find 75 *livres* of the purchase price as an initial downpayment. The rest could be paid in twenty monthly instalments, taking the total price to 550 *livres*. Credit proved to be the fuel which caused the share price to rocket. Even before the second monthly payment was due, the share price had reached 1,000 *livres*, producing an instant profit of 450 *livres* from a downpayment of only 75. In this way, Law raised the best part of 25 million *livres* for his expansionist plans. He was aided in his enterprise by the government, which recognised his success on the markets by granting him exclusive rights to the Alsatian salt mines and to trade with the Barbary States, as well as by selling him the entire profits of the Royal Mint for nine years for the sum of 50 million *livres*. To pay for his purchase of the right to mint coins, Law issued a further fifty thousand shares at 1,000 *livres* each, double their par value. They were still good value.

As enthusiasm grew for the prospect of the Mississippi Company's success in the rich mineral fields of Louisiana, rumour became inside knowledge and inside knowledge became fact, and fact then conspired with Law's offer of easy credit to drive hundreds of thousands of ordinary citizens to the bustling alleyway that was the rue Quincampoix in anxious search of wealth and profit before it was too late to invest. Meanwhile, Law offered to pay off the entire national debt of 1,500 million *livres* and, to do so, duly issued another 300,000 shares of 500 *livres* each, to be paid in ten monthly instalments. He also bought the right to collect taxes for 52 million *livres*.

England was forced to sit up and take notice. 'The King's [Louis XV's] revenue will be augmented near a hundred millions, and the people will nevertheless pay a hundred millions less in taxes,' reported the *Weekly Journal*. 'An infinite number of new families are raised to new fortunes; so that eight hundred new coaches are set up in Paris, and the families enriched purchase new plate, new furniture and new clothes. Money flows like the water of the Seine.'

Law had insinuated himself into virtually every aspect of the French economy. He had bought up so many of the government's debts that he was effectively its only creditor. In total, since he had launched his trading company, he had issued more than 600,000 shares worth just over 300 million *livres* at their par value. From the countryside as well as from Paris they came to buy the shares, and then as word spread they came too from abroad – from England and Holland, Germany and Spain. In the rue Quincampoix, they traded day and night in Law's great invention, paper, until the din became too much and guards cordoned off the street at night to allow its weary residents some sleep. Property prices, too, matched the mighty rise of shares, as the wheeler-dealers fought for a space to pitch their new business, share-selling. Humble artisans could make good money renting their rooms: a cobbler even rented his bench for 200 *livres* a day, and others rented chairs for weary investors – or the just plain curious – to rest their limbs. Genoese merchants were held to have bought £29 million worth of stock, merchants from Milan £28 million worth. 'The confluence of strangers to Paris is incredible,' the *Weekly Journal* told its readers in London.

With the property boom, too, came a building boom, with the rue Quincampoix expanding skywards as builders quickly added an extra, ramshackle, storey to existing houses. Fact and fantasy became one. With the genuine tales of sudden riches that befell many, came tales of the ridiculous which matched the giddy times: a humpback was held to have rented out his hump for 150,000 *livres* for use as a space-saving desk.

The frenzy was witnessed with growing alarm by the British Embassy in a series of situation reports for London: 'The rue de Quinqempoix, which is their Exchange Alley, is crowded from early in the morning to late at night with princes and princesses, dukes and peers and duchesses etc. in a word all that is great in France. They sell estates and pawn jewels to purchase Mississippi.' Through-out history, throughout the world, wars had been fought over valu-able minerals, over gold and silver. But a new invention, properly applied, had shown how backward were such ages. France was now living in modern times, amidst a financial revolution. Law had, as if by conjury, demonstrated that paper, simple, humble paper, was more valuable than gold.

How long, feared England, would it be before Law's schemes led to a revival of France's military ambitions? How long before it asserted its economic supremacy and crushed British business overseas? The watchful Earl of Stair, in the British Embassy, was far from sanguine about developments. 'By the success of Mr Law's project the public debts of France are paid off at a stroke,' he declared in one of his regular reports for London. 'The French king remains master of an immense revenue and credit without bounds.' Britain had to do something, and fast, to eradicate the national debt. Otherwise, warned Stair, Law would 'raise the trade of France on the ruins of our trade'.

With his share price soaring, Law now took steps to acquire the trappings of big business. The bank moved to the plush Hotel Nevers, with a separate office in the rue Quincampoix; the Company, to the magnificent Mazarin Palace at a cost of a million *livres*. Another half-dozen buildings were bought with an eye to the future, to try to create a bourse. But there were hairline cracks in Law's system, which were widening by the day: paper was running out of control. Some 380 million *livres* had been unleashed into the economy, and there simply weren't enough coins in the bank to pay for all the paper if its holders turned up and demanded hard cash.

Not that anyone saw it that way at the time. An era of prosperity seemed to have dawned, and Law was putting in place his long-held economic plan. His intellectual certitude led to an increasingly centralised control of the economy, and at a stroke he abolished the thousand and one different taxes levied in the country, aiming to replace them with a single national tax and in the process abolishing the measurers of cloth and coal, the meat inspectors, the examiners of pigs' tongues, and every other branch of petty officialdom whose jobs depended on the innumerable imposts levied by the government. Such a step was popular: the price of staple foodstuffs, and of basic necessities such as coal and wood, fell by a third. The poor received help from the government; the University of Paris was endowed. Public works were started, to provide barracks for troops, to create bridges and dig canals. Law even wanted to turn Paris into a port.

He had brought the country back from the edge of bankruptcy; now he was transforming it.

All the while, the Mississippi shares went on rising. From the early heights of 1,000 *livres* in the summer of 1719, they rose to two, then three, then four thousand *livres* until, in August, they reached the unheard-of heights of *five thousand livres* a share! At this point, Law made a final issue of 324,000 shares at the nominal price of 5,000 *livres*, but they were effectively auctioned to the highest bidder. Those who had bought at the bottom of the market, for a few hundred *livres*, could not believe their luck; those who pocketed the profit went on spending sprees which forced up the price of land and houses. They bought horses too, and furniture, books, works of art and jewellery. Parisian theatres were packed with the nouveaux riches; crowds swelled around the shops. Law himself bought vast tracts of land: the duchy of Mercoeur from a princess; at St-Germain, a million *livres*' worth of overpriced land belonging to a marquis, and then an estate in Normandy. At the height of the boom, the child-king Louis XV is said to have complained, when shown the latest map of Paris, that the rue Quincampoix was not marked in gold.

'All the news of this town is stock jobbing,' reported the British Embassy, gloomily, in its next dispatch. 'The French heads seem turned to nothing else at present.' To which the ambassador, the Earl of Stair, added: 'Mr Law tells them that their first returns from the East Indies will bring them fifty millions profit.'

Up and up soared the shares, so that by the end of 1719, 500-*livre* shares were selling for thirty times their original value, at 15,000 *livres*. In one month alone they rose 1,000 per cent. The term 'millionaire' was coined during these heady times, but it was a status which, as John Law was proud to recount, was within the reach of many. 'What make of people and what profession has not shared in the riches that have arisen from the new System?' he asked proudly. 'Lands and houses are at double, nay treble the value to the seller, and will increase considerably in revenue . . . the merchants and workmen have not enough to answer the demand of the buyers. The common people, and even those who by the meanness of their fortune can scarcely be ranked in any class, all of them in short find a way of life to thrive and enrich themselves.'

There are many tales of instant wealth, their common thread the power of money to disrupt the mind, combined with a mixture of envy and admiration of that instant wealth, and a mischievous delight in the overturning of the established social order. Inevitably, it is impossible to separate fact from fiction. But the prevalence of such tales illustrates the vibrancy of Law's System, and all show how even the professional classes forgot themselves when money was at stake. The Regent's physician Chirac was said to have heard a rumour at some point that the price of Mississippi shares was sliding. The shock of such news so dominated his thoughts that, while holding a patient's wrist to take her pulse, he exclaimed, 'My God, it falls! It falls!' It was a while before she and her family could be convinced that she was not in fact dying.

The stories also show a world which, if it was not exactly turned upside-down, was certainly levelling out. At the Opéra, ladies were surprised to find themselves sitting next to bejewelled servants who had made their fortune. Some servants became rich, it was said, because they were sent to the rue Quincampoix to sell shares for their masters. With the price rising by the minute, they would wait for the shares to rise beyond the selling point laid down by their masters, then take the extra profits for themselves. One was said to have sold shares at 10,000 *livres* rather than the 8,000-*livre* target he had been set, and by speculating with the profits made a million *livres* for himself. Another bought shares which, in the time it took him to buy a meal, rose by more than 10 per cent. John Law's own coachman, made wealthy by his speculation in the Mississippi stock, resigned from his master's service and, as a final gesture of goodwill, presented him with two men who might serve as his successor. When Law protested, saying he needed only one coachman, his departing servant replied, 'But I will engage the other myself.' An impoverished widow from the provinces had been forced, some years before the Mississippi madness, to accept state bonds in payment of a debt; by exchanging the bonds for Law's stock, she amassed a fortune of 100 million *livres* within three years.

Women, literally, threw themselves at Law in their desperation for shares. One lady who failed to win an invitation to a dinner party Law was attending even forced her servants to shout 'Fire!' outside the house where he was eating, so that she might grab his attention as the guests tumbled out in alarm. 'Mr Law came in person some days ago with the Duke de Antin to Quincampoix Street,' reported the *Weekly Journal*. 'He was no sooner discovered but the whole street was in tumult, and the throng was so great that several people were trodden down in the mud. This hurry was increased by Mr Law throwing several pieces of gold among the crowd, which set them to thrusting and pushing one another with intolerable violence.'

The extraordinary events of the year were also recorded by the Duchess of Orleans, Charlotte-Elizabeth, or 'Liselotte', mother of the Regent and the second wife of Philippe, the brother of the late king, Louis XIV. Blessed with a keen eye and a sharp wit, she always saw herself as an outsider, a German princess who never quite settled in her adopted country, whose marriage never worked because of her husband's homosexuality, and who became one of the greatest chroniclers of her age – prejudiced and opinionated, a spontaneous and sometimes bawdy observer of the social scene. In a letter from St Cloud of 23 November 1719, she wrote:

A lady whom M Law didn't wish to see thought up an astonishing way to speak to him – she ordered her coachman to turn her carriage over in front of M Law's door, calling out, *Cocher, versez donc!* At first he refused, but then he obeyed his mistress's command and overturned the coach in front of M Law's front door, so that she couldn't go in or out. He rushed up to her in a fright, thinking she might have broken her neck or her legs, but as he approached the lady told him that she had done it on purpose to talk to him.

On another occasion, a woman of a certain age tricked Law into meeting her and used the occasion to beg him for *une conception*, when she meant to say *une concession*; to which Law replied that he would certainly oblige, but she had perhaps left it a bit late. Liselotte watched duchesses kissing Law's hand as they begged for shares that would make them even richer, and amused herself by wondering which parts of Law's anatomy were kissed by people of lower social rank. They would, she eventually surmised in language not fitting to her social position, willingly kiss his arse.

As the share price in Mississippi stocks rose, so Law's truly intellectual invention gave birth to ever more fanciful ideas in the chase for the next idea that would bring even more instant wealth. In August 1719, Law's Irish friend Sir Richard Steele, a member of parliament, wrote to his mentor to advise him of his own brainwave. 'The King has given me his letters patent, for the sole use of bringing fish alive and in good health, wherever taken, to any other part however distant,' wrote Steele, 'and it is well known how ill Paris and other parts of France are supplied with that commodity . . . and the thing itself is a service to the world in general.' It was, nonetheless, admitted Steele, an idea which had attracted 'a great deal of ridicule and contempt' from the 'greater, unthinking part of the world'. But then, a sixty-one-ton floating pool which would roam the seas for fresh-fish markets was simpler to understand and laugh at than the great System which had brought such stunning wealth to so many and which was the mystical product of Law's incisive mind.

In the British Embassy, the Earl of Stair harboured such fears over Law's ambition that he could no longer be restrained by diplomatic convention. Without permission from London, he warned the Regent that, through his vanity and presumption, Law would cause trouble with England. Law, he declared, was 'doing everything that lay in his power to destroy the good understanding between the King [George I] and the Regent; and I bade the Regent beware how he trusted the reins of his chariot to that Phaeton Law, because he would overturn it'. Secretary of State Stanhope, made fretful by his ambassador and anxious to appease the Regent, voyaged to Paris to undermine Stair and apologise in person. But Stair reported back to Whitehall his repeated fear that England's economy would be ruined by her old enemy:

> Law in all his discourse pretends he will set France much higher than ever she was before and put her in a condition to give the law to all Europe; that he can ruin the trade and credit of England and Holland wherever he pleases; that he can break our bank when ever he has a mind, and our own East India Company. He said publicly the other day at his own table, that there was but one great kingdom in Europe, and one great town, and that was France and Paris.

On 5 January 1720, Law was appointed Controller-General of Finances, the highest administrative post in the country, awarded, he was told, in honour of his success. He was, effectively, prime minister and almost as his first gesture he gave 100,000 *livres* to the Church of St-Roche, which had received him into the Roman Catholic faith and in so doing had made his appointment feasible. Law's native city, Edinburgh, from which he was still exiled, sent him the freedom of the city in a gold box. The *Weekly Journal*'s Paris correspondent reported to his readers in London:

Had you been an eye-witness, as I have been, of what France was before Mr Law's administration, and what it is now, you would be astonished at the stupendous change . . . By his wise management, in a very short time, the national debts have been paid, taxes removed, art encouraged, commerce improved, and credit restored: in one word, the nation rescued from ruin.

This is what Mr Law has done for a *foreign* country; and I doubt not but that time will come, when you will see him as forward, as he is able, to serve his *own*.

But Stair did not share such enthusiasm. Law had told him that he would sell £100,000 of East India Company stock at 11 per cent below its market rate in order to force down its price and disrupt the London stock market: 'You may imagine what we have to apprehend from a man of this temper, who makes no scruple to declare such views and who will have all the power and all the credit at this court.' Law's apotheosis forced the British into action, persuading them to follow the example set by the man they had exiled a quarter of a century earlier. 'The Mississippi Affair goes on to an unaccountable height,' reported the *Weekly Journal* again; 'the monstrous things that Mr Law has done for the advance of public credit are looked upon with astonishment, not by us only, but by all the world.'

The rue Quincampoix, all madness and money, proved to be the precursor of England's equally febrile fate at the hands of the South Sea Company. It was but a short step from the rue Quincampoix to Exchange Alley, where the stockjobbers touted for trade in the shadow of Wren's magnificent cathedral. Dire warnings from its diplomats in Paris would spur the British government into action. Stair's colleague there, Daniel Pulteney, warned that France would declare economic war against the country:

> Mr Law says he shall now gain the most important point in his System, which was to draw into his Bank all the gold and silver of the Kingdom; to suppress entirely the use of the gold coin, and to allow no more silver than is absolutely necessary for small payments. The gold is to be sent abroad to turn the balance of the exchange and to purchase all the silver that can possibly be got; commissions for this purpose are to be sent to Genoa, Cadiz, Amsterdam and London.
>
> I am told that Mr Middleton, the Goldsmith in the Strand, who is Mr Law's agent and banker has already heaped up in his house very considerable quantities of silver.
>
> *Mr Law has said that he will drain us of all our silver.*

The British government should not have been so worried. Law's alchemy was not as effortless as it seemed. 'No one could be cleverer than M Law,' commented Liselotte, drily. 'But I wouldn't change places with him for all the world: he is being tormented like a soul in hell.' For Louisiana had been forgotten by investors in the headlong rush to make money. Instead, it was money that was making money, based on credit, rather than a realistic analysis of the Mississippi Company's trading prospects. To bolster Louisiana's population, in a second phase of his colonisation policy Law decreed that prisoners should be released from French jails, providing they first agreed to marry. They were lined up and ordered to choose their partners at first sight. Squads of troops in blue uniforms roamed the countryside and the towns in search of new recruits for the benighted land abroad. Well might the Earl of Stair world-wearily remark: 'There can be no doubt of Law's catholicity since he has established the Inquisition after having first proved transubstantiation by changing paper into money.'

The warnings to the British government about Law's stunning success, however, now came more frequently, and with greater urgency. A diplomat at the British Embassy in Paris told ministers in London that Law planned an all-out assault on England's stock market, and was already buying shares:

> I am assured that Mr Law has great dealings in them on account of his Company; that thirty millions of livres have been sent to Holland and employed this way, besides what has been done directly from hence to London. Mr Middleton, the goldsmith in the Strand, is Mr Law's chief agent in these matters. I am assured likewise that the value of £200,000 in gold is to be sent from hence tomorrow for London consigned to Mr Middleton.
>
> *You may depend upon it that Mr Law's design is to make such a strong and sudden push on our stocks as we may not be able to stand and he thinks himself sure of success.*

Within days, vast quantities of gold were shipped from Paris to Amsterdam, en route, it seemed, for London.

The situation was intolerable. Britain was under attack from the new French wealth. Something had to be done.

CHAPTER VI

The New Economy

*Japanese investors are in the throes of an e-commerce boom
that destroys the old adage: 'Once bitten, twice shy.'
Need an example?
The stock of Yahoo Japan – the Japanese offshoot of the
Silicon Valley-based web company – is currently trading on the
Tokyo exchange for over one million dollars per share.
That's right, dollars – not yen. For every share of this risky
Internet stock, an investor could buy 50 shares of Warren
Buffett's famously expensive, but universally coveted Berkshire
Hathaway shares. Nobuo Tanaka, Japan's representative for
trade, industry and energy affairs at the embassy in Washington,
reports that only four or five shares of Yahoo change hands each
day. Then, in another sign of Internet-induced mania, Mr
Tanaka himself – abandoning his carefully chosen diplomatic
language – had just one word for Yahoo's stock price.
Insane, he said, insane.*
the Globalist.com, 25 February 2000

George I had opened Parliament in November 1719 in sombre
mood. He spoke of the 'extraordinary expense' that the country's
wars had caused and declared that, with prudence, the government
could establish, upon a lasting foundation, both peace in Europe and
trade across his kingdom. Then he moved to the root of the difficulty:
Parliament must sort out the country's finances. 'I must desire you,'
he appealed, 'to turn your thoughts to all proper means of lessening
the debts of the nation.' The House of Commons dutifully assented,
but the way forward was far from clear.

The national debt was greater than ever, a corrosive element
undermining the Whig ministry and eating into its credibility. The
subject was like the weather; it was shared by everyone and talked
about with frequency, especially by the country gentlemen who
debated its impact and argued over solutions without necessarily
understanding the complexity of the topic. The economy itself might
be intrinsically healthy, not least because of England's rich agricul-
tural land and continuing trade with India and Africa, but most
speeches and newspapers described the 'heavy burden' of the interest
payments the government was forced to carry, the financial mill-

stone round its neck. Everyone had an opinion about the debt and such opinion mattered: the vote of the country gentlemen had to be kept sweet by any government, as Harley had discovered to his cost.

The national debt was now so large that nobody could accurately calculate its size, but it would cast a shadow over the century that the next generations could not escape. Nothing, it was feared, could grow in the shade of the annuities the government had been forced to grant to pay its way in the never-ending struggle against Louis XIV. Some annuities were to run for the best part of a century, so the government was locked seemingly for ever into making these irredeemable annual payments: a short-term fix to bring in cash had succeeded only in forcing it deeper into the financial mire. The Treasury faced an annual bill of more than three-quarters of a million pounds simply to service its debt, on top of which it owed the same amount again each year in interest on a whole raft of one-off redeemable debts that it did not have the wherewithal to quit. *A million and a half pounds* in interest payments alone, at a time of peace, when money was cheap again, and all this when Law was presiding over a resurgent, resplendent France.

'They write to us from Paris,' reported one journalist, 'that the people went dancing about the streets, as if they were distracted for joy; they now pay not one farthing tax for wood, coal, hay, oats, oil, wine, beer, bread, cards, soap, cattle, fish, or, in a word, for anything'. In England, as if in contrast, thousands of wool- and silk-weavers in London and Norwich were taking to the streets to protest against poor pay and conditions, sometimes tearing foreign silks and calicoes off women's backs. As if to rub it in, John Law had set up his own manufacturing base in France to process English material, backed by generous government grants. 'Many thousands of our manufacturers are now out of work,' complained the *Weekly Journal* on 5 December 1719, 'and one half of those at present employed are kept at work only upon the hope of some relief from this session of Parliament. As the riches, strength and power of Great Britain are owing to the manufactures which we, by our neighbours' folly, got from them, it is to be hoped we shall not be so infatuated as to throw them back again.' No wonder the country members of Parliament were so restless.

The King was still deep in debt, too, and ready for any measure that could dig him out of his financial hole. After the Restoration, Charles II had been granted more than £1 million a year in taxes by a Parliament seemingly anxious to make amends and grateful for a return to traditional, royal stability. But by the time William III took the throne, the politicians were more cautious about allowing monarchical freedom to spend. Conditions were laid down to circumscribe the cost: if there was to be a monarchy, it was to the good if it existed on the cheap.

George at least had a guaranteed income, of £700,000, voted through by Parliament in May 1715. But there was *so much* to spend it on. It wasn't that he was particularly sociable – indeed, for the most part he kept himself to two rooms, where he was waited upon by two Turks he had captured during one of his military campaigns; and while he enjoyed gambling, he played cards privately rather than at court. But the upkeep of the royal household was expensive, its running costs totalling more than a quarter of a million pounds a year. The household below stairs cost an average of £87,000 a year; there was the King's wardrobe – another £23,000; bedchamber staff cost at least £15,000 a year; then there was £10,000 a year spent on stables; another £33,000 on buildings and gardens. On top of which, while George lived quietly at St James's Palace from October to May, in the summer months he entertained on a grander scale, moving between Kensington Palace, Hampton Court and Windsor before returning again to London for the winter. The summer's entertainment alone could cost an extra £15,000. A king could not live like a pauper, but George, through little or no fault of his own, was haemorrhaging money, and the bills were kept down only when he left the country, as he did frequently, to visit his beloved Hanover. He had even accepted a deal brokered by Walpole to make peace with his son, provided the government paid off the royal debts of £600,000, a proposal which had helped Walpole win back his place in government, in June 1720, as Paymaster-General of the Forces again.

In all, the annual deficit in the first half of George's reign was probably more than £100,000. The King, therefore, came to an agreement with the Chancellor of the Exchequer, John Aislabie, to sell royal favours. The expedient he struck was a simple one. In order to live within his means, and as part of the peace deal with his son, he proposed selling royal charters of incorporation, specifically to two insurance companies which were prepared to pay £300,000 each for the privilege. The windfall would be used to pay for the gathering royal debt, and also to line the pockets of Walpole who had a large shareholding in both companies. In this way, from a murky background of financial dubiety and political chicanery, two of the country's most prestigious and reputable financial institutions came into being: the London Assurance and the Royal Exchange Assurance Companies, which were incorporated in June 1720.

But more was needed, and the success of France in eradicating the national debt and catapulting itself into the position of a leading economic power could hardly be ignored. There was so much money in France that it was flowing out of the country, and crossing the Channel to wash up on English shores. Forty million pounds' worth of new projects were being launched, backed by French money and attracting wealthy investors like the Duke of Portland and Joseph Gage, who had made so much out of speculating that it was said he wanted to buy a kingdom for himself. This rush of projects in England, and applications to patent them, were signs that there was too much money in the French economy, that the holders of excess share-dealing profits were blindly chasing ideas in which to invest. Nothing, it seemed, could halt the inexorable rise of the Mississippi stock in Paris. 'You, Mr Mist in England,' scoffed Daniel Defoe from his observation post in France, directing his wit at the Jacobite Nathaniel Mist, who ran the *Weekly Journal*, 'you are a Parcel of dull, phlegmatick fellows at London; you are not half so bright as we are in Paris, where we drink Burgundy and sparkling Champaign.'

Nearly a decade after the launch of Robert Harley's first scheme to swap £9 million worth of government debt for stock, the South Sea Company and the government sat down behind closed doors to discuss a similar deal, but on a much larger scale. The deal mirrored, too, the debt-for-shares exchange of 1719 which had appealed to the country gentlemen, both because it had lowered the national debt and because the Company had paid half a million pounds for the privilege. As the two sides talked, however, it became clear that the size of the Treasury's indebtedness, and therefore of the share scheme that Blunt was about to propose, was almost beyond imagining. The calculations were complex, but when the sums were done, it appeared that the government owed £16 million on the redeemable debts it should have paid off, but couldn't because it had no money to its name; and another £15 million in the irredeemable annuities which it couldn't pay off even if it wanted to, because it was locked into the annual payments. In reality, the government was so deeply in debt that it couldn't even calculate how much it owed: £15 million was an artificial figure, based on cutting down the term the annuities had to run to between fourteen and twenty years, rather than the ninety or more some of them should have run, and on fixing a compromise rate of interest somewhat to the disadvantage of those who had bought the deals with the longest terms. *Thirty-one million pounds* was now, or so it seemed, the true size of the national debt: no wonder the government was anxious to strike a deal with Blunt to shed the burden which so dragged it down politically.

Blunt, for his part, was just as anxious to come to an agreement. In the persuasive but intrinsically nonsensical analysis he put forward, he made it clear to his fellow directors that, as surely as night follows day, the bigger the debt, the greater the profit. Blunt was offering to pay the government for the right to own the national debt – and then aiming to float it, by selling shares in this vast, multimillion-pound liability in order to make a profit. It was as implausible a way of trying to make money as had ever been invented, but the dazzling promise of prosperity that Blunt held out blinded those present at the meeting – as it would blind the whole country – to the reality, which was that he was cooking up a financial nonsense.

What sounded complicated was actually very simple: the key ingredient was the gap between the price Blunt aimed to pay the government for buying the national debt, and the price he would charge to investors for taking shares in it. He planned to purchase the national debt at par – that is, creating a single £100 share for every £100 worth of debt – and then to persuade the government's creditors to exchange their annuities for shares in the Company at a higher market rate. So, for example, if the shares went up in value tenfold, to £1,000, then Blunt only needed to issue a *single* £100 share to redeem £1,000 worth of annuities. What's more, he would have nine of his original £100 shares left over (worth £9,000 on the market) for his own profit. The shares had to be issued at the highest possible price, so that, from the Company's viewpoint, as few as possible would be needed to buy up the existing debt, and then it could sell the rest for its own enrichment. How much stock actually needed to be issued was down to the market price, not to an exchange rate fixed by the legislators. This was the essential part of Blunt's calculations, the missing link in Parliament's handling of the affair.

The plan, like many strokes of financial genius, was both attractive and deceptive. The higher the shares rose, the greater the profit for the Company, so within the huge boundaries of the £31 million national debt the profit margin was potentially enormous. Therein lay Blunt's financial alchemy: his carefully thought-out plan to make serious money out of the nation's perpetual debt crisis, a crisis that threatened to stretch across the century, well beyond the lifespan of the politicians and their capacity to solve it.

Human greed was the other key to the affair. Logically, it was absurd to sell shares in a concern whose sole business consisted of servicing the national debt; but by making the debt the responsibility of the South Sea Company Blunt was wiping the Treasury slate clean – which was irresistible to the ruling classes – while investors, lured by the rising share prices that he came to engineer, were drawn, moth-like, to the flames. An investor who had lent money to the government would have to be sure that Blunt was offering a much better deal than he already enjoyed from the Treasury before he agreed to swap his guaranteed government income for shares in the Company. Blunt aimed to convince him that there was a quick profit to be made in a rising market, that a rise in the share prices was beneficial to him, even though that very fact would *reduce* the number of shares the investor would be offered if he converted his annuities or loan. It was at this precise point that Blunt would start to make his fortune. But his calculations depended on a booming stock market. Unless the company's shares went on rising, he could not make his profit.

Blunt knew that any proposal to take over the national debt, however welcome, faced political difficulties, not least because if the Company converted the entire debt into shares, then with a capital base of £31 million it would overtake the Bank of England to become the country's largest financial institution, and the Bank was bound to fight for its future. So the South Sea Company formed a subcommittee to plot its strategy. On it were Blunt himself, the Company cashier Robert Knight, the sub-Governor Sir John Fellowes, the Deputy Governor Charles Joye, and the directors Edward Gibbon, Richard Houlditch and Robert Chester. These seven men formed the group whose tactical acumen, underhand dealings and lack of scruples were well suited to exploiting the baser aspects of human nature. But Blunt and Knight were the key figures. It is hard to resist the notion that the pair were hard-headed businessmen who saw in the South Sea Company another money-spinning venture, who went into it less for the riches it might bring them than for the thrill of the chase and, above all, out of a spirit of competitiveness with the Scotsman across the Channel.

They were helped by the fact that neither of the government's leaders fully understood finance. Sunderland and Stanhope were simply out of their depth, even if Sunderland was, in name, First Lord of the Treasury. When Blunt first suggested his plan to them, he was rebuffed not by lack of interest but by their ignorance, and was told to approach the Chancellor of the Exchequer, the ineffectual Yorkshireman John Aislabie. Aislabie had been around long enough to realise the fierce opposition such a radical plan would raise. Just as Harley had found with his creation of the South Sea Company itself, there were too many vested interests that wanted to strangle financial newcomers at birth. Aislabie's political antennae told him that the East India Company and the Bank of England would fight the Company every inch of the way, rather than yield institutional and establishment supremacy to a parvenu. Astutely, therefore, he suggested Blunt should approach the Postmaster-General James Craggs, the father of the Secretary of State at the Foreign Office.

The elder Craggs was a political fixer, a tough politician who had made it to the top from humble beginnings as a footman in the service of the Duchess of Norfolk. He had made a small fortune twenty years earlier by creaming off the profits as a contractor supplying clothes to the Army. The Tower had claimed him for his dishonesty, as it had claimed Walpole, but George I had pardoned him. Aislabie knew full well what he was doing in propelling Blunt towards Craggs the elder; the clear message was that for the Company to overcome the inherent establishment opposition to its proposals, then a price had to be paid, and Craggs would determine the scale of the largesse that was needed and to whom it should be given.

In consultation with his son at the Foreign Office, Craggs set the political tariff for support and, like the fixer he was, declared who needed to be bought. Parcels of money, of £10,000 or more, or promises of shares in the newly expanded Company, were quietly dispensed to those who mattered. Secretary of State James Stanhope was deemed to be incorruptible. But his cousin Charles Stanhope, who was Secretary to the Treasury, was more open to persuasion. From the King's mistresses and their nieces, to a score and more politicians in the corridors of Parliament, share handouts were accepted and delivered. The Duke of Portland was allowed to convert his annuities on favourable terms; a quarter of a million pounds' worth of shares was handed out to ministers and their associates; twenty-seven members of parliament were bought up as well as six peers of the realm.

As the government and the Company negotiated, both sides extracted sweeteners to make the deal more palatable; for its part the Company would be paid £1 each year for every £1 the government saved on interest payments on the debt (though a lower amount was agreed for some of the annuities). For the government, the interest rate it would still pay on the national debt once the Company had taken it over was to be reduced after seven years from 5 per cent to 4 per cent, saving it £400,000 or nearly the entire cost of the standing army. Aislabie calculated that the saving on interest payments meant that the national debt could be eradicated within his lifetime. The Company would also give the government up to £3 million in the first year after the deal was completed, either to pay any annuitants who did not want to convert into South Sea stock, or for the government to keep as a present if the money was not needed.

There was just one problem: Blunt had no money. The South Sea Company had barely traded in its life – indeed, had hardly been near the water – so the notion that it possessed millions was risible. Ironically, at the tail-end of 1719 Philip of Spain declared he would strike a peace deal with England, and the prospect of trade with South America once more became a realistic prospect. But the Company no longer had the heart for any commerce except that conducted on dry land, in the hidden corners of Parliament and in the coffee houses of Exchange Alley. The directors' prime concern was to sail close to the wind, not to foreign shores. Like the denizens of the rue Quincampoix, Blunt and his colleagues were hoping for, indeed staking their financial future on, an inexorable rise in share prices. Only then could Blunt siphon off the excess profits which lay enticingly between the par value of the Company's shares and wherever they peaked – only then, indeed, could he find the multimillion-pound handout he had promised the beleaguered government. Wrote the anonymous author of the contemporary *Secret History of the South Sea Scheme*: ''t'was his avowed maxim, a thousand times repeated, that the advancing by all means of the price of the stock, was the only way to promote the good of the company'.

The South Sea scheme was ready to be launched in all its venal glory; John Aislabie, the Chancellor, steadied his nerve by buying £22,000 worth of shares and selling them quickly at a profit as word spread that the Company stood on the brink of a big announcement. Then, on 22 January 1720, he stood up in the House of Commons and made the most important, and dishonest, statement of his dull political career, which was followed by a brief statement of support from Craggs the younger. Aislabie listed all the advantages which would accrue if Parliament allowed the South Sea Company to take over the national debt. Interest rates would fall; the government would save money on servicing its debt; indeed, within twenty-five years the debt might be paid off altogether simply from the yearly savings the government would make. What's more, the Company would actually *pay* the government for the privilege of removing the millstone from around its neck.

The House was stunned into silence. Those who came to the scheme afresh were too staggered to reply; those who knew kept quiet, lest their corrupt behaviour be held up to the light. But for all their planning and for all their bribery, the debate did not go entirely to plan for the South Sea directors. Despite the stupendous offer the Company appeared to be making, an offer which was too good to refuse (and, for the sensible, too good to be true), some of the MPs who had not been corrupted proved remarkably open-minded about the sudden turn of events, and would not be rushed into making a hasty judgement that they might come to regret. One of their number, Thomas Brodrick, kept a note of the debate and recounted what happened in a letter to his brother, the Lord Chancellor of Ireland. In it, he gave a clear indication of the way the government had orchestrated the proceedings:

> A profound silence ensued for a full quarter of an hour. I rose and was pointed to. I readily agreed with the two gentlemen who spoke, that till the national debt was discharged . . . we could not properly speaking call ourselves a nation; that therefore every scheme and proposal ought to be received and considered . . .
>
> The occasion of my now speaking was, that the first gentleman who spoke [Aislabie] seemed to me to recommend the scheme not only in opposition, but even exclusively of all others; and that the next [Craggs] had chimed in with him. I hoped, in order to make the best bargain we could, every other company, nay any other society of men, might be at as full liberty to make proposals as the South Sea Company, since every gentleman must agree, this to be the likeliest way to make a good bargain for the public.
>
> Our great men looked as if thunderstruck, and one of them in particular, turned as pale as my cravat. Upon this ensued a debate of above two hours. Our ministers (as they might in committee) spoke again and again; Mr Aislabie, in heat, used this unguarded expression – things of this nature must be carried on with a *spirit*; to which Sir Joseph Jekill, with a good deal of warmth, took very just exception; this *spirit*, says he, is what has undone the nation; our business is to consider thoroughly, deliberate calmly, and judge of the whole upon reason, not with the *spirit* mentioned.

It would be comforting to imagine that the opposition faced by the government was a consequence of independence and integrity among all the members of parliament who chose to voice their concern. But it would be wrong. The difficulties the ministry encountered were largely the result not of disinterested opinion, but of vested interest. The parliamentary supporters of the Bank of

England, only a quarter of a century old yet firmly wedded to the Whigs since the day it was born, rushed to its defence. They would not be hurried into approving such an extraordinary financial measure – not from any diligent critique of the palpable nonsense that had been dished up before them, but rather because they wanted to give the Bank time to rally its forces and protect a monopoly which was so clearly under threat. If the Company could succeed in nullifying the national debt, then it was hard to imagine that the old way of doing things, as represented by the Bank, would survive such an assault on its position in the establishment.

As the debate went on, the Bank's supporters and the Company's men argued their respective cases fiercely. Indeed, so sharp was the division between them that the central question – whether it was actually a good idea to sell off the national debt in this way – went unanswered. By extension, and by omission, the answer had already been tacitly given: the Company's scheme, or one close to it, would be accepted. The only question was whether the Company could retain control of the idea it had developed, or whether it would be forced to stand by and watch the Bank of England wrest the prize from its grasp.

When the debate was finally adjourned to allow both sides to make fresh proposals, a delay which was in itself a small victory for the Bank's supporters, two clear outcomes had emerged. The answer to Law's economic boom in Paris lay in handing over the British government's debt to a third party; and the Bank of England, far from being a pillar of financial probity and solidity, had shown itself to be built on the shifting sands of self-interest. It offered no considered opposition to the Company's proposals; no warning of the dangers to the country's financial system or to the economy passed its lips. Its motive was simple and selfish: if it did not win the forthcoming battle for supremacy, the Sword Blade Bank – constituting as it did one half of the South Sea Company – would be the leading financial institution of the day. Could the Bank of England, the national bank, allow itself to be cut down to size by a company that had started by making rapiers? It must not happen. The Bank decided simply and crudely, for political advantage, to try to beat the South Sea Company at its own perfidious game.

Urgent meetings were now held in three centres of power. MPs who were members of the Company hurried to its splendid new headquarters, South Sea House. At the Treasury, ministers gathered. At the Bank of England, the directors met.

In the Treasury, the Chancellor of the Exchequer meekly suggested dividing the spoils between the Bank and the Company; but Blunt, who feared his master-plan was slipping out of his hands, declared: 'No, sir! We will never divide the child!' The Bank was bolder. Its directors decided to try to trump the Company's offer. The purchase of the national debt had become, incredibly, the subject of a blind auction. Within a few days, the Bank tried to better the deal the South Sea Company had put forward, the Company responded, and the Bank increased its offer again. The Bank of England was now offering £5.6 *million* for the privilege of taking over the national debt, and would reduce interest rates from 5 per cent to 4 per cent in four years' time. The holders of long-term annuities would receive £1,700 in Bank stock for every £100 of income they were receiving each year.

The South Sea Company was slipping behind in the race. But, unlike the Bank, it had not set a limit on how much stock it wanted to create. This was the final crooked piece in Blunt's complex jigsaw. There were to be no legal or political restrictions to the Company's expansion. If the shares were in demand, and their price rose as sharply as those in Law's Mississippi venture, then Blunt could continue to issue shares to make fatter and fatter profits for a company which had no purpose except that of debt-holding. The Company's future was open-ended. There would be no limits to its growth, nor to the amount of money that could pour into its coffers.

This fatal, and distinctly profitable, idea persuaded Blunt to outbid the Bank of England at any price. With the help of Charles Stanhope, Secretary to the Treasury, but working without the knowledge of some of his colleagues in the Company, he put together an improved offer. The size of the Company's gift to the government was raised again, this time to £4 million, but on top of this Blunt proposed that the Treasury should receive up to a further £3.5 million, the actual sum depending on how much of the debt was changed into shares. *Seven and a half million pounds to buy up the national debt!* The country members in the Commons could hardly believe what was happening; the debt had been transformed into a commodity so valuable that the two leading financial institutions of the day were trying to outbid each other in its pursuit. The world had turned upside-down; insanity had become reason. A debt of unmanageable proportions, which had eaten into governments and royalty alike for as long as anyone could remember, was now more precious than any gold mine in the world, or any of the riches in South America for which the Company had been founded, partly, to discover.

In the absence of a contemporaneous record of the debate which followed the government's launch of the South Sea Bill, history has cast a kind glow on those who failed to support the Company, but much, again, was down to the Bank of England's influence over the Whigs. This was almost certainly the position of Robert Walpole, who backed the Bank's rival scheme. He saw nothing wrong in principle with the plan to issue shares in the national debt, despite a later tradition which has suggested he was the sole voice to declaim against stockjobbers and to warn of the ruin that would be visited upon the nation. Thomas Brodrick's account noted that 'Mr Walpole applauded the design [of the South Sea Company], and agreed in general the reasonableness of [it]'. Certainly, Walpole had bought thousands of pounds' worth of shares in the Company, though he had halved his holding to £9,760 in January 1720. But he was also buying government annuities, knowing that the South Sea Company would be seeking to convert them, and by the end of January he had somehow acquired, and sold, £18,000 worth of shares for £24,383.

But Walpole did use his keen political intellect to cut to the core of the South Sea scheme, the crucial component that was to provide Blunt and his associates with their greatest opportunity for profit. Walpole determined to force the Company to declare just how many shares it would give to the holders of annuities. He wanted to lock Blunt into a fixed rate of exchange, and Blunt, just as badly, wanted to play the market. Sensing the danger, Blunt spread his favours ever more liberally, buying up a dozen more members of Parliament by selling them discounted stock, worth more than £100 on the market, at less than £2, the *douceurs* duly noted in the green book carried by the Company cashier Robert Knight.

The Company's preferred method of bribery was to award notional stock to its friends at a heavily discounted price: but they didn't actually have to hand over any money. Instead, many were granted the rights to sell the fictitious stock when the market had risen, so they could pocket the profits for no outlay and no risk whatsoever. The two Craggs, father and son, and even Sunderland himself, who was allowed the right to make a profit on £50,000 worth of stock, were thus ensnared. Two lords, four more MPs and the Treasurer to the Navy joined the circle. They were all recipients of what was a magnificently clean bribe – indeed, in its own corrupt way, a thing of beauty. In all up to a million pounds' worth of notional stock was handed out to oil the wheels of politics. And because the great and the good were supposedly 'buying' stock, others quickly followed suit with real money – investors like the Earl of Halifax who bought £4,000 worth of shares, or the Duke of Chandos, who pulled his money out of France to invest in 'one of the best funds in Europe'. The Duchess of Rutland instructed her stockbroker to buy as much as he could with her money 'and sell it out again next week'.

When the second reading of the bill passed easily through Parliament, London found itself gripped by intense political speculation. The denizens of the coffee houses could talk of little else and the price of South Sea stock swung wildly according to the latest rumour – down to 270 when the news seemed bad, or up to as high as 380 when the prospects of Blunt and his colleagues were supposedly in the ascendant, at which point the directors could almost taste the profit they soon hoped to enjoy. But the directors knew they were far from home and dry (and the metaphor seemed appropriate given the Company's disinclination to ply the world's waters in search of trade). The prospects of a majority in Parliament for the final passage of the bill seemed to slip with each passing day, as the pamphleteers set to work to press Walpole's – and the Bank of England's – cause. From amidst the broadsides came a prophecy from one anonymous polemicist who predicted with unerring accuracy that the South Sea directors had been 'cooking up the project for seven or eight months past, under the pretence of paying off the public debts, but if they are let alone they will turn this great design into a private job; and when they have worked up their stock by management to an unnatural price, they will draw out and leave the public to shift for itself'.

On 23 March, Walpole mounted his final attempt to sink the South Sea Company's bill. His motion asked the House of Commons to 'receive proposals from the South Sea Company, whereby it might be fixed and determined what share or shares of and in the to-be-increased capital stock of the said company, the proprietors of the said annuities should be entitled to have and enjoy'. The debate lasted for six hours, as the two vested interests, the Bank of England and the South Sea Company, locked horns through their surrogates. Walpole exposed the dangers of allowing the Company free rein to set its own terms and conditions for converting the national debt. But the Company's supporters retorted, with straight faces, that fixing the price might 'endanger the success of so beneficial an undertaking'.

When the government won the vote by ninety-six, South Sea stock climbed steeply to 400 in celebration. The Earl of Halifax sold out quickly, doubling his £4,000 stake; Hoare's Bank sold its holding for a £7,000 profit, and Robert Knight showered another nine MPs and four peers with shares. In contrast, shares in the Bank of England slid downwards, reflecting its sudden and seemingly terminal decline as a national institution. In the House of Lords, Lord North and Lord Grey railed gamely against the inevitability of history, attacking with prescience 'the pernicious practice of stock-jobbing which produced irreparable mischief in diverting the genius of the people from trade and industry'. But it was in vain. On 7 April 1720 the bill received royal assent.

A week later, with London in a ferment, King George I, Governor-General of the Company, travelled to South Sea House and, with great aplomb, deposited £100,000 from his dwindling funds (though it transpired later that he had paid only the first instalment of the total amount). Like the Duke of Orleans in France before him, he was demonstrating his confidence in the financial enterprise that would quash the national debt, though unlike the Duke he was, in all probability, up to his neck in the scam. His shares had been given to him at a 300 per cent discount by Aislabie and the younger Craggs.

For the moment, however, all that mattered was that the old order had been overturned. The share price was soaring. The new economy was born.

CHAPTER VII

Greed Is Good

Jonathan G. Lebed was not shy about telling people that he found his suburban New Jersey hometown a singularly uninteresting place.

'Is Cedar Grove a boring place to live?' he wrote in a letter to the editor of the Cedar Grove Observer. *'To the younger generation of this town, the answer is most certainly "yes."'*

To help pass the time, Jonathan, like many 15-year-olds, used the Internet to manipulate the stock market, racking up almost $273,000 in illegal gains, the authorities charged. Jonathan, a junior at Cedar Grove High School in Essex County, became the first minor ever sued by the Securities and Exchange Commission. On Wednesday he settled with the agency, not acknowledging any wrongdoing but repaying a total of $285,000, including interest.

'He's kept his cool and his composure throughout the day – it didn't faze him too much,' Tom McCarthy, a classmate since kindergarten, said after school yesterday.

New York Times, *22 September 2000*

The ages of great financial speculation, which occur as irregular outcrops of fool's gold in the landscape of global economic history, have brought with them riches and ruin in almost equal measure. For every industrial or economic invention that sparks a gold rush, there are canny investors who spot an early opportunity and leave the fray as quickly as they entered it, with their profits safely banked. But there are just as many who, inspired by the possibility of quick riches, back a copycat project which has scant chance of success. So it was in 1720, when the South Sea Company rose to financial and political prominence and became the effective engine of the economy. Through political leverage and bribery, it so skilfully manipulated expectations that its share price was buoyed by optimism and corruption rather than by any realistic analysis of its chances of success. Like John Law's Mississippi Company in France, it captured the popular imagination through the daring of its enterprise. Just as Law had done, the South Sea Company won establishment approval by convincing the government and the King that its directors could eradicate the national debt; and that was enough to guarantee that its shares were traded at a premium on Exchange Alley. But unlike the Mississippi Company – however unsuccessful it would turn out to be – it had no intention of fulfilling its professed aim of trading with the world.

From its fine offices at South Sea House on the corner of Threadneedle Street, the South Sea Company helped create an economic climate where every new project seemed destined to make money and reap a rich reward for those willing to invest. The dash for cash in 1720 saw plenty of investors with more money than sense, and some with little of either. This was a time of apparent alchemy, when money could be made from paper. Inevitably, it seemed to many, any paper, any shares, would create a fortune. According to one newspaper of the time, some investors were gullible enough to respond to the following advertisement:

> Such Persons as are desirous to be Proprietors may on Thursday next purchase permits . . . at five shillings each, at Baker's coffee-house in Exchange Alley. N.B. No permits will be delivered for less than £1000 and not more than three permits to one person, to prevent their being engrossed by a few, as 'tis to be feared has been lately done.

When prospective investors duly appeared, they were issued with a permit to take up 'a certain subscription to be made some time or other, they did not know when; to some certain scheme or other, they did not know what; proposed by some people or other, they did not know who; for the insurance of ships, etc., they did not know how'. The permits were signed with fictitious names by the promoters of the so-called 'Great Undertaking'. Later, the promoters revealed the true nature of their enterprise and offered to return the money they had taken. They declared that they merely wanted to 'convince the public, with what Facility designing people, under Colour of an Advantageous Undertaking, may at any time impose upon a credulous Multitude'.

Such credulity was understandable, though at this stage it was far from universal. Word spread quickly that there were quick profits to be made, but many investors sold out early on in order to bank their money. Men like Isaac Newton, scientist and Master of the Mint, soon sold his entire £7,000 holding and doubled his money. His motive was clear: the discoverer of gravity knew that shares that went up might come down. Asked what he thought of the Company's prospects on the market, he apparently replied that he could predict the motion of the heavens but not the madness of people. The Age of Reason was not dead after all, despite the seemingly inexorable rise of the Age of Insanity, though later Newton was tempted, disastrously, to defy gravity with a further bout of speculation.

The battle between the two Ages was reflected in the Company's share price, as it began to fall below 300 in the spring. But Blunt was alert to the risk. Following John Law's example, he knew that credit was the fuel which would propel the South Sea Company ever upwards – thereby establishing the dominance of the Age of Insanity. On 14 April 1720, in what was called 'the First Money Subscription', Blunt offered £2 million worth of new stock, at the market price of 300, of which only 20 per cent had to be paid in advance, the rest every two months. The lottery he had spawned less than a decade earlier, 'the Adventure of Two Millions', had been superseded by a £2 million adventure on the stock market. For investors with an eye to a profit it was a gilt-edged opportunity: a succession of two-month windows in which to sell the stock for the full price, without a heavy outlay. To a nation reared on gambling, whose gaming instincts had been so honed and exploited by Blunt and Harley in the lotteries of earlier years, this represented not so much a game of chance as an opportunity to roll dice that were heavily loaded in its favour. Investors did not even need to be able to afford the full amount to take part – at least, not if the 'gamble' paid off.

Blunt, however, was gambling too. He was offering shares in a sliding market, and to do so he was stretching the letter of the law. Under the terms of the South Sea Act, he was not allowed to create stock until he had started the process of converting the national debt. But Blunt's political antennae proved to be as sharp as his financial acumen. The politicians made no protest, and the market snapped up the share launch. Secretly, Blunt expanded the issue so that more than £2.25 million worth of stock was sold. Despite the issue's clandestine expansion, the market was far from sated, and the price of the stock began to move inexorably upwards. *A million pounds was taken in the first hour!* Blunt was making money even before his scheme to convert the national debt had started. At this point he knew he was sure to reap the riches that Law was gathering across the Channel. As he had predicted, the stock was soaring on Exchange Alley, guaranteeing an instant profit to anyone who had bought shares, even though they had only part-paid for them. Who now needed hard cash, as Wren had so desperately needed the coal-tax pennies to build his cathedral only two decades earlier, a cathedral that stood silent sentinel over the hurried dealings in the narrow alleyways and coffee houses at its feet? For credit would provide all, and by judicious selling an investor could buy and sell, sell and buy, and make profit after profit without having to find anything like the true capital sum he was staking.

A decade earlier, in Robert Harley's time, Defoe had penned a pamphlet on the subject. 'Credit,' he wrote, 'is a consequence not a cause; the effect of a substance, not a substance; 'tis the sunshine not the sun; the quickening something, call it what you will, that gives life to trade; gives being to the branches and moisture to the roots; 'tis the oil of the wheel; the marrow in the bones, the blood in the veins and the spirits in the heart of all trade, cash and commerce in the world.' Credit was now, however, a substance in its own right: the very root of the South Sea Company's success.

Dazzled by the profits which could be made for a small initial stake, few who took part in the headlong rush to invest saw fit to question the basic profitability of the company that was driving such paper wealth. If they had, they would have realised what was going on: Blunt was simply exploiting the notional profits of his Company, before it had actually made a penny. But the stockjobbers didn't care. Rumours of improved trading prospects helped to bolster the share price. The King of Spain, it was held, 'would give up ports in Peru in exchange for Gibraltar'. Alternatively, the Company 'was poised to trade with South Africa'. It was just stock-market gossip, some of it promoted by Blunt and his fellow directors, which helped to camouflage the essential vacuum that lay at the heart of the South Sea Company: that it had no business plan and no market for its goods; indeed, it had no financial prospects whatsoever other than the self-fulfilling nature of its enterprise. It attracted investors because investors were attracted to it.

Blunt now decided to pour more fuel on to the bonfire. The

Company had taken in so much money that he judged he could afford to mount what was effectively an operation to support the price of its shares on the market. He persuaded a meeting of the Company's ruling body to back his view that the Company, awash with cash, could grant even more generous terms to investors. Blunt decided not just to offer them credit on their share purchases: he announced that, like Law, he would actually *lend* them money to buy shares, half a million pounds in all, up to an individual limit of £3,000. The share price rose again, and the General Court, already overshadowed by the considerable personality of John Blunt, melted away, destined not to meet again for many months. Blunt was on his own, successfully recycling investors' money to boost the Company's share price, while the Company itself carried out no business whatsoever, other than sucking up cash, to justify its pre-eminent market position. The more money it took in, the more it could support its own share price; the more the share price was supported, the more it would make money by offering less and less stock to the government's creditors.

Not only that: the more money it took in, the more spare cash it had to pay its promised bribes. Because the Company had actually taken in more money than it had been allowed on the First Money Subscription, by issuing excess shares, it had untraceable reserves of cash to pay off the politicians who had been bought with notional stock. Some £400,000 in cash was disbursed to just twenty-one beneficiaries, the first tranche of more than a million pounds' worth of bribes which were handed out to the great and the good. With an average of £20,000 in their pockets, the recipients of the Company's largesse were the equivalent of millionaires today. By fair means and foul, the Company appeared to be transforming England's fortunes, just as Law had changed those of France. No longer could Defoe pour scorn on the dullness of London life compared with the gaiety of Paris.

And the Company had triggered a rash of new projects, a host of imitations. It was the age to be alive, the age to shrug off past cares, the age to make money. John Blunt's vision was the fashion of the day, and such modernity would drive the share price every bit as hard as Blunt himself. The country, it seemed, had come of age and was embracing a glowing new future. 'The hurry of our stock-jobbing bubblers especially has been so great this week that it has even exceeded all that was ever known before,' reported one newspaper. 'The subscriptions are innumerable; and so eager all sorts of people have been to engage in them, however improbable or ridiculous soever they have appeared, that there has been nothing but running about from one Coffee-house to another, and from one Tavern to another, to subscribe, without examining what the proposals are. The general cry has been "For G—'s sake let us but subscribe to something, we do not care what it is!"'

New promotions were running at twenty, then thirty a month in these hectic days of spring. Ingenuity and fraud, intellect and corruption, were exhibited in almost equal measure. Some schemes were truly inventive, others madly speculative, still more were speculatively mad. Some aimed, quite simply, to take advantage of the gullible; others demonstrated the ingenuity of the age, even if the invention of the projectors, as they were known, was not always matched by the practical ability to realise their dreams. With money to spare, and an eye to a fortune, investors were invited to take their pick from hundreds of new ventures. Some were inspired by the South Sea Company's success; others had been formed earlier or, inspired by Law in France, created by the wash of money which had flowed from successful Parisian speculators. Many were insurance companies, promoted by a desire to reduce the cost of shipwrecks in an age of overseas trade, or to defray the cost of fire, or to soften the blow of premature death. The Sadlers' Hall Insurance Company, formed with a capital of £2 million, was created in February 1720. Several marine insurance companies were floated for more than £1 million each. Only in two known cases were companies formed with a capital base of less than a million.

But while England boomed, so too did the satirists who foretold disaster. As the year unfolded, the humorists, like the money-makers, were in their element. The world was divided into those who passionately believed in the new order, and those who poured scorn on it with ever greater, and more sophisticated, effect.

Wrote one correspondent to a newspaper:

The World of late has run into so many whimsical projects, prithee for once, publish the following to see how they will encourage a good one.

The Projector, by long Study, has attained to a certain method of melting down Carpenters Chips and Saw-Dust, &c. and running them into Planks and Boards of all Lengths and Sizes.

Hereby all Gentlemen, Builders and others, may, upon ten Days Notice, be furnished with Boards and Planks adapted exactly to the Dimensions they want, at least twenty five per cent Cheaper than yet has been known.

These Boards will be free from Knots and Sap, and delivered grained or not grained, as shall be desired.

The Projector promises himself, that he shall shortly be able to give them a Tincture of Marble shade, or any other fine Stone Colour . . .

The Composition in these Boards has a secret vertue which prevents their shrinking, and destroys all Bugs and Vermine that come near them.

Proposals for erecting a Company, and raising Joint-Stock of one Million five hundred thousand Pounds, on very advantageous Terms to the subscribers, will shortly be published, and the Projector will be glad (in the interim) of an Opportunity to confer with any Gentleman of Ingenuity upon so beneficial a Scheme; and, for that purpose, will give daily Attendance at Exchange Alley, at the Cock in Birchin Lane.

From this time on, the new investment schemes became commonly known as 'bubbles', a term which was effectively the creation of the South Sea period, although in fact it had been used earlier: Shakespeare, for example, describes a 'bubble reputation', and in Thomas Shadwell's *The Volunteers*, written in 1692, men cheated or 'bubbled' each other for profit. Certainly, the use of the word became commonplace in 1720 and contemporary illustrations suggest that it was understood literally: like their counterparts in soap and air, which probably provided the inspiration, financial bubbles were perfectly formed, and floated free of gravitational market forces. But the implication, of course, was that there would be a day of reckoning, a time when they would grow too large to hold their shape, leaving them to implode with spectacular, and messy, consequences.

Indeed, the sheer variety and improbability of the burgeoning companies inspired a printer called Bowles to bring out in June 'A New Pack of Bubble Cards containing 52 Copper Cuts of Bubbles; with a satirical Epigram upon the same; Price 2s 6d'. The Five of Hearts set the tone:

> They talk of distant seas, of ships and nets
> And with the style of Royal gild their baits;
> When all that the projectors hope or wish for
> is to catch fools, the only chubs they fish for.

But for all the sceptics, there were thousands of converts to the cause of instant wealth.

From his pitch on 'Lucky Corner', the confluence of Lombard Street and Cornhill, in front of the open space known as the Stocks Market, a humble bookseller watched the excitement unfold, and resolved to make his fortune.

Thomas Guy was the sort of man who might take a risk, but only after carefully weighing the odds and looking at all the angles. Perhaps the caution came from his relatively humble background: his father was a lighterman and collier, who brought sea-coal to London and the south. Or perhaps it came from an inherited grasp of business: his father owned barges which plied their trade throughout the Thames basin. He was born in 1644 or 1645 in a house in Pritchard's Alley, in Horsleydown, amongst the narrow streets of the poor district of Southwark. With his stern gaze and heavy jowls, Guy appears, from the portraits painted of him, to be a man who did not suffer fools gladly; but there was compassion, too, underlying his frankly appraising gaze. Both qualities, the no-nonsense man of business and the caring humanist, would be demonstrated over the years to come.

Guy had made some money from his shop near the new Royal Exchange, built after the Great Fire. Booksellers, in those days, were publishers too, and by 1684 Guy and his colleague Peter Parker had been appointed University Printers, a position they held until the vested interests of the Stationers' Company saw them off, though not before Guy had banked a healthy profit of more than £10,000. So Guy was not a poor man, but he lived frugally, and stories soon spread about his supposed miserly habits. He was held to use a newspaper for a tablecloth in his home in Lombard Street, and to light only one candle. Unimpressed by the reason for one caller's visit, he extinguished even this, declaring, 'If that is all you have come to talk about we can very well talk it over in the dark!' He was even said to have abandoned his intended wife because she extended the pavement outside his shop, for which he had to pay.

In the reign of Queen Anne, in the first decade of the eighteenth century, Guy invested some of his money in government securities. In all probability he bought 'seamen's tickets', which were effectively IOUs to the sailors of the Royal Navy, issued by the government because it could not afford to pay their wages while it was locked in the ruinous War of the Spanish Succession against France, the war Robert Harley had ended so ignominiously in order to launch the South Sea Company. The seamen were happy to sell these slips of paper, which promised to pay 8 per cent interest until the debt was paid off, but to do so they had to take a sharp cut on the sum they were owed – sometimes as much as half. A speculator like Guy bought the tickets at a low price and took the risk that the government would be able to pay him back at a profit if the Exchequer managed to replenish its coffers. When the South Sea Company took over part of the national debt in 1711 under Harley, Guy was one of the government's creditors who had handed over his stake in the debt for South Sea stock. Nine years later, over the course of a few months, Exchange Alley held out before him the enticing prospect of wealth, as he watched his £54,000 holding first double, then triple. He could not believe his luck.

Cautious man though he was, Thomas Guy was caught up in the excitement of the age.

John Blunt had steered the Company through the choppy waters of Parliament, and the wind was now set fair. So too was the prospect of making a fortune. He moved to a large house in the West End of London and, like many investors, bought himself a fine carriage which he drove to South Sea House in the City. The humble scrivener of old was not just a financial success but a social success too, a self-made man, fêted by London society as its leading businessman extraordinary. His attendance was required at the highest levels: at court, or at aristocratic balls. He was the man who made money, and, although it was not overtly stated as the reason for his social popularity, the man who could make it for his hosts.

Each day, the coffee houses rang to the excited chatter of promoters and speculators with money to gamble. As the South Sea stock began to rise, so the roads around Exchange Alley roared with the rush of traffic, with Cornhill and Lombard Street frequently blocked by coaches, and the Alley itself, like the rue Quincampoix before it, full of eager investors spilling into the passageway, packed shoulder to shoulder and barely able to move. Newspapers reported on the life and gaiety of Exchange Alley, where businessmen, dressed in fine cloth, with gold and silver upon their coats and on their shoulders broad ribbons of green or blue, gathered to buy and sell shares, their footmen waiting with their coaches until the deal was concluded.

Coffee houses such as the Fleece, Jonathan's and Garraway's often spilled on to the pavement as eager stockjobbers dangled subscription lists in front of prospective buyers. At the Three Tun Tavern in Swithin Alley, the company 'for a general Insurance on Houses and Merchandize' was trying to persuade backers to part with £2 million. At Garraway's, a million was being raised for building and buying ships to let for freight. At the Rainbow Coffee House in Cornhill, another million was sought 'for granting Annuities by way of Survivorship, and providing for Widows and Orphans'. At Sam's Coffee House, behind the Royal Exchange, yet another million was needed for 'lending money by the month on plate, watches, jewels or any other goods honestly come by, at a moderate rate'.

From the fashionable quarters of London, from Kensington and from Chelsea, from Westminster and Piccadilly, they came: the rich who wanted to be richer. Within a short while the less wealthy came, too, as they sought to better themselves, and so did people from outside London as news spread by word of mouth and by newspaper of the money that could be made. Even women were able to invest, the pace of change on the stock market exceeding the capacity of the law to rule against their doing so. Many of the women at the Princess of Wales's court were speculators, and at the other end of the social scale the women at Billingsgate market were said to talk of nothing else but buying and selling South Sea stock. For a country brought up on the national lottery and used to the penal taxation rates imposed by war, here were opportunities by the dozen, which were not to be missed. As in the lottery, everyone could win: the question was, how much? 'To speak in gaming style,' declared one observer of the scene, 'the South Sea stock must be allowed the honour of being the gold table; the better sort of these bubbles, the silver tables; and the lower sort, the farthing tables for footmen.'

A man like the bookseller Thomas Guy had a vast array of projects before him in which to put his money. In the month of January 1720 alone, companies with a nominal capital of more than £6 million were floated – constituting nearly *a third* of the total share capital of the joint-stock companies already in existence in England. There were proposals to buy land to build on in London; to build or rebuild houses throughout England; to erect houses or hospitals for illegitimate children; and to clean and pave the London streets. Merchants who sold their goods in the towns and cities saw an opportunity to expand. They formed trading companies for dealing in hogs; for buying naval stores; for supplying London with sea-coal; for supplying the London market with cattle; and for furnishing the cities of London and Westminster with hay and straw.

The bubbles also reached into the countryside. The release of pent-up energy and ideas at this time provides a clear indication of the state of rural Britain and of its inhabitants' enthusiasm for improving their lives. Countrymen wanted investment to improve lands in Flintshire and the Lincolnshire fenlands, to buy forfeited estates, and to buy lands for the corn trade. Other projectors aimed to improve the breeds of cattle and horses, to improve tillage, gardens and church lands, to erect turnpikes and wharves.

Inventors and engineers jostled to find backers. There were ventures to bring water to London by a new canal from St Albans, to bring fresh water to Liverpool; to make an engine to supply fresh water to Deal in Kent; to make the River Dee navigable, and the River Douglas. A host of enterprises sought investment underground, from the tin and lead mines of Cornwall and Devon to the copper mines of Wales and the lead mines of Derbyshire. One company produced a patent for heat-resistant paint; another company made fire-engines; there was a company for raising hemp and flax in England; for improving malt liquors; and for drying malt by hot air.

A bewildering array of outfits aimed to sell oil, and salt and sugar; to make rapeseed oil and beech oil, and to make oil from poppies, sunflower seed and radish seed; there was the Salt Project, the Rock Salt Project, and the Saltpetre Company; and schemes for refining sugar, and for bleaching coarse sugar 'without the use of fire or loss of substance'. There were companies to make sail-cloth, or cambric and muslin; for improving silk and cotton manufacture; for preparing tobacco to make snuff; for making glass bottles and glass coaches; for making pitch, tar and turpentine; for making china and delft-ware; for making paper, pasteboard, packing paper, starch and soap. There was even an improbable project for the transmutation of silver into malleable fine metal and for extracting silver from lead.

The fishing industry tried to catch investors, too. Naturally, there was Sir Richard Steele's project, which he had pressed upon John Law, to create a floating pool to bring fresh fish by sea to London. But money was also sought for the North Sea Fishery; the British Fishery; Garraway's Fishery and the Orkney Fishery. The Royal Fishery Company, incorporated after the Restoration, took in a new subscription of capital; and the Grand American Fishery proved so successful it attracted £1.5 million. The Two of Spades in Bowles's 'New Pack of Bubble Cards' summed up the enterprise, and in doing so provided an appropriate, and enduring, metaphor for the year:

> Well might this bubble claim the style of grand,
> Whilst they that raised the same could fish by land;
> But now the town does at the project pish
> They've nothing else to cry but stinking fish.

Of the 190 companies launched in 1720, only four survived. The *Daily Post* was one of the newspapers that invented their own rival versions: in one issue it declared that projectors were trying to raise money 'for an engine to move the South Sea House to Moorgate'. Other newspapers claimed, variously, that projectors aimed to import jackasses from Spain to improve the breed of British mules; insure all masters and mistresses against the losses they might sustain by servants; insure marriage against divorce; and invent a wheel for perpetual motion. Later, one pamphleteer published a broadside entitled *The Battle of the Bubbles*, with a list of increasingly implausible companies:

An Hundred Offices of Insurance against the *Venereal Disease*, by what Title soever dignified or distinguished, each to raise Five Hundred Thousand Pounds.

Fifty different Offices for *Speedy Cure*, if the Insurance fails.

As many more to Cure the *Gout*, *Stone* and all other Diseases.

An Hydrostatical Air-Pump. To draw all manner of Wind and Vapours out of Human Brains.

Five Hundred Thousand-Pounds for Building Automatons, i.e. Carriages for conveying single Persons, thro' and about, the Cities of London and Westminster, and all other pav'd Places, without the help of Four-footed beasts; the Motion is to be perform'd by the Person carried, who is to wind up his Wheels every two Thousandth yard.

It is propos'd that every proprietor shall be able to ride in his own Coach and Six, in Nine Months, by the Profits arising from this Machine.

N.B. A *Flying-Engine* is under the Consideration of the Author of the *Automaton*, and is speedily expected to be seen in the Air.

Where invention ended, and absurdity began, was hard for people to tell in this year of the bubbles. Many of the ideas seeking investment were genuine attempts to improve people's lives, as well as to make money for their promoters. Other projects were nonsensical, either because they were ill thought-out or because they had been proposed by charlatans. But how could an ordinary citizen, caught up in the excitement of the boom, tell which was which and decide where to put his money? As technology advanced, even some of the flights of fancy promoted by the satirists came, in time, to be true, making rich men of the inventors of horseless 'Automatons' for the road and of the 'Flying-Engine' for the sky above.

Despite the written barbs, and in the absence of any organised political opposition to the South Sea Company's influence, the power of money and the fear of debt proved to be irresistible forces. Some of the speculators who had made money in Paris had begun to transfer their dealings to the London market. They were an aristocratic crowd, and to any who might have been wavering, likely to impress: among their number were counts and abbots and the sons of the Governor of the Austrian Netherlands, but the Scottish Whig nobility invested too, including the Earl of Rothes who celebrated his elevation to Lord High Commissioner to the Church of Scotland by cashing in his notional 'stock' in the South Sea Company at a profit of £18,500. Army officers, who had to buy their own commissions (the going rate was £7,000 to become a colonel), gambled on the stock market too.

Their money told. Share prices began to rise sharply and out of all proportion to their basic worth. Shares in the Company for the Navigation of the River Douglas soared from £5 to £70, in the English Copper Company from £5 to £105 and in the London Assurance from £5 to £175. Other companies fared even better. Shares in the Orkney Fishery rose to ten times their initial value, the Kent water-engine project to twelve and a half times, the freight-shipping company to fifteen and the Welsh Copper Company to twenty-two. York Buildings Company shares jumped thirtyfold, from £10 to £305, London Assurance thirty-five-fold, and General Insurance reached a massive sixty-four times its original price. Even shares in Puckle's machine-gun company, supported by a new weapon, a supposedly potent sword of which, sadly, no details remain, rose from £4 to £8.

But none of these companies could compete with the South Sea Company. It issued thousands of standard share forms, headed with its motto *A Gadibus usque Auroram*, 'From Cadiz to the Dawn', forms which in their wording and appearance reinforced the monumental trading deceit that lay behind the Company. Inscribed on the document was the figure of Britannia, and all the Company's supposed appurtenances: a ship, the globe, crossed fish, and a fisherman and net. The Company had a single-minded dedication to manipulating the market. On 30 April, Blunt promoted the Second Money Subscription, hoping to push the Company's price beyond 400 by offering another £1 million worth of stock. Again, shares could be bought in instalments, with credit. The King and the Prince of Wales were reported to be among the investors.

But, for all the excitement, Blunt had yet to lay the foundation stone of his absurd and magnificent structure. The conversion terms for the national debt had yet to be announced: Blunt had still not declared his exchange rate – the level at which he would price the Company's shares when he came to offer them to the government's creditors in return for the debts they held. It was the next crucial step, the key to the whole enterprise. The higher the price, the lower the number of shares Blunt had to hand over, and the greater the number he could retain, to siphon off and sell. He knew he could pitch them high. The market was in a ferment over the Company's shares.

John Blunt and his South Sea Company stood on the brink of great riches.

CHAPTER VIII

Paper Fortunes

*After months of anticipation and hype, the Internet shopping
business Lastminute.com finally joined the stock market yesterday
and immediately crystallised a £150m paper fortune for its
founders, Brent Hoberman, 31, and Martha Lane Fox, 27.
Mr Hoberman and Ms Lane Fox, who have become pin-ups
for the new breed of net entrepreneurs, were in their Mayfair
offices early yesterday to watch the newly floated shares soar from
a sale price of 380p to 555p in minutes, valuing the
19-month-old company at £835m at one stage.
'I'm not quite myself today,' said Ms Lane Fox.*
Guardian, 15 March 2000

John Blunt should have been worried by the spurt in the share prices
of the rival projects, which were quietly siphoning off money that
otherwise would have been pouring into the South Sea Company's
coffers. But he felt only confidence. Investors at home and European
brokers abroad could not buy enough South Sea stock. From Geneva
and Bern and from Holland, the orders for shares poured in. 'The
South-Sea-Stock is now become the General Talk of the Town and
Country,' declared one newspaper, which despite its general air of
scepticism dropped its readers' letters to provide space for a detailed
page of calculations on the Company's latest offer to investors.

The proliferating bubbles offered the tantalising prospect not just
of wealth but of social mobility too: the means to gain greater status,
of the sort which it had taken Blunt a lifetime's work to acquire
(and even his rise was exceptional, in the stratified, enclosed ranks
of British society which had only reluctantly clutched a foreign king
and his mistresses to its political bosom in order to protect the established order). In the early months of 1720, however, it was very
much an establishment bubble that captured the attention of the
great and the good, rather than the lower social classes. At the outset
the Duke of Chandos became Governor of the York Buildings Company; the Duke of Bridgewater and the Earl of Westmorland signed
up with rival projects; the Duke of Portland poured more of his
money into South Sea stock; and the Prince of Wales became Governor of the English Copper Company, despite Walpole's objection
that the project would henceforth be known as a 'royal bubble', with

all the dangers that might entail if the scheme went wrong. 'The Speaker and Mr Walpole could not dissuade the Prince from being Governor of this Copper company,' wrote Craggs the younger to Secretary of State Stanhope, 'though they told him he would be prosecuted.'

While rival projects moved swiftly to gather in the cash they needed, Blunt was considering the critical decision he needed to make to fulfil the terms of the South Sea Act. There had been an enormous flow of money into the Company's reserves – £1 million in April and nearly £4 million over the next two months. But crucial to the future of the Company was the rate at which Blunt would strike the conversion for the national debt. A hundred extra staff were taken on in South Sea House to cater for the expected rush when the terms were declared, and as the countdown started, excitement in all things South Sea spread across the country. The rise of the South Sea Company and the movement of its stock price were charted daily in print, both in London newspapers and in the provinces. Meanwhile in France, Law's great scheme was faltering, leaving the way clear for the Company to capture investors across Europe.

On 19 May Blunt announced his deal. The terms were complicated, and depended on the exact type of government debt which each annuitant held, but most were offered the South Sea Company's £100 stock valued at 375. Even at this conversion rate, the shares were a bargain because they would go on rising, Blunt put into place the next stage of his operation, flooding the market with money to support the share price. A million pounds' worth of Exchequer bills were poured into the system; so too were the Company's reserves of cash, and, for good measure, the Sword Blade Bank offered credit too. This great wash of money was turned into a tidal wave of credit to enable speculators and investors to buy Company stock for a lower initial stake than ever before. For every £400 invested, Blunt decided to lend £300. His aim was to lower the entry price for investors in order to have the *opposite* effect on shares – to push up their price to the highest level he could, through the very demand he had excited. For the annuitants who were hesitating over whether to accept Blunt's terms, his offer looked irresistible. 'We hear that the South Sea Company have at length agreed to offer the Annuitants

£700 of original South Sea Stock for every £100 a year Annuity,' reported the *Weekly Journal*, 'which being more by some Years Purchase than the Annuities would sell for at Market, 'tis not doubted but it will be readily accepted.'

As the share price rose, more annuitants rushed to cash in their government debt. Overtaking the offer price of 375, the shares broke the 400 barrier and, seemingly unstoppable now, sold for 450, then 460, in Exchange Alley, pausing only when they neared the 500 barrier. Sheltering in his office from the great onrush of annuitants, the Company accountant John Grigsby handed out more than £3 million worth of stock before the week was out. In this way more than half the national debt, controlled by the Company, was rapidly transformed into its shares, in an exchange which saw the government's creditors turning their annuities or loans into South Sea stock at the high share price Blunt had decreed. The effect of Parliament's failure to fix the price at which Blunt should swap stock for debt was clear. By being allowed to exploit the rising market price for shares so as to buy the debt more cheaply, Blunt had captured half the national debt while keeping more than £20 million worth of stock in reserve at the current market rate.

Like France before it, the country was booming, flaunting the stock-market wealth that the Company was generating. The King celebrated his birthday with an enormous gathering, quite out of keeping with the parsimony previously inflicted by the need to run courts at home and abroad. More than a thousand bottles of claret were downed at his lavish party, and the Elephant trumpeted the value of her shareholding by wearing a dress covered in jewels which was valued at £5,000. The South Sea director Sir Theodore Janssen, with a million pounds' worth of share options in the Company, demolished a Tudor mansion in Wimbledon to build a new house. The younger Craggs was busy buying up a terrace of houses in Whitehall, which he too planned to demolish to make way for a splendid new residence. Another South Sea director was held to have compiled a fortune at the rate of £1 million a month, a total of more than £3 million in three months flat. Robert Walpole, fresh from arranging the reconciliation of King and heir, cleared a profit of more than £2,600 in sixteen days of hectic trading through his brokers, money which helped finance the never-ending decoration of his sumptuous Chelsea house and which enabled him to buy up wide acres of land back home in Norfolk.

For every millionaire, there were humbler investors who wished to raise themselves up, or to avoid the threat of debt which hung over them as it had the country. At his desk in the Office of the Commissioners of the Duties upon the Salt, a young man called James Windham had seen his chance. Windham, the son of one Ashe Windham, an easy-going squire of Felbrigg, Norfolk, hoped to better himself in life and become a royal equerry. The Bubble was giving him an opportunity to make his fortune, and he grabbed it with both hands. On 12 May – a week before Blunt announced his terms – he wrote to his father: 'We are getting in all we can; I have wrote to Sir Lambert Blackwell [a South Sea director] and I hope he will get you in 1000 pound of it.' Soon the whole Windham family – the son, his father, aunt and grandmother – would overcome their natural caution and start risking their savings to buy shares in Blunt's money-making machine.

But the paper fortunes of the investors were, unknown to them, already under threat. The sheer scale of the stock-market revolution the Company had created threatened its existence: it had, in effect, been too successful. Coupled with the new and emerging businesses, the South Sea Company's ascent gave the impression that the country was going through a financial revolution of the sort that Law had inspired in France; that a vibrant new energy was coursing through the economy, so that anyone with an ounce of business sense should climb aboard the new ventures or risk being left in the dark age of the old economic order. If the speculators, like the political leadership of the country, were ignorant of the actual economic forces which were propelling the country forward, they nonetheless moved sharply to embrace the benefits of this revolution without troubling to ask too many searching questions about the long-term merits of the course on which the stock market had embarked. For just as the politicians had been ignorant of financial theory when Blunt had persuaded Parliament to hand over the national debt, so investors were ignorant of the way high finance worked. It was a world inhabited by experts, and if the experts were creating wealth with support from the state, then the enterprise was presumed to have solid foundations.

Blunt's problem, however, was that, unlike John Law, he had not intended to unleash an economic revolution. Much like the company which sought to invent a wheel for perpetual motion, his plan depended on one vital but unachievable condition: the South Sea Company's share price had to keep forever moving, for if it was to stop, its shares would inevitably plummet. The rival projects that had gone such a long way to confirming Blunt's reputation as a financial genius were in danger of conspiring to do him fatal damage, by draining money from the market.

One speculator, up from the country, had his wallet stolen in Exchange Alley and appealed for its return in the *Daily Post*. His share-buying habits would not have pleased John Blunt:

Picked out of a Pocket Thursday May 5th about Jonathan's Coffee House, a black letter-case where was the following receipts. No 294 for Bricks and Tiles one share. No 1105 for Whale Fishing in Davis Straights £1,000. No 125 from the Grand Lessees of Mines Royal Mineral and battery and for smelting of Ores, £1,000. No 37 to Thomas Dyer Esq. For making raw silk, signed J Carleton £1,000. With several other papers of no use but to the owner. Whoever brings them to Mr Rowley at Jonathan's Coffee House in Exchange Alley, or to Jonathan Wilde in the Old Bailey shall have two guineas reward: N.B. They are all stopped at the books.

Abroad, too, the influence of the bubbles began to spread. Ships bound for Holland advertised the names of stockjobbing firms where orders could be placed before they sailed; in Amsterdam and other Dutch cities, stock markets sprang up to deal in a range of shares, but especially in insurance schemes. In Hamburg, too, eager investors poured into the Exchange. As far as Blunt was concerned, every pound spent on buying shares in alternative schemes was money which could have been used to shore up the South Sea Company's position. Something had to be done to puncture the smaller bubbles, while leaving the South Sea Company to float freely through the market. Plans for this eventuality had been prepared. Back in February, the Scarborough MP John Hungerford had persuaded the Commons to vote for a resolution condemning these rival flotations, and as a result he had been placed in charge of a parliamentary committee to investigate their growth.

In his youth, Hungerford had been expelled from the House of Commons for accepting bribes; and in all probability, although there is no direct evidence, the South Sea Company had paid him to press its cause. He now launched an inquiry of such startling favouritism towards the Company that it is clear he was either on the take, or that Blunt was considerably cleverer than his rival projectors at disguising his actions. There had been an outbreak of financial scandals across the City, Hungerford reported. Wherever he looked, it appeared that there was an iniquity that had to be addressed; but the South Sea Company emerged unscathed from his investigation. The result was a bill which aimed to regulate the City by clearing it of the bubbles that might threaten the Company. The King's proclamation, rich in unintended irony, declared that 'unwarrantable practices' had 'ensnared and defrauded unwary persons to their utter impoverishment and ruin, by taking off the minds of many of our subjects from attending their lawful employments, and by introducing a general neglect of trade and commerce'. Exchange Alley quietened down, and the South Sea Company acquired the business status which had been accorded John Law's Mississippi Company in France: it became a near-monopoly. Only a handful of rivals survived, thanks to a City solicitor, Case Billingsley, who used his legal knowledge to exploit loopholes in the Bubble Act, as it was known, which, he argued successfully, allowed joint-stock companies to escape closure.

In the wake of Parliament's move, Blunt scanned the stock market for signs of jitters and decided the time was right to offer another South Sea loan to buy shares, with advances of up to £4,000. Between 19 May and 14 June, the Company spent more than £3.5 million on lending money to investors to buy more stock. Once again, the impact was dramatic. On 29 May the shares stood at 500, but then the price began to leap prodigiously. The *Weekly Journal* of 4 June reported:

The Stocks since our last are as follows:
South-Sea

Saturday	508
Monday	555

Tuesday	605
Wednesday	765
Thursday	830

In total, the South Sea Company had spent £1.25 million on bribes; £2.75 million on annuities; and £4.5 million on loans, a total of nearly £8.5 million. It had £3.5 million in cash-in-hand, but in order to support Blunt's dictum that the only way to promote the good of the Company was to advance the price, by whatever means, the money was being spent almost as quickly as the Company was raising it. It was a hidden problem: the Company appeared to be thriving, and giving a boost to the wider economy. The Bank of England, although bested by the Company as the leading financial institution of the day, saw its share price jump from 150 to 220, and shares in the third pillar of the financial world, the East India Company, more than doubled.

In these circumstances, it was not surprising that the King, the Governor of the South Sea Company and possessor of thousands of pounds' worth of gifted shares, was prepared to put the seal of royal approval on the financial revolution. In his June honours list, John Blunt was knighted. The working-class man made good now stood near the pinnacle of British society; here was a baronet who had made millions for himself and for those who had the faith to invest in his project. The scrivener who had taken his first step up the ladder when the old established order gave way to Robert Harley's Tories was now the friend of the establishment, of royalty and of the ruling Whig elite.

Great things were planned for the South Sea Company. It drew up plans to move across London, to a splendid new South Sea Square in fashionable Piccadilly. But imperceptibly, one by one, tiny pebbles were being removed from under the foundations of Blunt's soaring, rotten enterprise. Wiser investors saw how much they had made on paper, and decided to take their profits. Like Isaac Newton, bookseller Thomas Guy, sensible and cautious fellow that he was, had already started selling, content to take a guaranteed profit even if it meant that over the next few months he would be forced to watch as the share price rose even higher. From April onwards he had started cashing in his shares in the South Sea Company. By June, he was out. The historian William Maitland, who published his *History of London* in 1775, records: 'Mr Guy, wisely considering that the great rise was owing to the iniquitous management of a few, prudently began to sell out his stock at about three hundred (for that which probably did not cost him above fifty or sixty pounds) and continued selling till it rose to about six hundred, when he disposed of the last of his property in the said Company.' Thomas Guy had made a fortune, a fact that he meticulously recorded in pen and ink in his personal ledger. He had converted his £54,000 holding in the South Sea Company into £234,428 in cash.

He was not alone in his exit from the Bubble. Sarah, Duchess of Marlborough, made and saved a fortune for her husband by forcing him to cash in his £27,000 holding, which was worth £100,000. Like Thomas Guy, she saw that the Bubble couldn't last. 'Every mortal that has common sense or that knows anything of figures,' she confided to a friend, 'sees that 'tis not possible by all the arts and tricks upon earth long to carry £400,000,000 of paper credit with £15,000,000 of specie. This makes me think that this project must burst in a little while and fall to nothing.'

By and large it was only the corrupt elite who understood what was going on. On 11 June the Secretary to the Treasury, Charles Stanhope, banked a profit of a quarter of a million pounds, although unlike Guy he had not paid for his initial investment and his profit merely represented the difference in the price of the notional shares when they were put down in his name and the price at which he 'sold' them. The Chancellor of the Exchequer, John Aislabie, also cashed in his shares. But the King, bound for Hanover for the summer and his mind already there, was not of the same persuasion. At a frosty meeting, the Chancellor tried to convince his King that the company of which he was Governor-General was not a sensible long-term investment: an accurate assessment, even if his rationale – that the stock had been carried upwards 'by the madness of the people' – was disingenuous in the extreme. But George was having none of it, and was only persuaded to think otherwise when the Chancellor pointed out that there was not enough money in the Civil List to pay for the next instalment on the royal shareholding, due within a week. Accordingly, George agreed to take his profit, which was a healthy one, of £106,000. Unlike his subject Thomas

Guy, however, he was not content to stop gambling. Instead, he insisted that the whole sum should be ploughed back into buying yet more South Sea shares.

Aislabie was appalled. The King was about to set off for his four-month sojourn in Hanover, and if the share price plunged then the royal finances would be wrecked. How could a leading politician, and one responsible for the Bubble, explain to his monarch that the company in which he, the King, had such an interest might be in such trouble? Aislabie simply could not find a way to put across his message without antagonising the King. The Chancellor, George declaimed, was a 'timorous' man, and he would buy more shares if he so chose. Eventually, however, perhaps through weariness and a desire to clear his head of all things English as he prepared to cross the Channel, the King reluctantly consented to a compromise. Some profit was banked, but some was reinvested. Thus was the throne, or at least its financial well-being, saved by a politician who had helped put in place the very scam he now recognised might destroy the country's future.

More important than this, however, was the sentiment of the stock market which Aislabie's attitude reflected. If it was time to buy (and many still thought it was), then it was also the beginning of the time to sell. Even as it neared the peak of its market popularity and even as the plans for the resplendent South Sea Square were being drawn up by a team of architects, a financial undertow was tugging at the Company. Despite Hungerford's partial success in banning the rival companies, the newly acquired riches of others were still being diverted elsewhere rather than reinvested. People had begun to buy land.

As the rich sought to spend their South Sea wealth, so the prices of estates soared to thirty, forty, sometimes fifty times their annual rent, and so the Company was deprived of the only fuel that could keep it flying high: money and more money. It was one thing to ban the rival bubbles, as the Company had successfully sought to do, but it was quite another to restrict the spending habits of a nation. In France, John Law had determined that land should be the ultimate guarantor of any country's paper currency; now, ironically, land became the very commodity which threatened to undermine England's strongest and most sought-after paper currency: South Sea Company shares. One stockjobber is even said to have given up his job selling Bubble shares to become an estate agent.

In mid-May James Windham, in the Salt Office, wrote a letter home: he was almost beside himself with excitement at the prospect of buying land, even though he himself acknowledged that, while his shares were increasingly valuable, he owed a large amount of money on them. He declared:

Dear Brother,
I am glad you have disposed of my horses, for I have business enough upon my hands. I grow rich so fast that I like stock jobbing of all things . . . Since the South Sea have declared what they give to the annuitants, stock has risen vastly. I have in mind to buy land, for I think land will rise in a little time, so he that buys speedily I take will have a pennyworth. I like to buy in Norfolk because land is cheap in comparison of nearer counties to London. I would not give much for a house because I don't reckon I should ever live in it. But I want an estate that will bring rent, if it is in a pleasant country so much the better . . . though I owe a great sum of money, I have a great deal of money at command. I would willingly buy a clever estate in land if it cost 10 or 15 or 20,000 pounds.

Windham had set his heart on buying the estate of Crostwight, near North Walsham in Norfolk, but in this he faced fierce competition from Robert Walpole. He continued:

You will see by this whole letter what a mind I have to purchase, so pray if you hear of any thing that is good, pray buy for me, for land will be dearer if stocks rise, so whether I buy land or stocks 'tis the same thing.
    The whole of my letter is, if you hear of a good estate near you, buy it for me, and don't stand about price. If we had bogled about your South Sea you would have lost £1000 by it. You are not to think I have got above 5 or 6000, but I have now a good deal of interest and power of money, and so I would buy an estate. As every subscription has immediately been worth above the price subscribed, so would I give £1000 more for that estate than he that buys it will pay for it.

The reason for the popularity of land investment was that both the newly enriched aristocrats and the nouveaux riches saw shares as a means to an end, and in perennially conservative England the end was the permanent status which land ownership could bestow.

Just as the King's mistresses had sought an English title to signify their new-found status, so too those who found their purses swelled beyond any reasonable expectation looked for a source of investment which they could pass on to the next generation. They were not alone: the directors of the Company themselves saw it as an essential accoutrement to their position in the financial world. The deputy cashier, Robert Surman, whose previous wealth had amounted to a field in Tewkesbury, bought twenty-seven properties in nine counties in 1720 and secured a grant of arms. John Blunt, too, was a serious investor. His property portfolio seemed endless: in London he bought up houses in Cornhill, Cloak Lane, Iron-Monger Lane and Tower Hill, a dozen houses at St Mary-Axe and more in Houndsditch; he also had a large house at Barge-Yard, Bucklersbury. In Middlesex, he owned a dozen properties; in Stepney, a house and dockyard, and more houses in Grays Inn Lane and Wapping; in Essex, he bought part of the manor of West Ham and a farm; in Surrey, he purchased a pair of houses in Southwark and the whole of the land called the Downs at Rotherhithe; in Norfolk, he acquired nearly a thousand acres of marshland. In all, Blunt spent £75,000 on land and property, the equivalent of several million dollars today. England's citizens were as traditional as they had ever been in the way they chose to express their wealth, even if the means of affording it were radically different from the past.

By early June, Blunt knew that if the Company was to stay afloat, there had to be another share launch. If he could successfully aim high with the price of the next share launch, then few would seek to question the intrinsic worth of his hollow enterprise and none would ask the most relevant question of all: how had a holding company for the national debt become such a valued asset? So on 15 June he pitched his Third Money Subscription at 1,000, some 200 higher than the Company's valuation in Exchange Alley. But he also made the purchase terms absurdly generous: 10 per cent down, and then 10 per cent in each instalment, spread over four years, with the second payment not due until July the following year.

The bargain was simply too good to resist. Even Robert Walpole, who had not traded in South Sea shares since March, had determined to buy his way back in, just at the point that Thomas Guy, a wiser man, banked his enormous profit. Walpole also tried to buy shares for his family and friends, and encouraged the Princess of Wales to do the same. The King invested again, in the name of Aislabie's brother-in-law, Vernon.

The rest of James Windham's family, so cautious in the early stages, now joined him in investing heavily: Ashe Windham, his mother and sister Molly all decided that no price was too high for South Sea stock. So popular were the shares that political contacts were needed to be sure of buying some. 'I am very glad you have written to Mr Walpole for £1000 Subscription,' wrote James Windham to his brothers. 'My mother spoke to my Lord Townsend on Sunday and he promised to get her in £1000 in the next. You need not put yourself to any difficulty for the money (but there is nothing so well as borrowing it in the country). If I have any spare money, when the time comes, I will lend it to you: if I have not, it is probable you may sell it out to advantage and pay no money at all.'

With such easy terms, even the relatively humble could make a profit. A porter in Exchange Alley was said to have made £2,000 in this way and bought a splendid coach. 'Our South Sea Equipages increase every day,' the *Original Weekly Journal* recorded. 'The City ladies buy South Sea jewels, hire South Sea maids, and take new country South Sea Houses; the gentlemen set up South Sea coaches and buy South Sea estates.' Another journalist reported that there were '200 new Coaches & Chariots in London, besides as many more now on the Stocks in the Coach-makers' yards; above 4,000 embroidered Coats; about 3,000 gold watches at the sides of whores and wives; and some private acts of charity'. Exchange Alley even became a venue for marriage, with Councillor Edwards of the Middle Temple plighting his troth to Madam Brand of Leicester-Fields, who, it was reported, was 'a lady of great beauty and Fortune, having got by the Rise of South-Sea Stock upwards of One Hundred Thousand Pounds'. A certain Mrs Barbier, the star of the Playhouse, made £8,000 and sang farewell to the stage. James Windham himself set his sights on an even grander estate than the one he had failed to capture, declaring that he wanted to buy the Heydon estate, also in

Norfolk, with its beautiful Elizabethan house. 'If that should come to be sold, I verily think I should bid like a South Sea merchant for it.'

Holders of government debt realised that they needed to move fast to trade in their annuities before the price went even higher, leaving them with fewer shares than they hoped for in exchange for their government holdings: 'It is impossible to tell you what a rage prevails here for South Sea Subscriptions at any price,' Craggs the elder informed James Stanhope, who was sticking close to the King in Hanover. 'The crowd is so great that the Bank [of England] has been forced to set tables with clerks in the street.'

In the Third Money Subscription, the general public was allowed to buy only a fifth of the shares, and the allocation was snapped up on the first day of issue. Politicians, too, invested as never before – at least half the Commons and half the Lords put their money into the share launch. Each director of the South Sea Company was responsible for marketing the shares, through their friends and political contacts, and the Company asked some of its favourite politicians to do the same, including Sunderland, Aislabie, and Craggs the younger. In this way, the Third Money Subscription saw the fortunes of the South Sea Company become even more tightly enmeshed with those of the political elite. Craggs raised nearly three-quarters of a million pounds in subscriptions, a tribute to his clubbability. More than one hundred and fifty MPs, three dukes and eighteen other peers signed up; and from the arts, Alexander Pope, the portrait painter Sir Godfrey Kneller and Vanbrugh. So too did Black Rod, the door-keeper of the House of Lords, and the Lord Chancellor, who put down £23,000 for his shares – an investment which presupposed payments of a quarter of a million pounds over the next five years. The poet John Gay received £2,000 worth of shares from his patron, and with Pope planned to buy land in Devonshire with the profits. Jonathan Swift, whose own investments were being supervised by Gay, wrote in a letter: 'I have enquired of some that have come from London, what is the religion there? They tell me it is South Sea stock. What is the policy of England? The answer is the same. What is the trade? South Sea still. And what is the business? Nothing but South Sea.' The summer roads were full of country gentlemen and rich farmers, travelling to London to buy stock.

Blunt had caught a bigger haul of subscribers than in any previous share issue, raising £5 million which should have gone into the Company's purse but much of which was instead spent on loans to help even more investors buy shares. The Duke of Portland was lent £78,000; Lord Castlemaine £41,000; Lord Hillsborough £31,800; the Marquis of Winchester, £24,500; Lord Rothes, £18,500; the Earl of Dunmore £26,500; Lord Chetwynd, £12,500; the Duke of Montrose, £13,800; Lord Belhaven £10,000; Lord Archibald Hamilton £10,500; the Duke of Montagu, £9,000; Lord Fitzwilliam, £8,000; Lord Londonderry, £8,000 and Colonel George Churchill, £7,000. No one wanted to miss out. On 29 July the Duke of Newcastle, anxious to ensure he would get his shares, wrote a self-serving letter to Charles Stanhope at the Treasury:

My dear Charles,
Being always assured of your particular goodness to me I have taken the liberty to enclose to you the names that I have given in to Lord Sunderland and he has promised to take care of them for the next subscription. I beg you would take care that he does not forget . . .
I really believe I shall by this get quite clear and by that means be better able to serve my friends.

South Sea shares were the rage, the fashion, the only subject of conversation among the upper classes and the country squires, the politicians and the bankers, where once before the national debt had been their favoured topic. When the Company closed its books for a month to sort out its accounts, the stockjobbers engaged in such a fever of speculation that the future price of the shares rose still higher, while Aislabie's stockjobbing son-in-law, Edmund Waller, quoted the highest price the stock ever reached, 1100. At that level, the Company was valued at more than £300 million the equivalent of many billions of dollars today and ten times the size of the debt it was holding. Yet its ships had not sailed anywhere near the South Seas.

Truly, the country had gone mad.

★   ★   ★

England now stood on the edge of a precipice. Few realised the danger: not the political leadership of the country, which had scattered from London in the wake of the King's departure for the summer break; nor the stockjobbers in Exchange Alley, though at its peak the Company's price began to tremble, and slip slowly downwards to 900. The summer party season had started, and the money which had been made, both in reality and on paper, was spent by many in the pursuit of pleasure. Great sums were won and lost at the races on Epsom Downs. The housekeeper to Sir Theodore Janssen, the sub-Governor of the South Sea Company, was married to a customs officer – a marriage made possibly for love and certainly for money: she had gained £8,000 from her South Sea shares. Great crowds gathered at a house in Hampstead for nightly gambling and a weekly masquerade. The Duke of Newcastle paid for a sumptuous banquet to mark the anniversary of the King's accession, and was held to be spending £2,000 a week while he was on holiday. 'They write from Nottingham,' a journalist reported, 'that the Duke and Duchess of Newcastle went to visit the Earl of Halifax at his seat of Horton, near Northampton, where they stayed two days; and, when they came away, the Duke left 100 Guineas to be distributed among the servants.'

Walpole left for Norfolk on 28 July, to contemplate the new estate at Crostwight which he – not James Windham – had bought for £21,000; and over the course of the summer, just as prices reached the very top of the market, he made a dozen land purchases, also in Norfolk. Janssen was given a diamond ring by the Prince of Wales, and was busy building his vast new house in Wimbledon. Secretary of State James Craggs the younger, telling friends that the South Sea Company would set him up for life, was effectively left in charge of the country, but his duties were far from onerous and he partied heavily in Twickenham. Even the pickpockets were thriving: among the possessions reported stolen in July were Bubble permits and receipts worth £12,000 and seven diamond rings of great value, 'one of them a Brilliant weighing 30 grains, and for which a reward of £200 has been offered in the papers'. London's investors, gorged on the excesses of the past few months, were content to catch up on some rest and to dream of future riches. Even as the summer passed its peak, James Windham was still writing optimistically: 'Stocks are much on the rise. I fancy it will be 1200 soon; if that happens [the new] subscription will at least be at 1500.'

Only Blunt was restless. Because the Company's share price had risen so high and because it had given such generous terms of credit to investors, its shareholders owed it some £60 million, which was *twice* the level of the national debt it had taken on. Quite possibly it was more money than the entire kingdom possessed, for these were not the days when a nation's economy could be measured, as America's is today, in trillions upon trillions of dollars. Even as he departed from London for his family holiday in Tunbridge Wells, his magnificent new coach proudly displaying his coat of arms, Blunt was ordering the Company to buy back its own shares in another share-support manoeuvre.

It was at this point that the monarchy and the government, entwined in the Company's unfortunate embrace, made their fatal move. Acting from the best of intentions towards its corrupt colleagues in the South Sea Company, the government banned its remaining rivals, the joint-stock companies run by City solicitor Case Billingsley. Public confidence was shaken. 'Blue-chip' insurance companies plummeted in price: within a week, Royal Exchange sank from 250 to 60, and London Assurance from 175 to 30.

It was, in retrospect, the turning-point, a defining blow against the whole psychology of bubbles, a blow which punctured the illusion that a new economy had been created, and with it an investment opportunity not to be missed by anyone looking for a rapid return on their money. Ashe Windham's aged mother wrote to him on 23 August that 'the fall of stocks and bubbles will make land do so'. But even then there was no panic among the investors in the biggest Bubble of them all. Ashe Windham's mother merely thought that falling share prices meant James might be able to buy his estate more cheaply than before. 'If Jemy does not purchase Heydon, he thinks he shall like Honingham,' she went on.

In fact, the South Sea Company was afloat without a rudder, and was heading for the rocks. It was small comfort, and perhaps no coincidence, to learn that France was already there.

CHAPTER IX

Bonfire of the Vanities

A landslide of selling crushed the markets today, sending stocks down across the board as Wall Street reacted to higher consumer prices that they fear will make sharply higher interest rates a certainty. The tickers on trading floors across the city were bathed in a sea of red — the color that announces declining prices.
The blood bath was most dramatic in the technology area as the momentum selling in overvalued high-tech stocks continued. The Nasdaq composite index crumbled, losing 355.49 points . . .
The stock market rout burst at least one bubble — the sense of invincibility among new investors, those who were sucked into buying stocks by the lure of what looked like easy money.
Washington Post, 15/17 April 2000

At the beginning of 1720, John Law had faced the same financial forces that eventually attacked John Blunt. Caught up in the excitement of the rival enterprise they were launching, the English had chosen to ignore the warning signs, not least because, as Law struggled on, money was pouring out of the rue Quincampoix and into South Sea stock. The investors who deserted the Paris market and moved to London brought with them their gold, rather than banknotes. France's ambassador in London, Destouches, observed the startling success of Blunt's enterprise and reported: 'French people are flooding in here with as much as they can carry and subscribing for or buying shares. Thus I see two things at the same time — the total collapse of our credit and the rise of the British credit.'

The reason for Law's difficulties would have been clear to anyone who had chosen to look carefully. The French bubble might have been inflated with the fresh air of genuine intellectual conviction, but it was a bubble none the less. In Paris, Law had created a kind of financial biosphere where economic life could thrive in perfect conditions for growth, with a shield of government regulation and control to protect the economy from the unrelenting struggle against the outside elements. Continued protection was essential if the green shoots of the new economy were to survive. The problem was that real life had a nasty habit of intruding into Law's carefully regulated System. As in England, credit was both the strength and the underlying weakness of the economy, supporting the share price of Law's

Mississippi Company just as it supported that of the South Sea Company.

The catalyst for Law's downfall came when he put in place the next stage of his economic dream. Where, before, his banknotes had been backed by the specie in the vaults, now he moved to eradicate gold and silver from the country's economy, so that instead it was paper, untrammelled by the link to precious metal, that reflected the country's financial strength. At the beginning of 1720, his paper banknotes were trading at a 10 per cent premium above the coin of the realm. As in England, paper was used to buy property, or land, or precious jewellery. This was flattering to Law because it showed his vision had succeeded, but it had the side-effect of restricting the full circulation of money. Worse still, some investors were selling shares to buy more tangible assets.

'Most people,' he declared righteously, 'surprised at their own gain, thought they might turn it into heaps of gold and silver, which they call realising.' In Law's eyes, these people were effectively turn-coats who had rejected his System by failing to understand that the shares they held were more valuable than precious metals. 'They did not consider,' he went on, 'that the advanced price of stocks did not so much represent current money as capital funds . . . for the stocks actually surpassed in value all the gold and silver which will ever be in the Kingdom.' For Law, this startling confession was of no consequence because of his belief that the true wealth of the country was represented by its land. 'The lands of France are worth more than all the gold which still lies hid in the mines of Peru,' he declared. But his arguments, not surprisingly, failed to convince leading inves-tors, wary of the widening gap between the increasing value of shares and the gold and silver they once relied on, and anxious to exchange their stock for coin. The Prince de Conti, the son of one of Law's early patrons, cashed in all the gains he had made through speculating in the rue Quincampoix, sending three wagons to the bank to take away all the gold he was owed.

Law knew that drastic action was needed if he was to control the economic conditions he had created for his System. To prevent a run on the bank, and to support the credit economy he had created, he was forced to move quickly, via a series of government edicts. Between the end of January and the end of February 1720, he issued some of the most draconian orders France had ever known to try to stop his banknotes being spent. By order of John Law:

1. No one could wear diamonds or any other precious stones without permission.
2. No goldsmith could make or sell gold-plated objects, nor import them, apart from churchmen's rings.
3. No payment above 100 *livres* could be made in coin.
4. No one could keep more than 500 *livres* of gold or silver.

It was almost totalitarian. France was turning into a police state, with rewards being paid to informers. Many servants turned against their masters, and in at least one case a son is said to have given information against his father. The police were often seen responding to a tip-off by tearing up a hoarder's floorboards or digging over a garden in their search for hidden treasure. One bank clerk, whose hoard of 10,000 crowns was discovered, had his savings confiscated and was forced to pay a 10,000-*livre* fine. 'Money rules the world,' decided the Regent's mother, Liselotte, philosophically, 'but I can't think of another place on earth where it rules people more than it does here.'

There were even tougher measures to come. In a series of edicts, from March to May, Law banned the use of gold and silver in financial transactions. A country which for centuries had depended upon the mines of South America for its precious metals was cutting itself off from the rest of the world by refusing to accept the traditional form of currency. Next, Law merged his bank and the Mississippi Company, and closed the company's office to share-dealing. His aim was to bolster confidence in his banknotes while allowing the share price to drop. Within a fortnight, however, he had changed his mind, and decided that there were too many notes in circulation to maintain their value. Instead, on 5 March, to support the share price of the Mississippi Company, Law issued a decree which declared that the company would buy back stock at a fixed price of 9,000 *livres* for a share, well above the market rate. But ominously, queues of sellers began to form, eager to convert their shareholdings into banknotes. So many investors wanted to cash in that more than two billion *livres'* worth of banknotes had to be issued to pay them. Law later defended his curious change of plan, arguing that he could no longer support the value of his banknotes because there were too many in circulation, but that he had a duty to help the shareholders who had provided the money to enable him to eradicate the national debt.

It was a costly, and disastrous, miscalculation. There was only one way for Law to find the money: he had to print it. All his life he had campaigned for his belief that paper currency reflected the value that supported it, and that it was not intrinsically valuable. Had he not said, in the early days of his exile, that money was a means to an end, one which ultimately reflected the strength, or weakness, of a country's underlying economy? Had he not declared that money was not the value *for which* goods are exchanged, but the value *by which* they are exchanged? Already, however, he had started to break his hitherto indissoluble link between paper money and metal. He now compounded the error, and severed the monetary connection for ever. Law ordered nine presses to work flat-out, so that they could print, at break-neck speed, two billion *livres'* worth of banknotes. It was financial madness, the last throw of the gambler's dice, with the odds stacked heavily against him.

To make matters worse, the country was slipping out of his political control. The ruthlessness with which he directed the economy, as he tried to shore up his failing enterprise, could not control the growing crime wave which had been sparked by the rush for riches. As prices rose, there was an increase in gambling, and an outbreak of robberies and violent crimes. The gamblers gathered on the left bank of the Seine, near the Latin quarter, where they sometimes bet as much as 60,000 *livres* on a single throw of the dice. They were exhibiting the same compulsion as the speculators who had crowded into the rue Quincampoix.

The roads to the provinces were now patrolled by masked highwaymen, on the lookout for travellers with jewellery or other valuables whose worth was more constant than the paper money which was blighting the nation. They were joined by gamblers, keen to make good their losses. Over the course of a few days, eleven people were robbed and killed in Paris. The corpses of these victims of theft were washed up by the River Seine. And so, too, was a grisly assortment of severed limbs: the arms and legs of Parisians who had been murdered for their money and then cut up, as if the times had become so violent that it was not enough merely to rob or kill. In response, in a despairing attempt to restore law and order, the state acted almost as viciously. Public hangings and torture became commonplace, with the victims left hanging on the Pont Neuf. There were torchlit executions, too, as if to remind citizens that the forces of justice never slept.

In the end, John Law's System was broken on the wheel that crushed the Count of Horn.

The Count was a dilettante nobleman, twenty-two years old, who was distantly related to the Regent, the Duke of Orleans; but despite his connections he had a history of petty crime and fraud. When the rue Quincampoix started booming, he quickly left his army career behind to gamble on the stock market. But his greed had overcome him. On the night of 18 March 1720, at L'Épée de Bois, an expensive restaurant on the corner of the rue de Venise, he and two accomplices lured a broker, one M. Lacroix, to dinner, ostensibly to sell him shares worth 150,000 *livres*. The broker brought his money with him in paper currency.

The murder happened very quickly, and it almost went to plan. The Count threw a napkin over M. Lacroix's head to disconcert him while the Count de Mille stabbed the unfortunate victim with a dagger, a task completed by Horn himself. But their escape was foiled by a quick-thinking innkeeper nearby, who heard the dying man's cries and locked the door on the murderers, while he ran to find help. In a week of eleven murders, the crime was less of a shock than the sentence. The Count was sentenced to be broken on the wheel. He might have suspected he would die, but not in such an unrefined manner. An upper-class murderer such as he could expect to be hanged or decapitated – but executed *on the wheel* along with men of lower birth in front of the common *mob*?

To be put to death on the wheel was a terrible form of execution. In concept, it was similar to a crucifixion, for in the hands of a skilled executioner it was one of the slowest and most agonising ways to die. It was also a spectator sport, an intricate ritual designed to reinforce the power of the King, in which the crowd was required to participate by chanting prayers to his health. The executioner dressed elegantly and wore a powdered wig, and conducted himself with great airs, before large crowds. The punishment was inflicted in public so that ordinary citizens could take pleasure in seeing criminals suffer, and so that they might heed the lesson too.

The wheel itself resembled a giant barrel. The prisoner was stripped of his clothes, tied to the wheel and stretched around its frame. The device was then rolled slowly over the ground, so that it gradually crushed its victim as it turned. A good executioner, who understood his art, could crush the condemned man's bones without even breaking his skin. Once the prisoner was on the verge of death the executioner upended the barrel, so that the spectators could see him die more clearly, in the crucifix position. But this was not necessarily the end of the victim's agonies. If his death throes were so slow that the onlookers became restless, the executioner might strike the dying man's chest with a metal bar until he could breathe no more. In extreme cases, prisoners were beaten so savagely that their bone marrow splattered on to the eager crowds.

Such a degrading spectacle was clearly a fit punishment for commoners, but not for the nobility. What was society coming to? It was the question much of France was asking as it saw Law's grip weaken to the point of collapse. It was as if the aristocracy itself had been condemned by the court that had sentenced the Count of Horn. For shareholders to grow wealthy and pretend to be upper-class by investing their money in estates was one thing; but for the upper classes to be treated as common criminals was quite another. They were under threat! Some of them appealed to the Regent himself for justice. The Count must die, it was agreed, but his body must not be broken on the wheel – or France herself might be crushed.

Day after day his relatives made their pleas for clemency, but always to no avail. They enlisted the support of the Duke of St-Simon, who argued that France should take note of Germany's example, where the law insisted that no relative of a person broken on the wheel could succeed to any public office for a whole generation. For this reason he thought the Count's sentence should be reduced to beheading, a far less infamous punishment. But John Law was resolute in his view that the Count should be put on the wheel and, still firm in his determination to exercise an iron grip over his adopted country, he refused to let the Regent weaken. The murder had taken place too close to the exchange market for any kind of mercy. The public must have confidence in the rule of law, and in the rule of finance. The two were inexorably entwined, he declared, so that the very future of the centrally controlled economy was at stake if the Regent yielded. Less than a week after the murder, on 22 March, the sentence was carried out in the Place de Grève.

The Count of Horn took his punishment like an aristocrat, refusing to take the poison which was brought to his cell by two noble friends. 'I deserve the wheel,' he told the prison chaplain. 'I am resigned to the worst in order to obtain God's pardon for my crimes.' Then he asked, naively, 'Do you suffer much on the wheel?' The Count had never witnessed such a barbaric death himself. The chaplain knew, but could not tell him, that a man had to bear the most unimaginable pain and horror before his body finally broke. He could almost time the process. As he had expected, it took half an hour, in the Paris afternoon, to crush the life out of the Count of Horn.

With the execution, Law started to clamp down on speculation, which he now regarded as an evil. The life was draining out of the rue Quincampoix, leaving thousands ruined. The Count's agonising death merely reflected a greater truth. The rule of law, and the rule of Law, were both breaking down.

The System itself now stood on the brink of ruin. The rue Quincampoix was closed by royal decree. Hyperinflation gripped the country in which, only a few months earlier, Law had cut the cost of living by abolishing many taxes. More than 3,000 million *livres* in banknotes were in circulation (the equivalent of £200 million). Food became increasingly expensive. 'The working people no longer want to work,' wrote Liselotte dismissively. 'They put a price on their goods three times higher than they are now worth because of the banknotes. I have often wished that these banknotes were consigned to hell-fire. It is impossible to describe all the evil that has resulted from them. I should like to see Law go to the devil with his system and I wish that he had never set foot in France.'

On 21 May, Law took the only step he could. He acted to deflate the economy, by devaluing both his currency and his shares. The value of a 100-*livre* banknote was to be halved by the year's end, and the Mississippi Company's price on the stock market was cut from 9,000 to 5,000. But it was not enough to control the runaway inflation, which gripped the country as tightly as share mania had seized it before. Nor was it enough to dampen down the hysteria among the holders of banknotes. Where speculative fever had taken hold before, now came its mirror image, a desperate rush to sell paper. So great was the rush that Law's bank was forced to close for ten days after the publication of his edict, and when it opened again it refused to exchange anything bigger than a 100-*livre* note so as to conserve its supplies of coin. But still the customers queued. From the small hours they waited outside the bank until, with its vaults close to exhaustion, it was forced to limit its exchange dealings to *one* 10-*livre* note per person, and to shut its doors after half a morning's work. But the queues grew ever longer, and ever more bad-tempered. Fights broke out as customers tried desperately to push their way to the front.

Paris was now a tinderbox. Each night the crowds gathered in their thousands near the bank in the rue Vivienne to demonstrate against the foreigner who ran their country. 'I have never in my life seen an Englishman or a Scot appear so foolish and terrified as M. Law does now,' noted Liselotte in her diary, with the detachment which came from her privileged position and her sense of being a foreigner in an adopted land. 'Wealth breeds fear, and no one likes to abandon his belongings, but I believe there must be times when he wishes himself in Louisiana or Mississippi.'

The government itself appeared to be in danger. The troops on the street did not appear to be fully behind the Regent. On the night of 17 July, fifteen thousand protesters gathered in the rue Vivienne, which was far too narrow a street for such a large crowd. Sixteen demonstrators were crushed to death, and the soldiers stood by while the crowd, in its anger, marched on the Palais Royal carrying three of the bodies. Thousands then pushed through the gates into the outer court, and their angry shouts could clearly be heard inside. Bravely, the Secretary of State for War came out to talk to them; the Governor of the city, more patronisingly, threw them some coins, and was nearly lynched for his pains. Where Law had once been fêted, now the crowds had come to jeer him and to exact revenge. His house was attacked, his coach surrounded and destroyed. At one point, the wife of the Under-Secretary at the Foreign Office was mistaken by some peasants for Madame Law and was nearly drowned in the local duckpond.

For more than a week, Law was forced to seek refuge with the Regent. The ruler who had bound himself so tightly to John Law and his System, who had supported the itinerant economist where others had rejected him, now had to act as the protector of his life. So strong was the Regent's support, even at this late stage, that he forced the Parlement into exile outside Paris when it refused to sanction the Mississippi Company's request to withdraw 50 million *livres'* worth of banknotes from circulation every month. With its departure, Law was free to act in the way he liked best, untrammelled by restrictions, and he desperately tried to withdraw the banknotes he had printed at such speed.

Over the course of the summer he removed from circulation 700 million *livres'* worth of banknotes. In June, a great cage was set up outside his bank, and in it he held regular public bonfires of the paper money, trying to convince a sceptical public that the notes which remained in their pockets had been rendered more valuable by the flames. But Law had lost his touch. He had effectively set fire to his whole System, thoroughly convincing people who held banknotes that their money was good only for the inferno. As the summer wore on, the queues outside the banks, demanding to change paper into coin, lengthened. From Lyons to Nantes, the banks were surrounded by investors anxious to cash in their paper money.

By October the country's disastrous paper chain had been cut. Fifty per cent of the banknotes had been burned along with two-thirds of the Mississippi Company's shares. The economy was effectively back to where it had been in March, before Law had made his ill-fated move to start the presses rolling. With fewer notes in circulation, and the earlier devaluation, inflation should have been tamed; with fewer shareholders, there should have been a larger dividend for investors. But the psychological damage had been done and pyrotechnics alone could not restore economic equilibrium. By merging his bank and the Mississippi Company, Law had effectively linked his paper money to the company's shares: they were seen as an interchangeable commodity, with a common price. But the French people had not just invested money in his System, they had invested *faith* too, and their confidence in his enterprise had been shattered. Now they wanted the solidity, the reassurance, of metal coins. The Mississippi stocks continued their decline, to below 5,000, and the banknotes slid further into unpopularity and disuse. 'In France,' reported Liselotte sardonically, 'we no longer have two penny pieces to rub together, but we have (by your leave, and in good Palatine language) paper arse-wipers in plenty.'

The satirists had a field day, putting out a range of new publications including *Dissertation on the Philosopher's Stone by John Law*, and *The Mirror of Folly*, which showed the depth of despair in Holland, the very country Law had cited as the example of an enduring economy but which had been hit hard by the fall-out from France's collapse. *The Mirror of Folly* was an extraordinary book, consisting of seventy pages lampooning the bubbles, accompanied by inventive, and cruelly accurate, cartoons which blamed Law for the disaster. There were sketches of the supposed mountains of Mississippi, of Law as Don Quixote, of a golden calf that burped coins when Law applied a pair of bellows to the animal's rump, and, even less decorously, an illustration of the use to which Liselotte felt his paper money was best put.

A popular refrain charted the rise and fall of Law's financial rule:

> My shares which on Monday I bought
> Were worth millions on Tuesday, I thought.
> So on Wednesday I chose my abode;
> In my carriage on Thursday I rode;
> To the ball-room on Friday I went;
> To the work-house next day I was sent.

Prices soared again by as much as 60 per cent, despite the Regency Council's attempts to impose a freeze, but merchants had already begun hoarding so as to force prices up again. In October, the Council could take no more. It announced that it was withdrawing notes from circulation on the grounds that they were hindering trade. Gold and silver would be used instead. Law's System was dead.

So too, of course, was Law's political career. Even the Regent could no longer afford to stand by him if the government's stability was to be restored. But he acted decently to the end. On 12 December 1720, the Duke took Law and his family to the Opéra, next to the Palais Royal, and invited them to share his box as a final gesture of friendship. 'Sire,' Law told him, 'I agree that I have made grave errors. I am only human and all men err. But I have always acted without malice and dishonesty ... The South Sea directors have worked *against* England; I have worked *for* France,' he declared, with passion.

Two days later, stripped of power, Law was driven along the cold, muddy roads to his château on the outskirts of Paris to start the long journey into exile.

At about the time that Law's System was collapsing, the *Grand Saint-Antoine* came stealthily into port in southern France, bearing a secret cargo. Two passengers and four crew had already died on the crossing from Beirut to Sardinia, but her captain insisted on making for Marseilles.

Within a month of the ship's docking, plague had gripped the workers' quarter of Saint-Rémy. It appeared to many that the sins of the past year were being punished, the excesses of the rue Quincampoix crushed by a vengeful God. One observer of the terrible scene sent back reports to his master in England.

Marseilles, Sept. 15 1720

I arrived here on the 8th and entered the Gate of Aix which leads to the Cours, which has always been esteemed one of the most pleasant prospects in the Kingdom, but that day was a very dismal spectacle to me; all that great place, both on the right and left, was filled with dead, sick and dying persons. The carts were continually employed in going and returning to carry away the dead carcasses, of which there were that day above four thousand. The town was without bread, without wine, without meat, without medicines, and in general, without any succours.

The father abandoned the child, and the son the father; the husband the wife, and the wife the husband; and those who had not a house to themselves, lay upon quilts in the streets and the pavements; all the streets were filled with clothes and household goods, strewn with dead dogs and cats, which made an insupportable stench.

The people die, and are buried without any ceremonies of the church. The religious orders have almost all perished. It is accounted that there have died 50,000 persons.

The sickness however, is of a very extraordinary nature. It is the assistance of heaven we ought to implore and to wait for a blessing from thence upon our labours.

The enemy had to be confined to Marseilles, to stop it spreading to the capital. The port was put in quarantine, and every scientific nostrum of the day applied to protect Paris from the plague. But the most powerful measure of all was invisible: it was the change in people's minds. They had learned their lesson: some forces were too powerful to control. Desperate faith in God's mercy supplanted their year-long belief that an individual could control and radically improve the condition of their lives. 'When the plague evidently spread itself,' wrote Daniel Defoe in his *Journal of the Plague Year*, 'they soon began to see the folly of trusting to those unperforming creatures who had gulled them of their money'.

The plague struck, too, in Louisiana, where some two hundred and fifty souls clung tenaciously to the mosquito-ridden swamp to which Law's rule had consigned them. In January 1721, more than a thousand prospective colonists sailed for the New World aboard four ships. The epidemic struck at sea and barely two hundred survived the journey.

Law's great vision of a mercantile nation, trading across the world, had brought not riches, only death.

France, the economic superpower, was rotting from inside.

CHAPTER X

Time and Tide and a Fall from Grace

Oh fatal Blow to loose at once what through Artfull Charms I've got these many Years-Undone, Undone

A Broker went to let a Lady know,
That South Sea Stock was falling very low;
Says she, then what I gain in my good Calling
By rising things, I find I loose by falling.

At 30, Tetsushi Nakamura is a seasoned stock investor. The system engineer from Hibarigaoka, Saitama Prefecture, got his hands on stocks when he was in his fourth year of elementary school, buying shares of a construction company on his dad's advice. Nakamura now has about 3.5 million yen invested in various companies, despite a recent downturn in the nation's stock market that has caused the value of his stocks to shrink by some 500,000 yen since the beginning of the year.

'The loss doesn't shock me,' Nakamura said. 'I actually wish I had more money now because this is the best time to buy stocks.'

Japan Times, 4 September 2000

The dire financial news from Paris added to the enormous pressure on John Blunt when he returned from his summer holiday in Taunton. Professionally and socially he had made it to the top. Thousands of investors, large and small, had put their faith in him. He was still praised as a man whose financial acumen was unrivalled, an entrepreneur who could do no wrong, a businessman of magical skill who had created fortunes for his clients. It would have been comforting for Blunt if he had believed his own publicity, but as he boarded his coach for the drive to the capital, it was clear that he faced a struggle to hold his business together. He realised that unless he could keep the South Sea Company's share price moving ever upwards, he would lose it all, even the fine coach proudly displaying his coat of arms. Financial ruin and social disgrace lurked in the dark corners of Exchange Alley, ready to drag him down. Outwardly, like many a businessman after him facing the abyss, he had to remain calm, confident and in control, but inwardly he must have been in turmoil. The newspapers, which had built him up, were now more sceptical, and the *Weekly Journal*, which had once devoted its front page to the details of the First Money Subscription, was back to its cynical best:

Sir Isaac Newton has reduced that long amazing phenomenon, the tide, to order and rules of geometry. Now all the turbulent motions of the other seas are pretty well solved by his general principle; but I have not yet heard of any venturous Cantab, that has aimed at accounting for, and reducing to, any settled

Principle, the motions and phenomena of the South Sea. Sir Isaac's main movement, which causes the ebbing and flowing of the seas in all other parts of the world, is the moon.

I would give one hint to my very good countrymen (whom for the future I shall call the men of the moon . . .) that they would observe the different position of the stars before they buy and sell stock; and then if the tides rise or fall at uncertain times, they may have something to blame for their losses.

By mid-August London was readying itself for a week of partying to celebrate the festival of St Bartholomew. With the end of the month, however, and the imminent onset of autumn, the temperature in the market-place was changing. The warm summer months of giddy speculation in Exchange Alley were giving way to a brisker, more realistic assessment of the value of shares, more in keeping with the season. The change was at first imperceptible except to those who could sense the slightest shift in the wind, for on some days the barometer would point to a further fine spell for the markets, but it would always settle back at a slightly lower pressure than before. Blunt was in trouble and he knew it. That few others could smell the danger was a tribute to his continuing skill at manipulating the market.

The crisis was, effectively, one of his own making. The legal moves against the joint-stock companies of Case Billingsley, which the Company had launched in league with the government in the middle of August, had left investors with large debts, and they quickly realised that selling their South Sea Company shares was the only way to pay their dues. A sudden eruption of selling was depressing the Company's share price. The confidence of Exchange Alley had been shaken and Blunt needed to show that his business was built on firmer foundations than Law's failed project in France.

The problem for Blunt was, of course, that his company had been built on no foundations whatsoever. Unlike Law, he had no trading empire and no intellectual basis for his solution to the country's overwhelming debts. He had simply annexed the national debt and turned it into a specious profit-making machine. Worse still, Blunt was the victim of his own stock-market methods. The Bubble had been inflated by credit, which had meant investors did not have to pay the full share price; and so long as the share price remained high, they had been eager to buy. But they were also anxious to sell before they had to find the money for the next instalment on their shares. The prospect of riches at no cost was, for many, irresistible. This meant that the cycle of investment and upward share movement was, inevitably, followed by the exact opposite: a cycle of disinvestment, which could only be prevented from gathering pace by a new money subscription and another offering of credit. The higher the price rose, the greater the downward pressure, and the harder Blunt had to work to drive the share price upwards again.

He had no cure to offer, other than applying more of the same medicine: he had to try to support the share price of the Company once again. To this end, he ordered that more than £2 million should be siphoned off from the Sword Blade Bank to prop up the price of the Company's stock. Ominously, however, thousands of investors, faced with falling prices, had already rushed to register stock transfers at the Stamp Office. The crowds were gathering as they had in Paris, ready to pull out their money at the first hint of trouble. Clearly, more drastic action was called for.

Blunt knew that any sign of weakness on his part would puncture the Company's reputation for good. He had to maintain an air of optimism, and shore up the market position, even though he knew that the odds were stacked against him. *The Secret History of the South Sea Scheme*, the anonymous account which was probably written by a director of the Company who was hostile to Blunt, reports:

> he visibly affected a prophetic style, delivering his words with an emphasis and an extraordinary vehemence, and used to put himself in a commanding posture, rebuking those that durst in the least oppose anything he said . . . uttering these and such like expressions: gentlemen, don't be dismayed: you must act with firmness, resolution, with courage. I tell you, 'tis not a common matter you have before you. The greatest thing in the world is referred to you. All the money of Europe will centre amongst you. All the nations on earth will bring you tribute.

Blunt's preferred solution was to try to pump up the share price, and the bubble, with a fourth and final share launch. Provided that enough investors were gullible enough to buy at the top of the market – and again he fixed the price at 1,000 – a strong signal would go out that the market had deemed the Company to be in as robust health as ever. Blunt aimed to raise £1 million by this, his Fourth Money Subscription, which he launched on 24 August. It was perhaps the most cynical of all his marketing operations, not least because he was busy offloading shares himself. He was publicly promoting what he knew privately to be a failing enterprise. The chances of anyone making money by buying at this level were non-existent; and Blunt knew that, unless he was extremely lucky, the enterprise was doomed.

At first, though, his luck held. So successful was the power of the Company's hold over popular imagination, and so convincing was Blunt's display of confidence, that there were soon enough sub-scribers to fill the Company's list. Few investors saw through the impossibility of the Company's position, but one who did was the banker Robert Jacombe, who warned his client Robert Walpole: 'South Sea is under 900 and all the subscriptions are proportionally fallen . . . We are told that when the present subscription for annuities etc. is over we shall see a great turn in stocks, but I see so many watching to get out on another rise that I cannot consider they can carry it much longer by any art.'

Walpole would not be put off, however, and, after selling the stock he had bought in June, he ordered Jacombe to invest in the new subscription. He even encouraged his friends to invest in it. But all politicians need luck, and Walpole had it in abundance. His banker, a wiser man than his client, delayed buying until the pattern of the market became clear, telling Walpole, 'ready money is a valu-able thing.' Jacombe was no ordinary financier. He was also Under-Secretary of War, and had connections with the Treasury. Financially, Jacombe saved Walpole from losing a small fortune. Politically, he left Walpole's reputation untarnished by the gathering storm.

Despite the gullibility of the investors and the apparent success of the share launch, however, Blunt was facing a severe cash-flow prob-lem. Without an even faster inflow of money, there simply wasn't enough cash within the Sword Blade Bank to support the share price, and if the share price could not be supported then the illusion he had created for the last six months would be shattered. Accordingly, he found a new way of demonstrating his supposed confidence in the Company's future. On 30 August he persuaded the Court of Directors to vote for an absurdly generous Christmas dividend of 30 per cent, accompanied by the astonishing promise that the annual dividend for *a decade* would be 50 per cent. The offer of a such an extraordinary dividend was an attempt, though far too late in the day, to persuade investors to keep their money in the Company for the long term, rather than indulging in the short-termism that had marked the attitude of shareholders in the other bubbles. But to be in a position to pay such amounts, its shareholders could calculate, the Company would have to make at least a £15 million profit each year.

The effect was not as Blunt had intended. It was as if someone had thrown a bucketful of cold water over the investors, who had so blindly followed his charismatic financial leadership. They stood blinking and disbelieving at what they saw before them: a company whose trading prospects had been nonexistent in the past, and would be nonexistent in the future; a company whose proposed dividend implied such extraordinary annual profits that anyone with any sense could now see that it simply could not trade on the multimillion-pound scale which the offer to shareholders suggested; a company which was, quite nakedly, a machine for making a profit out of debt reclamation, and not a trading enterprise at all; a company which still had a third of the national debt to sell, and whose chances of doing so were receding by the hour. 'Sir,' wrote a sceptical correspondent to one newspaper, 'South Sea is very sick, a premium of 50 per cent has been applied as a cordial for revival, and it won't do; the old woman droops still.'

As in France, investors began to turn paper into metal again, and as shares were sold for cash the flow of money into the country, which had bolstered the Company's rise, began, inexorably, to reverse direction and return across the Channel. Agents for France, the Netherlands and Switzerland began to sell their stock. With a growing sense of inevitability, the Company's share price began to slide below 800, touching 770 on 1 September. With each fall, Blunt's powers seemed to ebb a little further. His colleagues, previously under his sway, vetoed his next proposal – to launch yet another million-pound share subscription to shore up the Company's crumbling position. And the share price went on slipping, its fall remorselessly charted by the *Weekly Journal*:

London, Sept. 10

The Stocks since our last are as follows:

Saturday South Sea Stock was 370
Monday South Sea 300
Tuesday South Sea 300
Wednesday 190
Thursday 180

Then in the middle of this fateful week, shareholders were summoned to a special meeting at the Merchant Taylors' Hall in London in an effort to persuade them to remain calm, to keep their money invested in the Company. When the meeting started, shareholders were treated to a public-relations exercise which starkly demonstrated the close relationship between government and the Company. Craggs the elder, the Postmaster-General, spoke at length and soothingly about how investors should be reassured by the directors' prudent management. Hungerford, the MP who at the Company's behest had promoted the Bubble Act to clamp down on rival promotions, was even more fulsome, declaring passionately that the South Sea managers had 'performed such wonderful things in so short a time'. He insisted:

I have seen the rise and fall, the decay and resurrection of many communities of this nature; but in my opinion none ever performed such wonderful things in so short a time as the South Sea managers have brought to pass. They have done more than the Crown, the pulpit, and the magistrate could do: for they have reconciled all parties in one common interest, and thereby laid asleep, if not wholly extinguished, our domestic jars and animosities; by the rise of their stocks the monied-men have vastly increased their fortunes: the country gentlemen have seen the value of their lands doubled and trebled in their hands; and they have, at the same time, done good to the Church, not a few of the reverend clergy having got great sums by this project.

In short, they have enriched the whole nation; and I hope they have not forgot themselves.

The proceedings were concluded by the Duke of Portland, who claimed that he 'did not know what reason anybody had to be dissatisfied'. Given that the Duke was known to have a large shareholding in the Company, and so had a sizeable fortune at risk, his intervention was crucial, helping to convince doubting members of the audience that the Company was still in safe hands and that it would weather this temporary setback. But talk alone could not save the South Sea stock now. Exchange Alley echoed to the sound of the stockjobbers as they hastily offloaded shares in a day of hectic trading.

London was now in the grip of a full-scale financial storm. A gale was tearing through the City, howling round the dark alleyways, blowing away thousands of scraps of worthless stock-market paper. It circled round the long-established financial institutions, and swept through the corridors of power. It blew into the coffee houses and sent a chill through the warm fug of drink and tobacco, silencing the eager chatter. The year of easy money was over. In its place would come a year of anxiety and apprehension, a year of dismay and doubt, a year of rack and ruin for the thousands who had allowed themselves to be swept away by the foolhardy optimism of the age. 'Exchange-Alley sounds no longer of thousands got in an instant,' reported the *Weekly Journal*, 'but on the contrary, all corners of the town are filled with the groans of the afflicted; and they who lately rode in great state to that famous mart of money, now condescend to walk the streets on foot.'

Investors all around the country watched their paper fortunes collapse, or – worse still – their share debts mount. So precipitously was the share price falling that Blunt's generous terms of credit, and his instalment plans, meant that they owed more than their shares were worth. Among their number were two bankers in Cornhill, who had agreed to purchase £14,000 worth of stock at 1,100, *an outlay of more than £150,000 during the next month for shares that were in free-fall!* There were investors who saw their profits falling, and wanted to cash in; investors who had bought at the top and were now caught between blind belief and fear, not knowing whether to sell at a loss or hope against hope that, given time, the share price would pick up and enable them to recoup their losses; and investors who had promised to buy stock in the future and who could not wriggle out of their commitment, but who watched in horror as the share price slid further and further away from the level at which they had volunteered to buy. Only the King, safely tucked away in his Hanoverian retreat, remained blithely ignorant of the ongoing financial destruction of his kingdom, lulled into a sense of security by his leading ministers, who failed to report what was going on until the stock-market crash was fully upon them. George I's own £60,000 holding was worth barely a fifth of that sum.

No longer was Blunt the commanding figure in the City, the man who never failed to deliver; no longer could he hold sway over his fellow directors in the Company; no longer would they look up to him and be dazzled by his drive, his energy, his golden touch. The man who could do no wrong stood revealed as a mortal, after all. Emerging from Blunt's considerable shadow, the South Sea directors knew they had to act, and they turned to the one institution that could save them: the Bank of England.

It was a moment for the Bank to relish. For the greater part of the year, it had been forced to sit and watch an upstart organisation steal its clothes to become the main financial player in the land. Since losing the battle to convince Parliament to back its own reckless proposals for taking over the national debt, it had shrunk into the shadows just as the South Sea Company had emerged as the apparent saviour of the country and the driver of the new economy. Within the space of a few terrible weeks for the Company, the Bank itself was being invited to come to the rescue, hailed by both fraught South Sea shareholders and government as the steadying hand, the exemplar of all that was solid and respectable about the old economy. Investors had short memories: the Bank's abortive bid for the national debt was forgotten. It was enough that it was untainted by the Company's collapse.

Two crucial meetings on the same day signalled the beginning of the end for the Company. On the morning of 19 September, its sub-Governor Sir John Fellowes asked the Company's General Court for permission to negotiate with the Bank of England, declaring with delightful understatement that affairs had 'taken an unexpected turn to the disadvantage'. The meeting went on to discuss how best it could repair the damage to the Company's reputation caused by the precipitous share-price fall within days of the launch of the Fourth Money Subscription. Of those who watched their losses mount, the purchasers of stock at 1,000 were by far the loudest in their protests, and had formed an action group under a journalist-turned-politician, Eustace Budgell. What redress could be given to Budgell and his vociferous complainants? The only option seemed to be to write off most of the instalments they owed the Company under the pay-as-you-go plan that Blunt had introduced, by cutting the cost of their shares to 400. This would slice the Company's fat profits in half, though its chances of success were slight: the price was still more than double the level to which the shares had plummeted in Exchange Alley.

On the afternoon of the 19th, a second meeting was held by James Craggs at the General Post Office, a gathering attended by representatives of the government, the South Sea Company and the Bank of England. The most important negotiator for the Bank was its former Governor, Sir Gilbert Heathcote. Heathcote, now seventy, was one of the richest men in England and a seasoned businessman. Chancellor Aislabie was there too, as were the two political allies, Viscount Townshend and Robert Walpole; and for the Company, the directors Sir John Fellowes and Sir Charles Joye. Heathcote was the key to any settlement that might rescue the Company. A Bank of England man to his well manicured fingertips, he would prefer to crush the Company; but he was a staunch Whig too, and it was the ministers' job to persuade him of the seriousness of the threat to the country's political stability if the Company was to fail.

For six hours, Heathcote stood firm, professing his reluctance to ride to the rescue of the enemy. Under severe pressure from the ministers opposite him, however, he reluctantly conceded to consider an arrangement which would put a floor under the Company's share price. Heathcote, in effect, was asked to name his own price for saving the South Sea Company, and he made full use of his strong position to unpick the web of relationships which had sustained it. He would not, he declared, rescue the Sword Blade Bank as well: 'If the South Sea Company is to be wedded to the Bank,' he insisted, 'it cannot be allowed to keep a mistress.' After a year of turmoil, the Bank of England had won its battle for supremacy, finally and for ever. The deal, which became known as the 'Bank contract', was drawn up by Walpole, and under its terms the Bank was to lend the Company £3 million, with nearly half a million to be paid straight away. At a second meeting four days later, Walpole drew up another document stating that the Bank would pay £3.75 million for South Sea stock. It represented a purchase price of 400 per share.

But the Bank, the Company and the government had all still failed to recognise the full extent of the Company's plight. So badly was the Bubble punctured that it was deflating at too great a speed for the Bank of England to repair it. Confidence had sustained the Bubble; now lack of confidence was destroying it, and no political or financial intervention, however powerful, could counteract market forces on this scale. The streets around Exchange Alley began to resemble John Law's Paris after *his* bubble had begun to burst. Crowds rushed to the Sword Blade Bank, trying desperately to turn their increasingly worthless paper back into metal. By 24 September, the Sword Blade Bank could hold out no longer. It ran out of currency reserves and closed its doors for the last time, though it posted a notice stating that it would meet its obligations in due course. If there had been any remaining confidence in the future of the South Sea Company, there was certainly none now. The Bubble had burst, and the Whig government was caught, inexorably, in the fall-out – even more damaged than it had been by the financial crisis under Anne that had cast its leaders out in 1710.

'All is floating, all falling,' observed the poet turned diplomat, Matthew Prior. 'The directors are curst; the top adventurers broke, and every man has a face as long as Godolphin's.'

CHAPTER XI

Not a Penny Stirring

A Famous Builder of Meridian Coaches,
To make each South Sea Drab, appear a Dutchess,
Had Fourty Coaches at one time bespoke,
But Falling Stock did Thirty Five revoke.

*Roll up for the 90 per cent club. It's the fastest-growing club
in business. Model entrepreneurs have joined it. Large numbers
of investors have shares in it. And the queue for membership
is lengthening fast. But this is a club no one wants to join –
and there's a scramble for the escape committee. The 90 per cent
club comprises those companies whose shares have plunged by
90 per cent and more in the torrid shake-out of hi-tech and
dotcom stocks.*

The Scotsman, 11 July 2001

In September 1720, England's investors resembled the half-drowned survivors of a shipwreck, washed up on dry land. The country's sudden transformation from a seaworthy vessel, capable of defying the elements, to a mass of flotsam tossed about by the waves, was deeply felt. Jonathan Swift was partly inspired by the Bubble's collapse to start writing *Gulliver's Travels* that same year, sending his hero to the South-Seas, where he was overcome by a violent storm. Like Gulliver, England's shareholders lay exhausted, gasping for breath and numb with shock, not knowing whether they would live or die after their terrible journey.

There was wreckage everywhere. Nearly every family of any social standing had been caught by the economic storm. The Duke of Chandos was £300,000 down, and would never quite recover. When he died, a quarter of a century later, his great house at Canons in north London, where Handel was composer-in-residence, was pulled down and its contents scattered, sold piecemeal by his son to pay the debts he had inherited. Today, its grand colonnade stands outside the National Gallery in Trafalgar Square, its gates at Trinity College, Oxford; the font and altar from the chapel stand in the parish church of Fawley, Buckinghamshire, while its stained-glass windows, ceilings, and the organ used by Handel, are installed at Great Witley in Worcestershire.

Of the other victims, Lord Londonderry owed £50,000 while Sir Justus Beck, a director of the Bank of England, went bankrupt, owing £347,000. The Duke of Portland was in terrible financial straits, his fall perhaps the most spectacular. His family was one of the richest in the kingdom, and on his father's death in 1709 he had inherited land, money and jewellery worth more than £850,000. He owned several streets in Westminster, and he had great estates all around the country, from Cumberland, Cheshire and Yorkshire, to Lincolnshire, Norfolk, Hertfordshire and Sussex. Now he was close to bankruptcy, and his family's power and influence were emasculated for a generation and more. Lord Irwin and Lord Lonsdale were both in financial trouble, too, as well as half a dozen Scottish peers, including the Duke of Montrose who had gambled heavily on the Bubble. Some investors had made such heavy losses they were deeply in debt, the victims of negative equity; others, more fortunate, merely saw their vast notional profits eaten up by the stock-market slide.

Politically, too, there were to be many victims in the weeks and months ahead. The government, like the South Sea Company, had been fatally weakened, creating an opportunity not just for the Bank of England to regain its pre-eminent financial position but for Robert Walpole – who had survived the trauma of the past few months relatively unscathed, thanks to his sceptical banker – to make his bid for power.

In London, the vibrant, noisy streets which had echoed so excitedly to the call of the stockjobbers lay silent. In their place stood a shattered city of sober introspection, a city whose citizens could only reflect on the madness and abandon of the year that had so carried them away, leaving them to shake their heads and wonder how they had been so deluded. Declared one poet in a newspaper:

> All things are hush'd, as law itself were dead;
> Poor pensive Fleet-Street droops its mournful head;
> The Strand's a desert grown; the town's undone;
> Some hang, some drown; and some distracted run.

All around, banks with long lineages such as Atwill and Hammond, Long and Bland, and Nathaniel Bostock, were closing their doors. Hoare's was busy offloading stock in great quantities, and bankruptcy proceedings were being taken against two bankers who had once been worth £300,000. Workers whose jobs depended on their wealthy employers found themselves with no income. Houses were left half-built; orders for ships were suddenly cancelled: at Lloyd's coffee house in Lombard Street not one person made a bid when several ships were put up for sale. The spectre of unemployment loomed. ''Tis almost unfashionable not to be a bankrupt,' complained one public speaker, 'the credit of our nation that has stood the shock of so many wars is at present on the very brink of ruin of a hundred families, and there is scarce a gentleman who hears me, but has felt the dismal effects of what has lately happened, either in himself, his relations or his friends.' Isaac Newton, who had been tempted to return to the Bubble after cashing his earlier investment, had lost £20,000, and it was said that for the rest of his life he could not bear mention of the South Sea Company. The nonconformist minister Samuel Chandler lost all his money and was forced to open a bookshop in the Poultry to earn a living.

Occasionally, through the coal-smoke air, there could be heard the cry of a salesman whose job it was to offer up baubles at a knock-down price to help staunch some aristocrat's dreadful losses. Where before Exchange Alley had been crowded with well-suited businessmen cutting their deals, now, the *Original Weekly Journal* suggested, it was empty, save for small groups of investors who stood wringing their hands and crying, 'I am undone, I am undone.' It was as if, the newspaper declared, 'some sickness was broke out in the place; and these walking ghosts were all infected with the Plague'. The *Daily Courant*'s columns were filled with advertisements for furniture and household goods: 'very good pictures, India cabinets and tea-tables, china and glasses, very clean bedding and kitchen furniture'. It was a day of reckoning, too, not just for investors in the Bubble but for all the luxury trades which had profited so mightily from the South Sea Company's rise. Overnight, the bottom had dropped out of the market for coaches, for jewellery and for fine clothes, all of them major employers of labour in the capital. 'There is to be sold,' the *Daily Courant* reported, 'a clean, plain Chariot, almost new, nothing the worse for wearing, with a whole fore-glass and a shield ready painted for any coat of arms.' One London yard saw twenty-eight out of its forty orders for new coaches cancelled. A newspaper correspondent reported: 'Weekly through the streets of London you may see second-hand coaches; second-hand gold watches, cast-off diamond watches and earrings to be sold; servants already want places who were, but a little while ago, so saucy and insolent, no wages and no kind of usage could oblige them; Long Lane,

Monmouth and Regent Fair are full of rich liveries to be sold, nay, and full of rich embroidered petticoats, rich embroidered coats and waistcoats; in a word every place is full of the ruin of Exchange Alley.'

England, having embraced the new economy, had few ideas on how to dig itself out of the mess into which it had been pitched. Without the Company at its helm, and ejected from a financial system which had promised so much stability and profit, the country appeared to have no economic course to follow. The days of inexorable stock-market growth, the buzz and excitement in the capital as projectors sought backing for their schemes and scams, now seemed so long ago. Credit, the modern economic fuel, had been defeated by the sudden appearance of a hitherto unsuspected arch-rival: debit. Overnight, as had happened in Paris, paper money seemed specious and insubstantial compared with the solid, permanent, traditional dependability of the once-scorned metal currency.

The trouble was that Blunt had created a snowstorm of paper. Quite probably there was not enough gold or silver in the country to pay for all the credit that had been created. There were hundreds of thousands of pounds' worth of useless notes in circulation, issued by the now derided Sword Blade Bank; on top of that, investors still held shares in a variety of companies that had escaped closure; and on the streets of London, in a wide range of private and illicit transactions, hundreds of IOUs had been issued privately by the denizens of Exchange Alley, whose capacity to settle their debts stood, at the very least, in question. As if this was not bad enough, the sheer pace of the stock market's expansion had vastly exceeded the capacity of the trading system to cope with the year's great rush of paperwork. When the Bubble collapsed, many debtors slipped quietly away in the hope that their promised purchases might be lost in the chaos of the time.

In the countryside, too, the impact of the Bubble's collapse was felt deeply, especially among the families who had spent their new riches traditionally, in acquiring vast estates which they hoped to hand on to the next generation. With the Company's decline came an inevitable slump in land prices, the very asset once seen by Law as the determinant of a currency's stability. Their value, pumped up by the attention of speculators with vast sums of Bubble money at their disposal, now declined almost as fast as the Company itself. As prices were forced lower and lower, many speculators refused to go through with their agreed land purchases, worsening the slump; others had borrowed heavily against the value of the lands they had bought, and their debts now outstripped their assets.

The Windham family, which had rivalled Robert Walpole for land speculation in Norfolk, was in deep trouble. Ashe Windham's brother, Colonel Windham, who was in the process of buying the estate of Earsham in the south of the county, wrote to him on 27 September:

> There never was such distraction and undoing in any country. You can't suppose the number of families undone. One may almost say every body is ruined, who has traded beyond their Stock. Many a 100,000 man not worth a groat; and it grieves me to think of some of them. I have no contracts against me, only they upon whom I have obligations are bad paymasters. If I get enough to pay for Earsham, it will be well ... Mr Walpole and the Managers give us hopes of better things in a few days. Not a penny stirring.

Not a penny stirring: for some, during this financial stasis, there seemed only one way out. One Sunday morning, in the first week of September, John Blunt's nephew Charles slashed his own throat with a razor in an upstairs room of his house in Broad Street, London, leaving behind a wife and several children and the ruins of an estate once worth £100,000. A stockjobber followed his example and killed himself in the same way; a certain Mr Wrexham, a noted mercer of Bedford Street, Covent Garden, threw himself out of a window, but lived to tell the tale; a lawyer left his house in Brownloe Street and drowned himself in the local pond – ''tis said on account of the calamity of the times'; a merchant blew out his brains; a West Indian trader, according to one newspaper, 'having lost the greater part of his estate by the South Sea business, had thereupon the misfortune to lose his senses and afterwards his life; for on Wednesday last he laid violent hands on himself at his habitation at Greenwich'.

Such incidents were common, and were widely publicised. One gentleman who had fallen on hard times hanged himself in his house near Golden Square, but was accidentally discovered by his servant who had the courage to cut him down, though it was too late to make any difference: he died the next day. The victim had clearly enjoyed a roller-coaster ride on the stock market, paying off his longstanding debts through his initial success in 'Change Alley and then managing to build a fortune – only to lose it all when stocks crashed. Such highs and lows were enough to drive a man mad. The coroner's inquest, the newspapers reported, brought in a verdict of 'non compos mentis'.

'They have dreamed their dream,' wrote Alexander Pope, who had made his own investment in the Company, 'and on awakening found nothing in their hands.'

The clamour outside Parliament was growing stronger, as if to signal that, like France before it, the country was becoming ungovernable. Angry shareholders, bitterly regretting having traded their government annuities for stock, formed noisy crowds which gathered on the streets of Westminster and called for their losses to be made good. They blamed the South Sea directors for duping them, rather than themselves for failing to realise that shares could go down as well as up. The newspapers, too, were in full cry, publishing heart-rending tales of honest citizens inveigled into investing in the South Seas. One account, quickly issued as a pamphlet, typified the pressure that was being placed on the ruling classes to placate the ruined shareholders. Even allowing for special pleading or invention, of which there was plenty, the *Letter from a Gentleman in the Country to his MP* demonstrated the temptation to which many citizens had succumbed, and caught the spirit of the times. It encapsulated, too, the frailty of human nature when the prospect of great riches is held out, but also the widely-held belief that it was innocent investors, rather than greedy ones, who had been trapped by the downright cunning of the Company and of the stockjobbers in 'Change Alley.

Wrote the *Letter's* anonymous author to his friend in Parliament:

Sir,

I think we have been friends and acquaintances for about thirty years, and as I have sat with you for some time in Parliament, have constantly given you my interest in this county, and am pretty nearly related to you by my wife, I cannot think of any person who is more likely to pity the deplorable circumstances to which I am at present reduced.

My story is this:

You know very well that I have, for some years past, retired from the busy part of the world, laid aside all thoughts of parties and politics, and contented myself to live in the country with my wife and children, upon that estate which has been in my family for many generations, and which, by my own improvements, I have brought from fifteen hundred pounds per annum to two thousand.

It was the 6th of last June in the evening, a day so fatal that I shall never forget it as long as I live; when I was sitting with my wife in the new summer-house (which you know I have lately built at the upper end of the canal in my garden). Our four youngest children were playing about us, and diverting us with those little wanton tricks, which are natural to youth and innocence, when my eldest boy (who was fourteen last August) came running to us with a great deal of joy in his looks, and told me that Mr S was just alighted at the gate. My boy had scarce delivered his message when I saw Mr S at the lower end of the garden. I went to meet him, and received him with that cheerfulness I endeavour to show to all my friends, and was somewhat pleased to think I should hear what was doing at London, from whence I presumed he came. Mr S told me that he hoped I would pardon the liberty he designed to take of being my guest for one night; and that he was to be the next day upon some particular business.

During supper, among other discourse, my wife happened to tell Mr S that she heard everybody was getting an Estate in London, and by the South-Sea; and that she hoped he had been a fortunate man: Mr S upon this shrugged up his shoulders and told her that to his great misfortune he had but little money to lay out, and consequently had only got such a trifle as was scarce worth mentioning. Upon my wife's asking him if she might presume to enquire how much, Mr S told her that the utmost farthing he had got yet would but barely amount to fifty thousand pounds clear gains.

My wife immediately gave a Look which sufficiently showed her surprise, to hear such a Sum called a Trifle; and as I could not help showing some signs of amazement at the same time, Mr S told us that he believed he could guess at our thoughts by our looks: but that if we knew what vast fortunes other people had acquired, and how certain a gain there was for everybody who had but money to lay out, we should not be at all surprised to hear him talk as he did: he proceeded with giving us instances of several people who had got five or six hundred thousand pounds, and even a million of money; concluding again with bewailing his own unhappiness that he had not more money to lay out at a time when so certain and considerable a profit might be made.

The letter's author then describes how he took a bottle of wine to his friend's room, and as they drank together into the night, their conversation turned again to the South Sea Company. Mr S suggested that his host should think about the future of his children, and that the best way of making a provision for them was to buy South Sea shares. It was, he opined, a certainty that his host would double his fortune within three months. But he must act quickly.

It was the time of the Third Money Subscription, which had been put on sale at 1,000. Mr S, who clearly understood the art of salesmanship and the appeal of a product that was in short supply, declared that all the shares had been reserved for friends of the directors and government ministers, so it might not be possible to buy any. But he would try to help his friend because 'it was as demonstrable as any proposition in Euclid that after the next subscription the stock would as infallibly be at 1500'. Not only that, but he might be able to help his friend buy shares at a bargain price – only 750! The country gentleman was tempted to let him go ahead, but mentioned that he had no spare money. It was here that his troubles started:

At this answer Mr S remained silent for some time, and seeming to be under a great deal of concern told me at last that he had so much friendship for me that he was resolved I should not, however, lose this golden opportunity; and that he believed he

had a particular friend in London who upon his recommenda-
tion would accommodate me with money upon a mortgage of
my estate. To make short of my story, Mr S thoroughly convinced me that I must infallibly double the money I took up,
in three months' time; and my wife, whom I consulted on this
occasion, was so much of the same opinion, that I agreed to
go with him to London, when he returned thither: he accordingly called upon me two days after; and when we came to town,
recommended me so effectively to Mr H that that gentleman did
me the favour to supply me with thirty thousand pounds upon
a mortgage of my estate.

I laid out this money in stock at 750; and my good friend
Mr S assured me he procured it for me considerably under the
market price. He told me from day to day that I had now
made a very noble provision for my family, and might give my
youngest son a better fortune than my eldest son was born to.
At the same time, he took care constantly to inculcate me to
this maxim, that I should not part with one farthing of the stock
I had bought, but should, if possible, buy more, though I
pawned my very coat for it. As I had resigned myself up entirely
to Mr S's management, I followed his advice in every particular;
and to my great misfortune, found my reputation and credit
were so good in town, that though I had no more ready money
to lay out, four several persons contracted to deliver me one
thousand pounds each, capital stock, on several days in October
and December last.

Inevitably, however, the country gentleman's investment went awry.
Like many, he had bought at or near the top of the market, in
instalments, in the hope that he could pay for the shares with the
profits he hoped to make by selling them when they rose in value.
When the share price, instead, started to tumble he was still under
an obligation to pay the next instalment of the purchase price, on
the next due date of the 'contracts for time' he had signed. He was
squandering his money on a declining asset, forced to pay out for
shares he no longer wanted. There was no legal way out of the
nightmare of his obligations, and no prospect that he could meet all
his debts now the shares had crashed. His best hope was that, rather

than cut his losses by selling his shares as quickly as possible, he should wait for the market to pick up. But he could not afford to hang on.

I need not acquaint you with the dismal turn of affairs the South Sea Company took soon after; that at the opening of the books in August, when it was generally expected our stock would have been at 1200 it fell to 800, after which fatal period it constantly declined. I thought, and was told, that it could not be advisable to sell upon a falling market, and that things would very soon change for the better; till at last, one of my contracts for time expiring, and the person I had contracted with insisting that I should either take in the stock or pay the difference, I began to awake out of my golden dreams. To preserve my credit in the Alley, which I had learned a man was never to forfeit, I was obliged to sell the Stock I had bought for ready money, to pay the difference of my bargain for time; and if you have never stockjobbed yourself, it is impossible to express to you to what deplorable circumstances I found myself on a sudden reduced: for at the same time that demands came upon me, the fortune which I thought myself in possession of, and out of which I was to satisfy these demands, shrunk to *nothing*.

The country gentleman had bought forty £100 shares at the market price of 750, at a cost of £30,000 – more than a hundred times the income of a well-off family. He had then bought a further forty £100 shares at 1,000, at a cost of £40,000. In total, he had acquired eighty shares, with a face value of £8,000, but for which he had agreed to pay the staggering amount of £70,000. He was assured that he could do this 'without the least danger of wading out of my depth'. But his investment was far from safe: soon, he was drowning. On 5 October, his stock was worth only 120, but he had to find £8,800 for his instalment payment. To help meet the demand for payment he sold the shares that had cost him £30,000 for just £4,800, even though this still left him with £4,000 to find.

I had nothing now left to hope for, but that the stock would rise as fast as it had fallen, and that I might still be a gainer on my bargains . . . but, alas, these were vain hopes! When my next contract expired, I found myself not only undone but involved in such a debt as I could never hope to pay.

I confess to you I was more than once under a temptation to have put an end to my misfortunes with my life. My wife sent me letters every post, in which the poor woman took it for granted that I had doubled my fortune, and was even contriving how to lay out some of our gains upon the embellishing of our house and gardens. I could not find in my heart to answer one of her letters till at last frightened by my silence, she came up to town herself. My heart is too big with grief to describe to you our first interview. The day after she came to town, one of my creditors to whom I could not pay the difference of our bargain took out a writ against me. Some people who I once thought my friends refused to be my bail for so large a sum, so that my wife was contented to give up joynture [the property settled on a woman at her marriage, to be enjoyed after her husband's death]. This was the only thing we had left to prevent my lying in a gaol, where I should have been now, notwithstanding her kindness, if she had not hurried me into the country by force.

I write this to you from a place which was once my home, but is now my prison, being confined to one room of it, to avoid the pursuit of bailiffs, who have been discovered, more than once, lurking under my windows. I am told that the equity of redemption to my estate will be foreclosed next term; and the person to whom I mortgaged my estate has already had the assurance to send down a surveyor, and a master builder, to see what additions can be made in the house, which, it seems is not large enough for him.

Even as he saw financial ruin visited upon him, the country gentleman was keen to pass the blame on to others for his misfortune. He convinced himself that he had been the victim of a deliberate fraud. To some extent he was correct, in that Blunt's money-making schemes were based on thin air. But the letter-writer suspected that the very man to whom he had mortgaged his estate had lent him money with the specific motive of gaining the property, and that he had conspired with Mr S with this in mind. It is an unlikely tale: for it to be true, the pair would have had to know that the stock was bound to fall. The country gentleman's letter reads like special pleading, an exercise in refusing to face up to his own role in the affair, in the hope that the government, by launching financial rescue, would extricate him from the consequences of his own stupidity. By the end of his appeal, he had wrung every ounce of emotion out of his predicament:

I have given you my unhappy story. I have not only lost all I had, but have still demands upon me for above twenty thousand pounds. Where will my misfortunes end! My poor wife, whom I upbraid myself with having ruined, is for her own part, half distracted, to think what I did was partly by her advice, and is in tears from morning till night. My youngest children hang about their mother; my eldest son keeps me company; the poor boy had the good nature to tell me this morning that if I would but put him apprentice to some honest trade, he would endeavour, at least, to support the family. Alas! The poor child does not know the depth of his father's misfortunes. I am pitied by all who knew me, but find no assistance; and am told, several gentlemen, my neighbours, are almost in the same circumstances.

Dear Sir, as you sit in the House, you can probably tell me what the Parliament deigns to do. Are we to have no relief? Are we to see no end of our miseries? If you have any good news to send me, for God's sake, do it quickly, to prevent me, and my poor family, from going quite distracted.

Postscript.
I hope you will pardon any expressions in this letter that may look a little like distraction, from a man that has not been in bed these three months.

The public, seeking revenge, turned its anger on the South Sea directors who, only a few weeks before, had been so highly praised for their success in business. Investors began to campaign against their underhand dealing, partly to help explain their own stupidity in believing in the Company, but also so as to try to obtain official sanction against the men by whom they had been ruined. One such investor, the splendidly named Captain Maggot, told a meeting of shareholders that he knew of a director who had sold more than £50,000 worth of shares from the Third Money Subscription at a 250 per cent premium. The truth, of course, was that many investors had known of, or had benefited from, the largesse of the directors, and when the Company was booming none had complained. Now that it had collapsed, many were calling for an official inquiry into what had gone wrong. Faced with such pressure, on 29 September the South Sea Company decided to cut, retrospectively, the price of the third and fourth subscriptions from 1,000 to 400, and to halve the going rate for exchanging annuities from 800 to 400. This course of action was designed to benefit shareholders who were paying in instalments for their stock – this way, they would have to find less money to pay fully for their shares. It would cut the Company's profits, but it hoped to stabilise the share price and to reduce the debts of the shareholders who had bought at the top end of the market, by bringing them in line with the first two subscriptions. As with the Bank of England's rescue scheme, the difficulty was that the share price was already below 400, so investors were still being asked to throw good money after bad.

It was not enough to placate the discontented shareholders, though. Investors were still pressing for a larger rescue package, and two weeks later, in Salters' Hall, they met in force to decide whether they should form an action group to tackle the government. One declared that the directors were a 'cabal of sharpers'. The terms of the Company's offer were insufficient, he insisted: 'Must we compound our debts with them? Where will be the honour of our King and the sanction of our laws in Parliament?'

The King, who had left for Hanover in June with the Bubble at its height, had planned to take the rest of the year off to recover from the rigours of ruling England. This was the only factor in the whole crisis that gave the government some cause to believe it might survive. George had been accompanied abroad by the assiduous Sunderland, which should have assured him some contact with events at home, but there is little doubt that the news of the Bubble's slide, which Sunderland regularly received, was diluted by the time it reached the monarch, partly because Sunderland did not relish telling his King the full horror of what was unfolding at home, but partly, too, because Sunderland possessed confidence, to an absurd degree, in the power of the South Sea stock to recover. On 23 September he had told his wife that he was 'very much concerned about the falling of the South Sea but do verily believe it will rise again'. It was, perhaps, the blind faith shared by many investors, for Sunderland possessed a large shareholding himself.

It took another week for Sunderland to tell the King what was happening in the country he had left behind. When he finally plucked up the courage, it was a miserable picture he painted. The booming economy had gone bust; the South Sea Company's shares seemed to be fixed on an inexorable path downwards; hundreds of citizens were bankrupt; and the country was seething with discontent. Parliament needed to be summoned. Sunderland wrote, disingenuously, as if to cover his tracks after all the delay:

Upon the first news we had of the unhappy turn the stocks and public credit had taken, we got the King to fix the meeting of Parliament for the 25th of November. Since then, within these three or four days, we have had the news of Credit's being lower and lower, and of things being every day in a worse condition, the King had taken the resolution of going over to hold the Parliament on the 8th of November, which is as soon as it is possible for him to be there, and orders are sent for the necessary notice. I myself should have set out as soon as we had news of this melancholy state of things, which was but three or four days ago, but that I thought the first necessary step was to fix the King's going as soon as possible.

Sensibly, in what was now a looming leadership crisis, where any action of a contender for power would be scrutinised and magnified, Sunderland's rival Robert Walpole decided to stay away from trouble, distancing himself both from the Bubble's collapse and from the ministry that had provoked it. Calibrating his actions perfectly in keeping with his chance of high office, Walpole took himself off to his Norfolk estate for a month and kept his head down, to wait and see if events moved in his direction when the King returned. Already, ruined investors were turning to him for advice, and his banker Jacombe wrote to him from Lothbury Street that 'they all cry out for you to help them. Everybody longs for you in Town'.

Wearily, with Sunderland in tow, and nearly three months earlier than he had intended, George I set off on the long journey back to his ruined kingdom.

Across Europe, as the King returned, dark clouds of economic depression gathered. France, in breaking away from paper money and condemning Law's experiment as a failure, tried to mend the damage by attempting to suck back in the very metal it had once been so keen to export, pulling out its investments from other European countries and causing their economies to falter. In Holland, shares in the Dutch West India Company collapsed with startling rapidity.

But far more insidiously than France's economic collapse, the outbreak of the plague in Marseilles infected Europe's spirit, eating away at a confidence already sapped by the year's financial disasters. In England, the great plague was only half a century distant, the devastation it had wrought still deeply imprinted on people's minds. It scarcely needed Richard Bradley, a Fellow of the Royal Society, to point out that the 'contagion now spreading itself in foreign parts has nearly the same symptoms that were observ'd in the late Plague at London'. Fear of plague was etched in the memories of those who could remember losing an immediate family member. Thousands of copies of a treatise outlining how families had supposedly been cured of the plague, or avoided it altogether, were given away free. The new generation would do everything in its power to avoid a recurrence of the deadly visitor to France.

The threat of a new outbreak, imported from abroad, had the effect of turning a previously exuberant country in on itself. England's ports were placed in quarantine, with dozens of ships unable to unload their cargo. But in its outlook on life, too, the country became introverted, for the plague loomed large without ever quite arriving, the unrelenting threat making its citizens daily more anxious about their future while giving them time to reflect upon their past conduct as they desperately sought salvation.

There was little practical help to hand, for science had failed to make any progress in its search for a cure. James Craggs the younger, the Secretary of State who was so deeply implicated in the unfolding financial scandal, found time to ask the leading physician Richard Meade to write a discourse on the plague, but Meade was more interested in the effect of coal-smoke on the health of Londoners. He was an enlightened man – one scientist, a Fellow of the Royal Society, wrote a treatise on the virtue and use of coffee in treating the plague, while another doctor issued instructions on how citizens could guard against the disease by wearing an amulet containing half an ounce of arsenic and two ounces of dried toads. The company directors and projectors who had sold quack financial remedies had been superseded by the medical men with their guaranteed cure-alls.

Offered a variety of nostrums, none of which bore any likelihood of success, and fearful for the future, citizens turned to God to protect them against disaster, and the Church moved quickly to regain ground it had lost in a year in which Mammon had been the main object of worship. Across the country, the churches rang to the sound of sermons blaming mankind's vices for the looming infection. William Hendley, chaplain to Lord Fitzwalter, wrote a discourse arguing that 'the Plague never proceeds from first natural cause, but is sent immediately from God, and that as a punishment to a people for their sins'. The plague, he declared, was God's handiwork 'as visible as was the hand-writing on the wall'. The *Post Boy*, a newspaper not given to understatement, agreed: 'The public calamities, which men naturally look upon as proceeding wholly from natural causes, ought to be considered by those who hold the faith as decrees of the providence of a just and merciful God . . . licentiousness and corruption, the fatal fruits of irreligion, reign everywhere; men give themselves up to insatiable avarice; usury and fraud are openly practised; there is no longer any curb strong enough to restrain covetousness.' Another newspaper published a poem entitled 'The Pestilence':

> Oh! England, England, then repent betimes
> Of your notorious, and unheard of crimes
> For judgement ripe; and which most loudly call
> For heavy vengeance on your heads to fall.
> No South Sea water can wash out the stains,
> Of which an injured nation now complains.

So great was the threat from the plague that the Privy Council issued a royal proclamation for a fast day 'to avert all those judgements which our manifold sins have deserved'. The link between the disease and the financial madness of 1720 was, in the Church's eyes and in the minds of many worshippers, explicit. Man was always sinful, and had demonstrated it again; repentance might persuade God to be lenient. What God had sent, in the form of the plague, He could take away, provided His subjects recanted. Quick action was called for. To protect the country from His wrath, the Church of England hastily issued an all-purpose prayer to be used by Christians in private:

> We have abused our plenty by riot and luxury, our liberty by licentiousness, our ease and safety by strive and envyings, and division amongst our selves . . .
>
> This, O Lord, is the sad and deplorable state of this sinful nation, which I unfeignedly grieve for and lament before Thee; and the more, because my own sins (with sorrow I confess it) have greatly increased the number of our iniquities.
>
> I confess, O God, that I have grievously offended Thee by . . . (Here you may name your own particular Sins).

A country which had once seemed so vibrant was living in a shadowland, assailed by the twin forces of economic collapse and imminent medical catastrophe. Its adherence to new financial systems had been shattered, its belief in scientific progress dulled. England no longer embraced the future with a bright eye and a questioning mind. Instead, it clung to the wreckage of its past verities by resorting to the power of prayer, appealing to a superior power to save it from the damnation which, it now piously conceded, it had brought upon itself.

CHAPTER XII

A Lasting Foundation

A Farmer sold a small Estate outright,
To Buy South Sea, but meeting with a Bite,
Purchas'd Sham Stock, paid down five Hundred Po.
And now would thank South Sea to Stock his Ground

Thirty years ago, nobody could have predicted an escalation of the war in Vietnam, wage and price controls, two oil crises, the resignation of a president, the collapse of the Soviet Union, a one-day 508-point drop in the Dow Jones industrial average, nor the fluctuation of treasury bond rates from 2.8 per cent to 17.4 per cent.
Well let me tell you, these events have had little impact on investors who chose to put their money in large corporations like Coca-Cola or Gillette. Whatever the state of the economy, people will always need to shave and quench their thirst.
Warren Buffet, 1994

The King slipped quietly ashore at Margate on 10 November at seven in the evening, a storm-delayed homecoming as inglorious as his country's predicament. Strong winds had blown him back to port in the Netherlands, as if to demonstrate that he was no longer in command of his own destiny. The Channel crossing took five days to complete and when he finally arrived, the bonfires that greeted him were lit more out of a sense of duty than celebration. For if George had hoped to reassure his subjects by his return from abroad, then they took no notice. In the coffee houses, the stockjobbers and shareholders blamed him personally for the fiasco, as titular head of the Company, and there was talk of his being forced to abdicate in favour of his son. As if to demonstrate indifference to the King's return to London, South Sea stock went on falling.

The foul weather which again greeted George when, at the month's end, he went to ride on the Downs, appeared to match the mood of the nation. A sudden hurricane blew up, of a ferocity which few had experienced before. It shook homes with such violence that their frightened inhabitants ran outside for safety. All around the capital, the wind felled chimneys and ripped up roofs, killing a woman and child at Shoreditch and sending hundreds of broken tiles spinning into the streets below. Not even the churches were exempt from the wrathful elements. At St Martin's-in-the-Fields, terrified citizens who had been seeking sanctuary were hit by falling masonry. On the river the damage was as great. The watermen, who had tied their boats together with rope, half a dozen at a time, could only watch from the banks as their craft were dashed against each other. Lighters laden with coal, and barges with corn, were tossed around by the hurricane and dispatched, dismissively, to the bottom of the fast-flowing Thames.

The storm ended as quickly as it began: within three hours the heavens were quiet again. But few investors could see a similarly swift end to their ordeal. The banking system had effectively collapsed, with credit sunk as easily as a waterman's boat. The Bank of England, which had promised a solution through its contract with the South Sea Company, no longer felt like keeping its side of the bargain. It had seen the precipitous fall in the share price, and its enthusiasm for the deal, which had never been great, had begun to wane. Time and again, the Company's directors sought to establish whether the Bank would keep to the terms of its contract, and buy millions of pounds' worth of shares at 400, to prop up the price. But South Sea shares stood at 200, half the price proposed in the contract Walpole had drawn up, and once the Bank had seen the full magnitude of the crisis unfold, it treated the Company's directors with barely concealed contempt. Day after day the South Sea directors, once the mightiest businessmen in the land, tried to make an appointment to see the Governor of the Bank of England, and day after day he loftily refused to meet them.

The Bank's attitude could be explained both by its desire for revenge and by its realisation, as South Sea shares hurtled ever downwards, that it would lose heavily through any operation to prop up the enfeebled Company. But the Bank had also faced, in secret, a financial crisis of its own. No sooner had it reclaimed its pre-eminence from the Company than, ironically, it too was threatened with collapse. Just as had happened in France, so great was the desire to cash in paper money and so great the demand for coins, that the Bank thought it might have to close its doors to customers. If the threat had become widely known, it would have fatally damaged the Bank's reputation and its ability to trade, leaving the country without an established institution to act as the foundation stone for recovery. Desperately, the Bank called in as many loans as it could, acting like a giant financial magnet to attract metal both from across London and from European capitals. It finally emerged from danger when a large sum of Dutch gold arrived to bolster its reserves, and only then did it consent to give the South Sea Company some of the money it was requesting: not the full amount, but merely £100,000, a sum granted as if on sufferance to keep its directors quiet.

By the time the Bank of England finally gave some ground and agreed to hand over a further £250,000 to the Company, its action was a clear sign of the government's growing weakness. It was only with reluctance that the Bank made the gesture, and with a letter which tried to draw a line under the affair by stating its formal refusal to do any more on behalf of its former enemy. So enfeebled had the Whig government become that its old ally in the City had grown beyond its powers of control, and from now on it steadfastly resisted all attempts by Sunderland and Aislabie to try to change its mind. The government had nowhere left to turn. Ejected from the Bubble, the financial mechanism which had cocooned it from reality for the best part of a year, the leadership had no new economic plan. It was offered plenty of advice from other quarters, including one suggestion from an erstwhile projector that a new royal coin should be minted by melting down, and debasing, all the money in the Treasury and in the Company's coffers. It seemed a suitable metaphor for a devalued economy and a shrunken monarchy, but not a practical solution to an unprecedented crisis. In the end, the recall of Parliament had to be delayed because no one in the government could think of a policy to place before it. The result was a leadership vacuum, one which Walpole could clearly see, and to take advantage of it he quickly returned to London from his Norfolk retreat.

Walpole knew it was greatly to his advantage that he had spoken out back in January against the terms of the deal that had handed over the national debt to the South Sea Company. Precisely because Walpole had made such efforts at the start of the year to force the Company to declare to Parliament how many shares it would offer annuitants, he was deemed politically clean, and, even if the truth was a little less clear-cut, he could portray himself as the man who had condemned the speculators. Walpole turned to his banker Jacombe, who in August had effectively protected his client's political career by refusing to buy more stock for him, and between them they tried to devise a rescue deal that would be very different from the Bank contract, so clearly doomed to failure. Even before the Company's formal demise, Walpole could see that the plummeting price of its shares rendered the rescue deal financially impossible; but it was in his cynical political interests, too, for the deal to collapse, in order that his own private scheme should succeed instead.

Walpole had calculated that he needed the crisis to run out of control, and for the anger of investors to grow and be heard ever louder, in order to pitch the ruling duopoly of Sunderland and Stanhope out of power, just as they had effectively wrecked his career so far under George I. This would leave him with a good chance of achieving higher office, and perhaps, indeed, the highest office in the land. If his rescue scheme succeeded he would be hailed by King and country alike as England's saviour. While he needed the crisis to grow, however, and to envelop the ruling elite, it was against his interests for it to reach the point where his own Whig party might itself lose power. He needed the country to be shaken to its foundations, but not destroyed.

Walpole knew he had the power to bring down the government, and perhaps even the monarchy, but if he swept corruption out entirely there was a risk that he would be swept out too. So he opted for politics above principle and began to plot his rise to power. The Tory opposition wanted blood, and so did the independent country landowners in Parliament, so it needed little action on his part for Sunderland and Stanhope to lose their jobs. But there the line must be drawn. The King was Governor of the Company and he held a large shareholding in the Bubble, granted on suspiciously favourable terms, so he was as deeply implicated as most of the leading politicians. But he was also the figure on whom the Whigs depended for their survival, and it was unlikely that he could be removed from office even after the Bubble's collapse, not least because of the thinness of support for the outcast Jacobites. In any case, no self-respecting Whig wanted to do anything that might enhance the prospect of a Catholic returning to claim the throne. The task for Walpole was to manoeuvre within these rules in order to extract the maximum political advantage. He needed to protest his loyalty to his King and party, but not to such an extent that either could again manage without him in the future. High office might best be achieved, and with it security of tenure, not by maintaining an overtly hostile attitude to the main players in the drama but more subtly, by protecting them. To take power would require consummate political skill

– to make use of public anger, but at the same time to control it.

For a week, in private, Walpole negotiated with his allies in the Bank of England about a new rescue deal, even before it had announced its refusal to honour the terms of its contract with the Company. It was deception on a grand scale between an institution which had lost power and a politician who wished to gain it. The country's rulers were effectively stitched up. When the Bank officially announced it had rejected the first rescue deal, Walpole kept silent for a few days. Then he casually announced to Sunderland and Stanhope that he had been working on an alternative plan. His rivals had no choice but to let him proceed. Sunderland called together Walpole, Townshend and half a dozen South Sea directors. Walpole, who informed the King of his actions in order to curry favour, met separately with the East India Company which was reluctant to help out in any way and told it that it was required to play its part in the new deal, even though its directors considered South Sea stock to be 'as fatal as goods from Marseilles'. The new economy which had so spectacularly failed had to be rescued by the representatives of the old.

Rather than try to support the South Sea share price on the market, under Walpole's new plan the Bank and the East India Company were both required to increase their capital to take over a quarter each of the doomed enterprise's shares. Nine million pounds' worth of South Sea shares would be grafted on to each company, and each company would have to offer some of its own stock to annuitants in exchange for some of the South Sea shares they held. In addition, further instalments of most of the different money subscriptions would be cancelled: investors no longer faced the awful prospect of having to throw good money after bad. Shareholders would still rue the day they became entangled with the South Sea Company. But investors would at least hold shares in two reputable representatives of the old economy, and have a reduced holding in the collapsed representative of the new. It would not please everyone, but it was the only hope. The Norfolk landowner, Colonel Windham, wrote to his brother Ashe: 'We are here in a most sad state between hope and despair. Mr Walpole is said often to declare he thinks his scheme will do, but . . . people are frightened. Poor Jemmy's [James Windham of the Salt Office] affairs are most irretrievable . . . Those devils of directors have ruined more fortunes in this world than I hope old Beelzebub will do souls for ye next.'

Parliament could not meet in the King's absence, and he had been away since June. For a half-year, therefore, MPs had been deprived of a political platform on which to debate the affairs of the South Sea Company. When Parliament was finally summoned, nearly a full month after the King's return, it would be an angry, bitter and controversial session, but at last there was a plan of action to put before the MPs, unsettled by the flood of anguished petitions which they were receiving. Already, however, the balance of power had shifted. A political leadership which had come up with no ideas of its own had been forced to look to the man it had kept at arm's length to get it out of the fix. But if Sunderland and Stanhope thought their fellow Whig would save their political skins if they backed the deal he outlined, they were being unduly optimistic.

It was barely a decade since Robert Walpole had sworn revenge for his incarceration in the Tower, and he had just taken the first big step towards keeping his promise to himself.

On Thursday 8 December, Parliament finally met to try to piece together the wreckage of the South Seas. It was only a year and a month since the King had appealed to the Commons to help lessen the debts of the nation. Now, as MPs gathered with peers in the House of Lords, he stood before them in very different circumstances, asking them to restrain the very forces they had helped to unleash. While foreign trade was flourishing, all their prudence, good temper and resolution would be needed, he declared, if order was to be restored, and he asked for their support in finding 'the most effectual and speedy methods to restore the national credit, and fix it upon a lasting foundation'. In reply, the Lords promised a zealous search for a remedy and the Commons, with conscious echoes of the King's request, declared they would certainly do their best to put public credit 'upon a solid and lasting foundation'. Ominously, however, they also suggested that they would inquire into 'the causes of these misfortunes'. It was the last message the King and the political leadership wanted to hear.

It was a vital point, and it had been hard-won. The evening before the King's speech, the government's allies had met to hear a rehearsal of the next day's proceedings – an outline of the King's speech and the address of reply – the usual cosy arrangement which saw the Lords gathering at Stanhope's house and the MPs in Craggs the elder's office. When the Commons' draft reply was read out and it became clear that there was no reference to an inquiry, any sense of complacency ministers may have felt about their ability to control the MPs quickly vanished. The howls of protest were led by the influential backbencher Thomas Brodrick, the man who had opposed the South Sea Act and who had written an account of the initial debate. So great was the threat to party discipline that the leadership, including Walpole, had been forced to give way and agree to the inquiry. It proved to be the defining moment in the history of the Bubble after its collapse. When Parliament began to flex its muscles, as the full scale of corruption began to emerge, Walpole would manoeuvre to undermine the actions of his parliamentary colleagues without leaving any evidence of his involvement in the cover-up he had orchestrated. The next few months were dominated by the unstated conflict between the parliamentary investigation into John Blunt and his Company, and Walpole's determination to limit the scope of the inquiry in order to protect those in power, so that he might seize it for himself.

There was little sign at first that the government was under threat. In the debate which followed the King's speech, most of the dissent came from obvious quarters which the government thought it could discount. The MP William Shippen put forward an amendment which demanded that the restoration of public credit should be carried out 'as far as it is consistent with the honour of Parliaments, the interest of the nation and the principles of justice'. In his opinion, he told the Commons, the directors of the South Sea Company were not the biggest villains, since 'there were those above them' – in other words, government ministers – who should have kept a check on their progress. Shippen, the government considered, could safely be ignored – he was a well known Jacobite who had been put in the Tower after the King's Speech of 1717 for remarking that ' 'twas a great misfortune that the King was a stranger to our language and constitution'.

Lord Molesworth, the Anglo-Irish radical, spoke with great anger, and would have impressed the government if it had not been for the way he chose to express his sentiments. The South Sea directors, he said, were like the sons who killed their fathers in ancient Rome, an act so vile that there was no law against it, because it was assumed that no one would commit it. Rome had been forced to invent a punishment, sewing the culprits into sacks and throwing them alive into the River Tiber. Molesworth declared: 'As I look upon the contrivers of the South Sea scheme as the patricides of their country, I should be satisfied to see them undergo the same punishment.' No one could tell whether he was being serious.

Next, the former Chancellor of the Exchequer, Sir William Wyndham, drew parallels with the demise of John Law in France and the powers of the French Parlement, which were less extensive than those in England. It would be a disgrace, he said, if MPs showed less vigour and spirit than their counterparts in Paris who had forced Law's removal from his post. But Wyndham had been close to Henry St John, Viscount Bolingbroke, who had fled to France and the Jacobite cause, so the government thought that he did not represent mainstream opinion either. Thus the warning signs were ignored. It was the first of its many misjudgements of the Commons' mood.

For his part, Walpole was biding his time, content not to reveal his rescue plan until Parliament had given full vent to its feelings. Instead, he was eager to side with Secretary of State Craggs and show full support for the Whig government's handling of the crisis. As he rose to his feet and stood before the Commons, his enormous bulk added to the sense that he was the dominant figure amongst his anxious colleagues on the government benches. He could not have chosen his words more carefully or to greater ambiguous effect. In his view, he said, it would be wrong to start the new session of Parliament with 'irritating' inquiries: if the City of London was on fire anyone with any sense would rush to put out the flames rather than waiting to ask how the fire had started. Only after the government had managed to staunch the 'bleeding wound' of public credit should there be an inquiry into its cause.

Walpole was pointedly making clear his agenda to both his friends and his rivals at the very top of the government. He reminded the Commons that 'for his own part' he had never approved of the South Sea scheme, but then, with considerable disingenuousness, he declared that 'since it could not be undone' it was the duty of all good men to help sort out the mess. He announced modestly that he himself had already developed some thoughts on a proposal to restore public credit, which 'in a proper time he would submit to the wisdom of the House'.

The political code did not need much deciphering. If the rescue plan worked, then he should receive the credit, and if political scalps were needed, then he was to remain untouched by the scandal.

The Commons, however, was not prepared to be as docile as it had been when the government had put forward the South Sea Company's plan to buy up the national debt. MPs, scalded by the scandal and their own role in it, wanted to demonstrate their newly discovered independence of thought by controlling the precise time-table under which an inquiry would be held. They no longer trusted the leadership to deliver on its promises and feared, correctly, that if the government had its way an inquiry might never be held. They were led by the merchant MP James Milner, who proposed that 'the authors of our present misfortune' should be punished, a motion which was seconded by Sir Joseph Jekyll. Milner was greeted with such an outpouring of support that the government was forced to concede the point.

With the government's retreat, Walpole could see the difficulties ahead for his own strategy. To side too strongly with discontented MPs would reduce his chances of gaining high office, if the King and his acolytes survived; but to side too strongly with the government would lower his standing in members' eyes. However much he emphasised his original opposition to the scheme, they might even tar him, by association, with the South Sea disaster. Already, several speakers from the opposition benches had rumbled his tactics, and attacked his resistance to an inquiry by accusing him of screening those in power.

The leadership, too, realised that its position would become increasingly untenable unless it could control the restive Commons. As if to confirm the fears of MPs, behind the scenes it was trying desperately to fix the parliamentary timetable so as to hold a quick debate on restoring public credit, as a way of deflecting MPs from their threatened inquiry. First Craggs the younger, who had his own dubious shareholding to hide, suggested that a grand committee should meet to consider public credit, a committee which would, he promised, then go on to hold the inquiry the Commons wanted. Again, Walpole fixed his colours to the government's mast by telling MPs that by following their proposed course of action they risked upsetting his rescue plan – even though he had still to reveal its contents. An inquiry would be 'odious', he protested, and if the Commons went on 'in a warm passionate way, the said scheme might be rendered impracticable'.

Sir Joseph Jekyll then rose to his feet and proceeded, in a magisterial speech, to demolish the government's position. An inquiry must be held without delay, he insisted, to examine whether the South Sea Company directors had followed the rules laid down by the Act of Parliament which had given them their powers. It was absurd, he suggested, for the government to attempt a cure before it knew what the illness was, while conversely an inquiry might inform the remedy. So powerful was Jekyll's speech, and so eloquently did he plead his cause, that the House barely listened to any more opinions. Sir Richard Steele, the inventor of the travelling fish pool, railed against the 'cyphering citts' who had brought the country to its knees and warned prophetically that, unless MPs acted, the guilty parties were going to be 'screened by those of greater figure'. The Tories had no need to say anything. The government was on the run. Jekyll had won the day.

An inquiry was not, however, the limit of Parliament's ambitions. It wanted the power to punish the guilty. Its desire for revenge was quickened by its anger over the degree to which it had itself been duped by the South Sea Company. Some members had been involved with the Company on straightforward terms, through buying and selling shares, and now saw, as the full absurdity of the country's position struck home, that their political decisions looked tarnished by their investments. In retrospect, they realised, they should have listened to the siren voices which had warned them that the Company could not make a profit out of the national debt, and that perhaps it could not even raise the millions it had promised to pay the government for the dubious privilege of buying it. But they were ranged against many others who had been bribed and who needed to disguise the depth of their corruption. In all, more than four hundred and fifty MPs had held South Sea stock at some time during the year, and 122 out of the two hundred peers had been shareholders.

There was a tension between members of Parliament who wished their infamy to remain hidden and those who simply regretted their misguided entanglement. Overall, Parliament was determined to root out corruption, if only because it needed a scapegoat for its own stupidity.

The result was that the Company directors found themselves on the receiving end of a series of sharp commands issued from the Commons. It ordered them to account for every action they had taken under the South Sea Act, and for all the money that had gone through their books for a year, since Christmas Day 1719. In particular, MPs wanted to uncover more about the practice of lending, without authority, large sums of money to investors; and, specifically, which people had gained from this illegal practice. The whole system which had first inflated share prices, and then brought them crashing down, now stood condemned as Parliament passed a motion declaring that 'nothing can tend more to the establishment of public credit than preventing the infamous practice of stock-jobbing'.

Parliament, like the Bank of England before it, had outgrown the government's control. The government appeared paralysed. When MPs went home for Christmas, Bank of England stock stood down at 142, and no price for South Sea stock could be quoted. Holders of the First Money Subscription could barely sell their options at half the price they had paid, and buyers of the later subscriptions could not offload their shares at all.

It would not be a season of peace and goodwill for ministers. The Jacobite William Shippen ignored the holiday period and continued, relentlessly, to ask questions. Why, he demanded, had the Company, only weeks before, declared a 50 per cent dividend when it knew it was in terminal trouble? The government knew that if the questioning continued, and if the threatened inquiry was even half as hostile as the previous session of Parliament had suggested, then the extraordinary extent of its complicity and corruption would soon be laid bare.

In fact, a vast archive of wrongdoing lay waiting to be discovered only a few miles from Westminster, an entire balance sheet of evidence meticulously recorded in the registers kept by the Company, noted down in line after line of entries in the cashier's green book. But it would not be there for long. Although the politicians did not know it, time was running out for any inquiry to succeed. For deep within South Sea House, the Company's cashier Robert Knight was orchestrating a cover-up. As each parliamentary demand was made for the directors to account for the money that had passed through their hands, Knight was taking steps to hide the full extent of the corruption that had propelled the Company's share price to its zenith. He knew that if MPs saw the ledgers which recorded all his dealings, their inquiry would discover that the Company had lent vast sums of money, far in excess of the individual limits set, to help investors buy shares. Quietly and efficiently, Knight ordered that scores of false names should be added to the ledgers, each entry recording the supposed recipient of a small, allowable loan, so that in this piecemeal fashion he could account for the total figure he had handed out.

Harder to disguise were the shares which had been handed out so liberally at the start of the year to buy support for the South Sea Act, the widescale bribery which had captured leading members of the government including Sunderland, Aislabie and the two Craggs, as well as the Secretary of the Treasury, Charles Stanhope, who had cashed in the fictitious stock he had been granted in the spring, thereby banking a quarter of a million pounds in all. Again, forgery was Knight's answer. False names of share purchasers were added to the register to disguise the true recipients of the South Sea Company's largesse.

A year which had started with corruption was ending with concealment. But Knight's subterfuges were nothing compared to the cover-up which Robert Walpole would soon authorise, the cynical screen he would put in place to prevent the newly found spirit of parliamentary democracy from discovering just how far corruption had eaten into the very heart of the British establishment.

CHAPTER XIII

In the Darkness of the Night

My sincere apologies for the predicament I have left you in. It was neither my intention or aim for this to happen but the pressures, both business and personal, have become too much to bear and after receiving medical advice, have affected my health to the extent that a breakdown is imminent. In the light of my actions I tender my resignation with immediate effect and I will contact you early next week to discuss the best course of action.

From a handwritten letter from Nick Leeson, who lost £869 million and broke the Queen's bank, Barings, 24 February 1995

The Christmas break concentrated minds. The government had time to take stock of its tactics, despite the barrage of questions fired at it by the obsessive Shippen, while the opposition considered its next move. The two sides were set on a collision course. Ministers, left bruised and battered by the parliamentary tempest they had endured, decided that their approach had been too tame. Equally, MPs resolved to yield none of the advantage they had gained. From now on, they launched themselves upon an increasingly savage pursuit of justice, as if they were trying to make up for their past quiescence with excessive zeal. The conflict between the government and its opponents was one of the most spectacular of the century. The head-on clash would leave the government reeling, several ministers destroyed, three more dead, and the South Sea directors under lock and key, with one more on the run. But despite the casualty list, it was a process skilfully stage-managed by Walpole so that the severity of some of the punishments handed down screened the guilt of those in higher places that he had resolved privately to protect.

When Parliament reconvened in January 1721, the government's first miscalculation was to propose, with a straight face, that the disastrous state of the nation's finances was not the most important business for discussion. Instead it suggested that the annual Mutiny Bill, which legitimised the standing army, should be debated first, a tactic which would give it an opportunity to wrap itself in the flag and to tempt the Tories into vociferous political debate, in order to delay any discussion of the emergency facing the nation. But if the government had any realistic expectation that its tactic would work, it rapidly found otherwise. The ruse was blown away by the same back-benchers who had given the government such a torrid time before.

Sir Joseph Jekyll, for one, would have none of it. There was only one way to serve the King properly, he said, and that was not by discussing the Mutiny Bill, or any other money bills, but to get on with punishing the people who had brought the nation to its knees. As a first step, he demanded legal action to prevent all thirty-three South Sea directors from leaving the country for a year, and to force them to declare their wealth. Walpole's brother, Horatio, seconded Jekyll's proposal by outlining the unfair methods by which the directors had become rich. 'Their pride and insolence,' he said, were inseparable from their 'upstart fortunes'.

The atmosphere in the chamber was already tense as the two sides launched their attacks, but within a few seconds it became explosive. The fuse was lit by William Shippen who repeated his claim, made before Christmas, that he knew of great men in high places who were as guilty as the directors. If he had left matters there, his intervention might have passed without comment. But what made his charge sensational was that this time he threatened to name names, and as he did so he turned his head slowly and deliberately to stare at James Craggs the younger on the government front bench. For the first time, a specific minister had been singled out for blame. Craggs was furious. He rose to his feet in a fit of temper and shouted angrily that he was ready to 'give satisfaction to any man who should question him, either in the House or out of it'. Lord Molesworth, though he was well past sixty, was quick to rise to the challenge, declaring as he did so that he had the whole nation behind him. 'I have been a member of the House upwards of thirty years,' he thundered, 'and never knew before any man bold enough to challenge the whole of the House of Commons, and all England besides. I will answer whatever he has to say within the House, and hope there are enough young members who would not be afraid to look Mr Secretary in the face out of the House.'

Loud murmurings of support rippled round the chamber. Craggs, conscious that the mood of the Commons was against him, knew he had gone too far. 'By giving satisfaction,' he explained weakly, he did not mean he wanted to challenge his opponents to a fight: 'I meant clearing my conduct.'

Craggs's retreat marked the government's climb-down, too, the point at which it was forced to give way in the face of overwhelming opposition, never to recover. It could only watch impotently as the Commons voted for an inquiry to be held by a 'Committee of Secrecy', so named because it was selected by secret ballot. The thirteen members of this committee, who had wide-ranging powers, were among the Commons' most independent-minded spirits. Their number included Thomas Brodrick, the most outspoken opponent of the South Sea Act; Lord Molesworth and Sir Joseph Jekyll, and Archibald Hutcheson, an economist who had campaigned against the Company in many learned, if incomprehensible, pamphlets. In Thomas Brodrick in particular, the government found a determined opponent who would not try to disguise any evidence of wrong-doing. The collision between the ruling elite and ordinary MPs had moved from the chamber of the House, with its fluid allegiances, to an inquiry of undiluted hostility towards the men who had launched the country on its misguided adventure upon the South Seas.

Such hostility could be found in a growing sense that the directors were guilty until they proved their innocence. After Jekyll's intervention, they were each forced to find £25,000 in bail money, to be handed over against the possibility that they might try to leave the country. But there was another sanction which was far more serious if the course of justice was to be properly observed: the directors were refused the basic right to appoint lawyers in their defence. Years later, Gibbon the historian campaigned against the iniquities of the Commons' action against the grandfather who shared his name, the South Sea Company director Edward Gibbon: 'The legislature restrained the persons of the directors, and imposed an exorbitant security for their appearance,' wrote Gibbon. 'Against a bill of pains and penalties it is the common right of every subject to be heard by his counsel at the bar; they prayed to be heard; their prayer was refused; and their oppressors, who required no evidence, would listen to no defence.'

Despite its draconian measures, however, the Commons had missed one trick. Lord Hinchinbroke had tried to convince MPs, as they started their inquiry, that they should take the directors into custody straight away, but his warning had fallen upon deaf ears. The MPs' decision not to take this final step rebounded upon them spectacularly.

It would allow one of the directors to escape abroad, with a vital file of evidence, thereby handing Walpole the single greatest weapon in his attempt to protect the established leaders of the country.

On 14 January 1721, the Commons' Committee of Secrecy began its hearings at the scene of the crime, South Sea House itself. For fourteen hours a day, six days a week, it proceeded diligently and methodically to lay bare the innermost workings of the state. The first session of the committee examined Blunt, and three fellow directors, all day, but they gave nothing away. 'The top directors have 100 things to answer for,' wrote James Windham in the Salt Office to his stockbroker. 'The town are very much rejoiced at this vigour in ye Commons, for it was shrewdly suspected the Court did design to screen ye directors for fear it might draw in Craggs. The directors have brought themselves into bankruptcy by being cunning artful knaves. I am come into the same state for being a very silly fool.'

The Commons did not have the field to itself, however, and this was to become another complication. Not wishing to be outdone by their emboldened colleagues in the Commons and risk losing the political initiative, the House of Lords decided to establish a parallel inquiry, their own grand committee. Many of the hundred or so members of the upper house who had tied up their money in the South Sea Company had taken heavy losses, not least because they had been so assiduously cultivated by the Company directors at the time of the money subscriptions. These were men of wealth and influence, and they were about to turn the very qualities for which they had been courted into weapons to train upon the government. In the light of this, Stanhope and Sunderland took stock of their position, and decided to change tack. Ministers rapidly realised that, rather than stand by their erstwhile business allies, they needed to shift the blame on to the directors as quickly as they could. Keen to distance themselves from the Company without delay, they mounted a full-scale damage-limitation exercise. In this, they employed two tactics. Their aim over the next few months was to use the Lords' committee of inquiry to spike the guns of the freelance spirits on the Committee of Secrecy, in case the MPs' findings caused too much damage. And they developed a face-saving formula to explain the government's role in the selling of the national debt. Ministers

drew a distinction between the South Sea *operation*, which they conceded, for the first time, had gone wrong, and government *policy*,
which had, in principle, been correct.

The ministry's two leaders took charge of selling the new message.
Secretary of State James Stanhope, one of the few members of the
ruling elite who had not been corrupted by the Company, told his
audience in the House of Lords that 'the estates of criminals, whether
directors or not, ought to be confiscated, to make good the public
losses'. Sunderland, too, surprised the chamber by joining the peers'
onslaught against the directors, delivering a *mea culpa* which managed,
at the same time, to deflect blame. He conceded that he had been
in favour of the South Sea scheme, because he thought it was in the
nation's interests to reduce the national debt and the 'encumbrance'
of the long-term annuities. But 'no man would imagine that so good
a design could have been so perverted in the execution, and in my
opinion no Act of Parliament had ever been so much abused as the
South Sea Act, and therefore I would go as far as anybody to punish
the offenders'. If Sunderland was in any doubt that the peers were
in a mood to find scapegoats, he did not have to wait long. The
Duke of Wharton, who had been a heavy loser in the Bubble, Lord
North, Lord Grey and the Earl of Abingdon all weighed in against
the handling of events, while the Bishop of Rochester compared the
South Sea project to the plague.

If the attacks on the government over the South Sea debacle had
gone no further than this exchange of political rhetoric, then the
tactic of blaming the directors might have enabled ministers to escape
unscathed. Still to be unravelled, however, was the creeping under-
growth of corruption that had entwined itself around the body politic.
One man, the Company cashier, Robert Knight, was to alter the
whole course of the investigation.

Knight had watched the two inquiries, in the Commons and the
Lords, get under way, and had become increasingly anxious about
the evidence piled up in his office. On 16 January, Blunt had been
called before the Lords' inquiry and had been subjected to some
searching questions about his role in the affair, although he had again
revealed nothing of importance. But Knight did not care for the
direction in which the hearings were heading. As the man in charge
of the Company's accounts, he knew that its records pointed to his

specific involvement in organising the fraud, and he also knew that when his turn came for interrogation he had only one weapon with which to defend himself, which was to argue that he was following orders, and to threaten to bring down others with him. As the days went by in the run-up to his own appearance before the Commons' inquiry, Knight desperately approached government ministers to try to blackmail them into protecting him. 'If I should disclose all I know,' he hinted darkly to his fellow director, Sir Theodore Janssen, 'it would open such a scene as the world would be surprised at.'

On Saturday 21 January, Knight's questioning began. The Commons' inquiry tackled him about the fictional 'shares' he had given to the great and good in order that they could cash them in when the price had risen, without any risk to themselves. Knight told them that he had given away a huge quantity of stock in bribes, and that he had camouflaged the absence of income by entering the transactions in the ledgers as loans 'to sundry'. But he refused to reveal the names of the recipients of his favours because otherwise, he said, he would have to give up 'forty or fifty of the Company's best friends'.

Knight was buying time while he considered his next move. In the absence of the political fix for which he had pressed, he was faced with a bitter choice: to take full responsibility, and bear the punishment for others, or to come clean and implicate the politicians he and Blunt had ensnared. Neither course had much to recommend it. Blowing the whistle on ministerial corruption was to be considered only if it would cause the government's downfall, or else if his freedom – and perhaps even his life – was in danger. Taking full responsibility was hardly palatable either. There was, Knight thought, only one solution. On the Saturday evening, as soon as his questioning had drawn to a close, he slipped silently out of London and headed for Dover, where he boarded a boat for Calais. Much like John Law before him a quarter of a century earlier, he was fleeing from justice, across the water, into exile. The nature of his arrival in France showed both the interlocking nature of the two rival Bubbles, and their symmetry. Knight was met by Law's son as he stepped from his yacht on to French soil.

Knight's disappearance appeared to be spontaneous, but that was the illusion he wanted to create. In reality, his flight had been carefully prepared for some time. Long before he left, Knight had sent some of his money abroad, and to protect the assets he left behind he put them in the names of members of his family. He may even have been helped to organise his escape by the government. None of this, however, was of immediate concern to the investigators: they were less interested in how Knight had managed to escape than in why he had done so, and the impact of the increasingly aggressive questioning his departure provoked was to prove catastrophic for the government. Knight had, by his action, stripped away the veneer of official respectability which had masked the Company's disreputable dealings over the past year, so that the Commons saw for the first time the true nature of the South Sea enterprise.

The first the Commons' inquiry knew of Robert Knight's departure was when it reconvened on the Monday morning. A self-serving letter from Knight to his fellow directors was handed in to his assistant Robert Surman at South Sea House. The letter made light of the cash he had taken with him, claiming it was just enough to make ends meet, and instead laid great emphasis on the burden the inquiry had placed upon him. Quite why he bothered to write the letter is unclear. It could hardly wipe away the stain of guilt that his flight indicated – though Knight did attempt to do this – nor was the inquiry likely to think kindly of his suggestion that it was itself to blame for his departure because it had been too hard on him. It is the unctuous letter of a man eager to blame anyone but himself.

Gentlemen

Though self-preservation has obliged me to withdraw myself from the resentment against the directors and myself, yet I am not conscious of having done anything that I can reproach myself for.

I have taken with me but little more than a sufficiency to maintain myself, and the effects left will more than answer for all deficiencies.

I have withdrawn myself only to avoid the weight of the inquiry, which I found too heavy for me; and I am sensible that it would have been impossible for me to have avoided the appearance and charge of prevarication and perjury, not from my own intention to do so, but from the nature and largeness of the transactions. I am sure, I am a good deal concerned to add to your present difficulties, though I must say that I have deserved better usage than I have had from the court the last week. But this I say without any resentment, otherwise than that it has been an addition to the weight I had before upon me.

I am pressed for time, so can only assure you, that I am, with all respect, in inclination, though not in power,

Sunday Evening
22d. Jan. 1721   Gentlemen,
                Your most obedient
                humble servant

                Robert Knight

The letter sparked a day in which political sensation followed political sensation, in which the hesitancy of the last two months was swept aside by the Commons' determination to seek revenge for the way it had been deluded. MPs were spurred into a fury of belated action, putting in place a series of measures which, if implemented earlier, would have prevented Knight's escape. On the Monday, as soon as Knight's letter had been read out to a hushed chamber, they fired off two missives to the King at St James's Palace, demanding that Knight be arrested, the coastline watched and all the ports sealed. Then the doors of the chamber were locked, and the keys were ceremonially laid upon the table. Four MPs who were also directors of the Company, Sir Robert Chaplin, Sir Theodore Janssen, Jacob Sawbridge and Francis Eyles, were summoned to the House immediately. The Committee of Secrecy sent its agents to raid the offices of South Sea House and the Sword Blade Bank in order to seize the paper-trail of evidence that Knight, they assumed, would have left behind; finally and belatedly, Blunt and his fellow directors were rounded up and taken into custody. Their homes were raided for evidence which might point to their guilt – though the key evidence was safe in Knight's grasp.

Theodore Janssen, who was rich but relatively untainted, and Jacob Sawbridge now stood before the Commons as if they were on trial for their lives. The MPs in the chamber were more like a baying lynch mob than a court of law, their anger whipped up by the Committee of Secrecy as it described its preliminary findings to the angry House. They had 'discovered a train of the deepest villainy and fraud that Hell ever contrived to ruin a nation', they said, and they promised in due time to lay the evidence before the House. But the Commons was in no mood to wait. It decided, on the spot, that Janssen and Sawbridge were guilty 'of a notorious breach of trust and thereby had occasioned a very great loss to great numbers of His Majesty's subjects, and had highly prejudiced public credit'. The pair were instantly expelled from the House and taken into custody by the Serjeant at Arms. Before the week was out, Francis Eyles and Sir Robert Chaplin were under lock and key, too.

That evening, there was more drama. The King issued a proclamation in which he belatedly ordered the ports to be sealed and his customs officers – and his subjects everywhere – to be on the lookout so that Knight, who was already in Calais, could be brought to justice. A reward of £2,000 was put on the cashier's head. Then the ministry stripped the Company's directors of their public offices. Francis Hawes was removed as Cashier of the Customs; Richard Houlditch, as treasurer of the Stamp Office; Arthur Ingram, as treasurer of the Duties upon the Salt; Sir Harcourt Master, as Receiver-General of the City of London; and Thomas Reynolds as a commissioner of the Victualling Office. James Edmundson was forced to resign as purser on the Navy's leading man-of-war, the *Royal Anne*. Society which had been so ready to embrace the directors of the South Sea Company when they were successfully generating wealth had now stripped them of their standing, and removed any sign of their connection with the state itself.

Finally, that day, came the first ministerial casualty. The Chancellor of the Exchequer, John Aislabie, who was close to Francis Hawes, saw which way the wind was blowing and resigned from the government. Aislabie was a charmless, unprepossessing man, an over-promoted politician who dreamed not of filling high office with distinction, but of the great riches which it brought him. Now he was forced out, to await the findings of the Committee of Secrecy on his share dealings and the inevitable punishment that lay in store. His departure was the first dent in the government's armour, the first sign that it might not survive the renewed onslaught from the two inquiries. If the Chancellor had resigned, where would the rot stop? Was the King himself vulnerable, as Governor-General of the Company? The very establishment itself seemed about to unravel before the astonished eyes of emboldened politicians.

If Monday's events had put the country on a political knife-edge, the next day was no less sensational, as the inside story of how the South Sea Company had falsified its accounts began to be revealed. Its Deputy Governor, Sir Charles Joye, thoroughly rattled by the parliamentary crackdown and fearful for his own position, began to tell the Lords' grand committee the story of how the South Sea Company had bribed its way to power. Acting on his evidence, the House of Lords ordered Black Rod to imprison five of the directors: William Chapman, Robert Chester, Edward Gibbon, Francis Hawes and Richard Houlditch. Their papers, too, were seized. But at this stage the government's opponents were lacking someone of authority who could point the finger at leading members of the ministry. Two directors, William Astell and Harcourt Master, gave evidence of ministers' culpability by naming several politicians both inside the government and on the back benches who had taken large quantities of stock in return for smoothing the passage of the South Sea Act, and the Lords quickly passed a resolution condemning such action as 'notorious and dangerous corruption'.

The evidence the Lords had gathered was, however, largely anecdotal, and in the absence of Robert Knight, Sir John Blunt himself was clearly central to uncovering the full story. Only months before, each day in Exchange Alley had brought free-spirited talk of new companies, crazes and inventions that had created opportunity for all, but now the only talk was of law and order, and of how quickly the country's rulers would impose their authority to crack down on the directors. On the streets, the demonstrators were still mounting their protests, and their mood was vile. A large rat had been nailed by its ears to a sign which read 'a director of the South Sea'. The Duke of Wharton, the president of the Hell-Fire Club, had driven a hearse through the capital, in a mock funeral for the South Sea Company. It was not an optimistic backdrop for a man in Blunt's position.

On 27 January, Blunt went before the Commons' Committee

of Secrecy and again refused to answer any of the key questions. But he was preparing to shift his ground in the most dramatic fashion. After Blunt had finished giving his day's evidence, Sir Charles Joye paid him a visit and was startled to find that the man who had fought so tigerishly to dominate the business world was thinking of surrendering, meekly, to his inquisitors. Blunt told him that he had concluded it was best to tell the whole truth, even though it meant implicating those closest to the King. 'What?' cried Joye. 'The truth about the ladies and all?' 'Yes,' Blunt replied, self-righteously. 'The examination is very strict and nothing but the truth will do.'

Blunt had calculated that the only way to save the wealth he had amassed was to cut a deal. Part of his consideration may have been the changing balance of power after Knight's departure. The two inquiries, in the Commons and the Lords, now held the whip hand and Blunt suspected the old order was doomed. It was in his interests, he thought, to throw in his lot with his Commons inquisitors, in the hope of a lighter punishment, one which might even preserve the grand estates he had acquired. So on his second day of evidence, in keeping with the tenor of his conversation with Joye, Blunt revealed that Knight had kept records of all the Company's transactions in two books, one of which, the so-called green book, had accompanied him across the Channel into exile. He confessed that these accounts contained false entries, to hide the names of leading ministers who had been on the take. Then, within the space of a few stunning seconds, he destroyed their cover and reeled off the roll-call of corruption.

More than £1 million had been spent on bribes, he recalled. It was an astonishing amount at a time when to earn £500 a year was to be wealthy. Blunt could not remember all the recipients; but certainly, he said, he had followed the instructions of Craggs the younger by paying the Duchess of Kendal £10,000 in return for her 'good offices' in bending the King's ear when the Company launched its scheme, with the same amount for Madame Kielmansegge and her two nieces. Senior members of the government had benefited too: Lord Sunderland had received £50,000 and Craggs the elder £30,000.

Blunt had betrayed his fellow conspirators in the government.

Word quickly seeped out from the Commons that senior ministers had been exposed as corrupt, that the government was in terminal trouble, and that the royal family might be engulfed in the scandal too. But it was still rumour, and this placed the government in a quandary. How could it shore up its crumbling position, when it did not know exactly what Blunt had told the Committee of Secrecy? Its only hope was that he would repeat his claims before the Lords, where the government could hope to exert enough influence to counter his allegations. But Blunt, though no longer in command of his mighty business empire, could still play an astute hand with the few cards he had been dealt. His compliance with the Commons' inquiry had strengthened, not undermined, his cause. When the time came to appear again before the grand committee, the Lords were optimistic that Blunt would reveal much more. But, to their surprise and anger, he refused to answer the Lords' questions, or even to take the oath. The reason, he insisted, was that he had given evidence 'in another place', and he did not have a record of what he had said. 'As no man is obliged to accuse himself, I would not run the hazard of prevaricating.'

The Lords were furious, and voted Blunt guilty of contempt of the House. No one was angrier than the one-time hearse driver, the Duke of Wharton. He accused James Stanhope, sitting grim-faced on the government front benches, of provoking divisions between the King and the Prince of Wales, and even suggested that Stanhope might be suffering from venereal disease. Stanhope was indeed unwell, but not because of the pox. He had been out the night before drinking with his friends, the Duke of Newcastle and Craggs the younger, and they had consumed rather too much champagne and burgundy – so if anything, he considered that he had a hangover. Furious at Wharton's allegation, he rose to defend himself, calling his opponent a degenerate who should have been sacrificed in the name of patriotism.

This was the last political intervention by one of the few incorruptible ministers in the government. Stanhope took his blinding headache home, and the doctors bled him. Strangely, he was little better the next day, and at six in the evening he was still in bed, sleeping, when he turned over, took one look at his doctors, and died – probably from a brain haemorrhage.

It was a devastating blow to the government, shattering its hopes of retaining power. At home, it was losing its grip on the nation, and abroad even the manner of Stanhope's death became the subject of ridicule. 'Lord Stanhope died as the result of a horrible orgy he had with four lords,' the Duchess of Orleans wrote in her Paris diary. 'I don't understand what pleasure people find in excesses which are really only suitable for beasts.' King George, realising the full depth of the new crisis, pushed his supper to one side, and retired privately for two hours to contemplate the death of the one man who could have helped shore up his own position. The omens were not good. In two days' time, it would be 30 January, the anniversary of the execution of Charles I seventy-two years earlier.

The King paid for Stanhope's funeral out of his own pocket, and it was a splendid affair. The slow procession through the City to the Earl's family seat at Chevening in Kent was led by ten of His Majesty's Horse Grenadiers, who cleared the way for another fifty grenadiers, two hundred Life Guards, the youngest battalion of Foot Guards, and then the eldest battalion of Foot Guards. They marched in step to the beat of muffled drums and to the lament of trumpets, from which fluttered black mourning banners. An officer of arms carried Stanhope's spurs and crest, another his shield and sword. His servants walked slowly, two by two, then came his hearse, which was covered with black velvet, adorned with feathers and his coat of arms, and drawn by six horses. It was followed by the King's coach, the Prince of Wales's and then the Archbishop of Canterbury's. Forty Horse Grenadiers brought up the rear.

But Stanhope's passing was not the end of the government's losses. Within a day of his death, James Craggs the younger began to feel unwell. Within a fortnight he was dead from smallpox, which carried him off at four o'clock on a February afternoon at the age of thirty-five, just as the first report on the South Sea affair was being presented to the House of Commons. Nothing became Craggs quite like his funeral: the government, keen to put on an outward show of establishment normality, buried him at Westminster Abbey with the full political obsequies, as if it could draw no distinction between his conduct and that of the irreproachable Stanhope. The Speaker, Spencer Compton, acted as a pall-bearer, and the Bishop of Rochester officiated, as Craggs was laid to rest in a vault which contained the remains of a general, a duke, a marquis and an earl.

It was prestigious company, and ostensibly appropriate. In death, a veil was drawn over Craggs's role in the South Sea affair. Pope wrote, in all seriousness, the following epitaph which was inscribed on his tombstone:

> Statesman, yet Friend to Truth! of Soul sincere
> In Action faithful, and in Honour clear,
> Who broke no promise, serv'd no private end,
> Who gained no title, and who lost no Friend,
> Ennobled by himself, by All approved,
> Prais'd, wept and honour'd by the Muse he lov'd.

In only one respect did the private funeral service appear out of the ordinary. It was held at night, in case the South Sea protesters tried to disrupt it. In its own way, the nocturnal ceremony was a fitting symbol of the government's failing powers. Its rule could not survive the scrutiny of daylight.

CHAPTER XIV

Hall of Mirrors

We regret having to conclude that, notwithstanding Mr Maxwell's acknowledged abilities and energy, he is not in our opinion a person who can be relied on to exercise proper stewardship of a publicly quoted company.
Department of Trade Report, 1971

The late Robert Maxwell was, by common consent, a monster. The publication this week of the Department of Trade inspectors' long-delayed report on the events that led to the collapse of his empire will reliably confirm that verdict. This was a man who had been declared unfit to run a public company in the early 1970s. Such a damning verdict should have put Maxwell beyond the pale for all time.
Why did the City of London allow him back?
Financial Times, 28 March 2001

For a year, the government and the South Sea Company had conspired to pull the wool over the eyes of the country's citizens, exploiting their blind belief in the power of the stock market to deliver them a fortune. None of the investors possessed such faith now, but nor did they yet know the full facts of how they had been defrauded by their political leaders. With Blunt's evidence in its pocket, the Committee of Secrecy was working towards the first of its many dramatic conclusions. Revenge was in the air. The best the government could hope for was to try to contain the damage, but it was so enfeebled that it had given up hope of trying to influence the committee through its agents in the Lords. Ministers resigned themselves to the fact that the inquiry would order political bloodletting within the government ranks. Their main concern was to make sure that the patient did not become so weak that the cure would kill it.

To this end, Robert Walpole pursued his strategy of simultaneously undermining ministers who no longer posed a threat to his ambitions, while shoring up the parts of the administration which, he calculated, would provide vital support if he was to succeed in his bid for power. Some of his colleagues he would save; others would be damned. Too many casualties would damage the establishment structure irreparably, and with it his own chances of heading a continued Whig hegemony;

too few, and he might be a casualty too. The calculation was a fine one, and complicated by the destabilising movements of the loose cannon he had failed to tie down: the Company cashier Robert Knight was still on the run with his green file of evidence, which contained the power to destroy the government.

The way forward required great skill and cunning, both qualities that Walpole possessed in abundance. The government, though weak at home, still held influence abroad through its network of overseas diplomats and the cooperation of friendly countries. British foreign policy, untrammelled by the domestic considerations of an unruly Parliament, was now to be diverted and perverted by Walpole so as to contain the danger posed by Knight. While Walpole publicly protested that he wanted Knight to be extradited, and that he was doing everything he could to make it happen, behind the scenes he had resolved to keep him abroad at any price, rather than bring him back to give evidence. Walpole was engaged in playing not one, but *two* games of chess. One was carried out in public, in front of a Westminster audience which watched him carefully, although he was always several moves ahead of his scrutineers. The other game was an altogether darker and more sinister affair, carried on behind a screen of political protection whose existence would be deniable. The consequences of this hidden game would only become clear when several centuries had rolled by. Once more, the wool was about to be pulled over the eyes of the country's honest citizens, to clear the way for political ambition.

Since his flight in January, after the Committee of Secrecy's first day of interrogation, Knight had journeyed in a roundabout way to Brussels, to avoid countries which had an extradition agreement with Britain. The city lay within the Austrian Netherlands, geographically equivalent to Belgium and Luxembourg today and an area which was controlled by the Hapsburg Emperor, Charles VI. On reaching Brussels, Knight lived under a false name in the most expensive hotel he could find, funded by the money he had been so careful to export before his flight. His plan was to join John Law, whose wanderings had led him to Germany, but his movements were being carefully watched by police spies and as a result his presence in the city soon came to the attention of the British chargé d'affaires. The chargé, Edward Gaudot, was deputising for the resident diplomat in Brussels,

William Leathes, and if Leathes had not been away on holiday in Suffolk the course of history might have been very different. As it was, Gaudot was determined to show that he was worthy of his caretaker role, and that he could be trusted as an honest servant of the Crown. The large reward which the government had placed on Knight's head was, to the enthusiastic Gaudot, a sign of the importance of his capture. He was not aware, as Leathes might have been, that the King and his government were living in a hall of mirrors: that their publicly stated intentions were in fact the opposite of what they wanted.

Quickly and quietly, Gaudot took out a warrant for Knight's arrest. Even as he set out to seize his quarry, events nearly worked out to the government's advantage. Knight was tipped off about the danger and left Brussels in a hurry, accompanied by his son and an aide in John Law's service. His future and that of the British government depended on the speed with which the trio could reach the eastern frontier, where the principality of the bishopric of Liège began and the jurisdiction of the Austrian Netherlands ended, as did the legality of the imperial arrest warrant that had Knight's name upon it. And Knight could afford not a moment's delay. Kicking up the dust on the road to the border, a few miles back, a detachment of sixteen dragoons raced towards him, headed by the eager Gaudot who was so keen to impress his masters back in London.

The chasing party tracked Knight to Leuven, the former capital city which lay twenty miles east of Brussels. His pursuers established from the burgomaster that English gentlemen had spent the night at the local inn but had left early in the morning. Time was running out: Knight had already completed half the journey to the frontier. Gaudot cut the size of his party to the four best riders, took fresh horses and set out on the road to give chase again. Just short of the border, Knight stopped at another inn, at Tienen, and it was here, twenty miles further along the road to the south-east, that Gaudot caught up with his prey. Knight was arrested on the spot and dispatched with his son to the impregnable Citadel of Antwerp, fifty miles to the north, while the documents he had filched from South Sea House were removed from his grasp.

The parliamentary cheers which greeted the news of Knight's arrest matched, in their intensity, the anger MPs had expressed over his escape in January. No one was more ecstatic than the government's old scourge, Lord Molesworth, who showered fulsome praise on his monarch. A humble address should be presented to His Majesty, he declared, 'for his great goodness in giving such effectual directions to his ministers abroad for securing Mr Robert Knight'. But Molesworth was sharp enough to ask whether the King would ensure that Knight was repatriated 'together with his papers and effects'. He was right to ask the question. The incriminating papers had already disappeared, probably secreted away by the government: they had been sealed and handed to the British chargé d'affaires by the Deputy Governor of the Austrian Netherlands, the Marquis de Prie, who possibly forwarded them either to Walpole or to Townshend. They were never to be seen again. Like many of his ministers, the King hoped that Knight would not be repatriated. But he replied that he would certainly give the orders that would deliver Knight to the Serjeant at Arms.

Inside the Citadel of Antwerp, it seemed a certainty to Robert Knight, too, that he would soon set out on the return journey to his homeland to face a heavy jail sentence. Any prospect of escape had vanished with his incarceration. A prison officer was stationed inside his cell, and another four outside. He could not even send messages beyond the walls of the vast fortress that enclosed him: the man whose ledgers had caused such trouble for the government was deprived by his jailers of paper, pen and ink. But Knight's extradition was, in fact, becoming far from inevitable. Outside the prison walls, the forces which wanted to keep him from justice were already secretly manoeuvring over his fate.

In England and in Europe, events were moving in opposite directions. At home, the Committee of Secrecy was bearing down on the errant ministers it had identified; but abroad the government was carrying out a diplomatic dance designed to keep Knight on the continent and to prevent him from giving evidence. The first sign of the move to prevent his return was a mission to Austria, engineered by Walpole. In the middle of March, while he was publicly protesting about the need for Knight's return and at Walpole's behest the King sent a special envoy, Colonel Charles Churchill, to Vienna, ostensibly to persuade the Austrian authorities to hand over their prisoner. But nothing was as it seemed. In reality, Churchill had been ordered to persuade the Governor of the Austrian Netherlands, Prince Eugene, that Knight's extradition posed insoluble difficulties for the British government. Even the choice of Churchill for this mission was an indication of the government's duplicitous intent, for he was a colourful character who had absolutely no qualifications for the task he had been set. He was cheerful and outgoing, a professional soldier and a ladies' man, and, by diplomatic standards, he was practically illiterate. The crucial ingredient was that he was a staunch friend of Walpole, who had chosen him to be his fellow MP in Norfolk, and he was entirely trusted by his ally.

A second diplomatic mission was undertaken, also orchestrated by Walpole, to try to secure the government's position. At the same time that Churchill set out for Vienna, the Brussels diplomat William Leathes was dispatched from his Suffolk home to give two messages to the Marquis de Prie. Leathes's two messages, like Churchill's, were the mirror image of each other. For public consumption, Leathes maintained that he had been given specific instructions by the King himself to demand that Knight should be sent back to London. But privately, he told de Prie, the King wanted a very different outcome. He asked the Marquis 'so to arrange matters that the prisoner should not be handed over', and to promise that he would keep the deception to himself. He was requested to do nothing that might cause 'the British Parliament or the British people to doubt whether the representations being made for extradition were sincere and unreserved'.

There was no doubt that matters could be fixed, if de Prie was amenable. Like Walpole, he could operate behind a screen, in his case constructed by the complicated constitutional make-up of his territory. While de Prie had imperial powers, he could seek refuge in the local charter privileges which had been granted to the duchy of Brabant, centuries before, and which gave it the right to try any suspected criminal arrested in the province's territory. The ban on extradition had been circumvented before, but it could clearly be activated again to resist the demands for Knight's return which were issuing daily from the British Parliament.

In launching his initiative, however, Walpole was risking everything. Discovery, or the Emperor's refusal to participate, would do him irreparable damage, as well as adding his name to the roll-call of political casualties which the Committee of Secrecy would demand. To guess which way the Emperor would jump was a gamble, but a calculated one. A deal with England would be hard for him to swallow, precisely because of the very web of deceit that had led to the South Sea Company's formation. The secretly negotiated, dishonourable peace with France, forged by Robert Harley in order to launch the Company, had left Austria to continue the fight against the French enemy alone. Subsequently, to try to forge a worldwide trading empire, England had again turned its back on Austria in order to repair relations with Spain. But, on the other hand, Walpole knew that the Emperor could plainly see that George I's throne was under threat, and that he would not do anything to encourage the King's replacement by a Stuart monarch, who would lean towards the French. On top of which, the British made it very clear that they would pay almost any price for the Emperor's help. Leathes stated that 'it was a matter of the very highest importance for the King of England and those in whom he placed his confidence and were implicated in the affair that he should recover from the unfortunate predicament in which he now found himself and had made his ministers objects of public hatred'. Furthermore, 'favourable management of this affair would be regarded by His Britannic Majesty as the most conspicuous mark of friendship the Emperor could possibly confer on him, which he would always bear in mind, and one for which he would demonstrate his gratitude at all opportunities'.

As the delay continued, it appeared to the Commons that its move against Knight had been stalled for no apparent reason other than the intransigence of a foreign potentate and his interpretation of legal procedure. One afternoon in March, becoming restless, a grand procession of three hundred MPs travelled in their coaches to St James's Palace, with the Speaker at the head of the procession, to present the King with a politely worded resolution thanking him for his help so far in trying to bring Knight to justice, and asking him to press their cause more strongly with the Emperor. They concentrated their anger on the obduracy of the Brabant leadership in hiding behind the 'pretence of their privileges'. Any reservations they may have harboured over the King's conduct were left unexpressed. Their diplomatic niceties were matched by the King, who chose to interpret the Commons' message as unalloyed approbation of his actions. 'I am very well pleased that the instances which I have made for obtaining the delivering up of Mr Knight have given you satisfaction,' he declared. 'I shall continue to employ my utmost endeavours for obtaining what you desire, and hope they will prove effectual.'

In the meantime, however, as the King well knew, Britain's foreign and domestic policy lay in the hands of a rival empire. So close was Austria's involvement behind the scenes in the manipulation of the political process, that Leathes's letters to London spelling out the apparent difficulties of extraditing Knight – which the government placed before an increasingly indignant Parliament – were drafted by the Deputy Governor of the Austrian Netherlands himself. The Emperor's excuses were deemed to be frivolous by MPs but, in their impotence, all they could think to do was to pass a motion banning the import of lace from the Austrian Netherlands until Knight had been handed over. But the Deputy Governor's subterfuge went further. He also helped draft Leathes's letters to the Brabant assembly (known as the States of Brabant) in which the diplomat spelled out, for public consumption, why Britain wanted Knight's return. But at the same time he held a confidential meeting with the Archbishop of Antwerp, who chaired the assembly, in order to persuade him to *refuse* Knight's extradition. Finally, he won over the three key Brabant municipalities of Brussels, Malines and Antwerp, so that they agreed to block Knight's return. After two days of debate, the assembly voted to block the British demand for Knight to be sent home to face justice.

None of this serpentine diplomacy was known to the anxious politicians in Britain pressing for Knight's return. All they understood for certain was the strength of Leathes's protestations at home and abroad which were published by the helpful editor of the *Edinburgh Evening Courant*:

Brussels, April 22 1721
Yesterday I presented a memorial to the Marquis de Prie desiring Mr Knight might be given up to justice. He has given me repeated assurances of his endeavours to persuade the states to comply with the King's demands. A little time will now bring this important affair to a conclusion, and I hope, such as will be satisfactory to his Majesty, and the whole nation.

The contents of Mr Leathes' Memorial to the Marquis de Prie:

That Mr Knight, instead of deserving refuge and protection, is by a pernicious conduct and such crimes as were never heard of before, become a public offender and enemy to mankind, so that he cannot claim any public right to the benefit of any nation in the world.

The late directors of the South Sea Company allege that Knight is the sole author of the great mischiefs done to the nation which have overwhelmed it and nobody but himself can lead the Parliament through the windings of a maze, composed of the most infamous contrivances that ever were practised.

Over the next few months, the two sides, the Commons on the one hand and the Emperor on the other, tested each other's strength, probing for weaknesses which might decide Knight's fate. Molesworth suggested that Knight could be granted a royal pardon if he returned to testify before the Committee of Secrecy, and, ominously for the government, Knight himself was said to be rather taken with the idea. The government had to move quickly behind the scenes to block the possibility, which it finally accomplished when de Prie sent a lawyer to the Citadel of Antwerp to inform Knight that even if he was given a pardon by the King, the Committee of Secrecy would still be able to prosecute him. Even then the government was not out of danger. The Committee of Secrecy decided to send one of its number to question Knight in prison, with the promise of parliamentary immunity. Once more, de Prie came to the rescue, this time by ordering the police to stop the MP at the ports. Knight, a suspected criminal who had escaped from justice, was being given the protection of the state while his pursuers were being treated as undesirables.

But these moves were not enough for Walpole, nor for the King. At any time, they feared, Knight might fall into the hands of the parliamentary forces, either by escape or because the Commons might establish some form of communication with him. To safeguard against escape or rescue, the Brabant authorities were persuaded to move Knight secretly from his Antwerp prison to the Luxembourg

Citadel, while an elaborate charade was performed to mask the fact that he was no longer where he was meant to be. Security was maintained as usual at Antwerp, food was sent in at mealtimes, dirty plates were removed, and visitors, who were in de Prie's pay, were sent into Knight's cell to 'talk to him'. It was a laborious and ridiculous routine and one which could not be kept up for ever. William Leathes assured de Prie that the ritual had only to be maintained until the summer, by which time Parliament would be in recess, the Committee of Secrecy would have completed its task, and pardons could be issued to both Knight and his son.

The desperate attempts to protect the monarchy, and Walpole's career, now became increasingly comic. Almost nothing went to plan to support the subterfuge. Parliament sat far later than anyone had anticipated – until August – giving time for rumours to circulate that Knight's Antwerp cell contained only a phantom prisoner. Still the Committee of Secrecy was unrelenting in its legal pursuit of Knight. There seemed only one solution. The British government concluded that the prisoner who was supposed to occupy a cell at the Antwerp Citadel must be brought back there – in order to be allowed to escape. That way his presence at the prison could be verified, and, even without an amnesty, he would escape the Commons' clutches. The Emperor agreed that if the British would help him in his fight against the growing Spanish threat in Italy he would go along with the plan. But there was one more condition: the British would have to acknowledge – formally – his help in the matter, to protect him against any reprisals if it all went wrong.

The details of this secret deal lay buried for the best part of three centuries, until a piece of paper was uncovered in the Vienna state archives, the smoking gun which some of Walpole's enemies suspected but none could ever prove. It was a letter, dated 11 September 1721, to the envoy of the Hapsburg Emperor from the British envoy, Leathes.

Sir,
The King my master, being highly gratified not only with the orders which Your Excellency has issued and the care you have taken to keep a secure guard on Mr Knight, former Cashier of the South Sea Company, but also, and more emphatically, for

the striking instances and continual diligence you have shown on His Majesty's behalf in relation to the States of Brabant to persuade them to consent to the extradition of Knight to England in accordance with the requests I was instructed to make on behalf of the King my master to Your Excellency to employ the Authority of His Imperial Majesty and his government in that regard; and having been informed, on unquestionable authority, that all the efforts so far made, or which could yet be exerted, would be completely ineffective owing to the special situation of the said States a breach of whose privileges could lead to serious consequences: His Majesty has found it appropriate no longer to insist on pressing for this extradition, bearing in mind the desirability of avoiding opportunities (contrary to the Emperor's interests) for ill-disposed persons to foment complaints and new troubles in the Austrian Netherlands.

His Majesty has commanded me to inform Your Excellency on his behalf, that since he takes a true and sincere interest in all that concerns the service of His Imperial Majesty, he is pleased to express the wish that Your Excellency should order the Governor of the Antwerp Citadel to enlarge Knight from confinement, allowing him not only to have liberty to walk on the Citadel, but to escape.

His Majesty relies upon the prudence of Your Excellency in carrying out these requests in such a manner that it shall not appear that this escape is authorised by His Majesty or this government.

I am, &c
William Leathes

It is a document which no diplomat would have considered writing unless he could take no other course of action: the preferred form would have been a nudge here and a wink there, a policy of plausible deniability. Even so, the tortuous prose in the letter's first unwieldy sentence tried to offer some sort of defence against the day when it would be unearthed, seeking, disingenuously, to shift the responsibility for the request on to the local extradition policy of the duchy of Brabant. But there the well of inspiration ran out. The British were in a bind, and had to accede to the demands of the authorities in Vienna for an exculpatory piece of paper as the price for the deed. Here was Albion at its most perfidious.

But at least the Emperor was as good as his word, aided by his remarkable second-in-command in the Austrian Netherlands, who was meticulous in the detail of the arrangements. Knight and his son were taken to the Ardennes and, to their evident surprise, released in the middle of the night. They did not know it, but they had broken through a solid wall to freedom. In the morning, at the Citadel, a hole in the wall was discovered, with a rope ladder dangling down. When the alarm was raised, the sergeant who was on duty that night was found to have gone missing from his post. Publicly, it was said that he was a deserter. In fact, the men who knew about the conspiracy had been bribed handsomely to keep quiet. The sergeant on the night-watch was paid, promoted, and moved to another regiment. The silence of a second officer at the Citadel of Antwerp was bought in the same way. The officer who had been sent specially from Vienna to supervise the whole operation was promoted and sent to Transylvania, far beyond the reach of rumour.

The political corruption which had inflated the South Sea Bubble had now ensnared Britain's foreign policy and its legal processes. Once more, Robert Knight slipped away from justice and into the darkness of the night. He would remain in exile, like John Law before him, for twenty years and more.

Walpole's secret manoeuvring was suspected, but never proven: it was not clear who was to blame for Knight's disappearance, though the affair clearly smelled. A popular cartoon of the time, called 'The Brabant Screen', pointed the finger at the Duchess of Kendal, one of the King's mistresses – she is depicted behind a screen in a handsome room, handing over money to Knight, who stands with riding-whip in hand, ready to escape. On a table are inscribed the words: 'Patience and Time and Money set everything to rights.'

By such devious devices, the established order was preserved and George I rested more easily on his throne. By the same token, Walpole was a step closer to his avowed aim of seizing power.

CHAPTER XV

Friends in High Places

New York – Former President Bill Clinton said Friday he takes 'full responsibility' for pardoning Marc Rich, the international fugitive wanted on tax evasion, fraud and racketeering charges. Clinton said he believes he handled the pardon in the 'most appropriate way,' but added he wished he had 'more time to work on it.'
'I take full responsibility for it. It was my decision. Nobody else made the decision,' the former president said after a meeting in Manhattan. 'But I handled it in what I thought was the most appropriate way.'
The pardon has outraged many lawmakers on Capitol Hill, especially Republicans, and hearings are expected on the controversial pardon. Rich's ex-wife, Denise Rich, has donated roughly $1 million to the Democrats.
CNN report, 2 February 2001

Protective barriers had been placed around the monarchy by Walpole just as surely as the country's coastline had been sealed against the importation of the plague. Already, the political cost of establishing the King's defences was clear. George and his coterie of hangers-on were in the debt of their saviour, whose rise to power seemed assured. Walpole's brother-in-law Viscount Townshend was promoted to take charge of foreign affairs as Secretary of State, a significant indicator of the pair's revived influence with the court. Times had, indeed, changed since they had been excluded from the inner circle, when ministers had been forced to dance to the tune of the King's mistresses. Now, it seemed, it was the royal family's turn to keep in step with Walpole, and provided he did not go too fast for them or trip himself up in his eagerness for power, a glittering political future looked certain. But, at the same time, there were still battles to be fought. While Walpole had managed to protect the monarchy through his devious activities abroad, he could not throw a similar screen around corrupt ministers back home. The two parliamentary inquiries were in full spate, and evidence of wrongdoing had become widely known. There still lurked the possibility that the established order could be brought down by over-zealous parliamentary investigators incapable of seeing the damage they might cause their country if they pursued their case too strongly. If that happened, then Walpole's future might suddenly look bleak, and the King's position might be weakened. In such circumstances, what was to stop the Jacobites from attempting to reclaim the throne?

Half a dozen years into his reign, George was more secure than when he had first arrived from Hanover, to face immediate, if small-scale, rebellions against his rule. But at no point since his accession had the wounds inflicted by the expulsion of the Catholic James II in the Glorious Revolution of June 1688 entirely healed. The first summer had been punctuated by rioting, which had marked the parallel lives of the King and his rival. In May of that year there had been conflict between Whigs and Tories in Oxford on George's birthday; then trouble in Somerset and the Midlands on James III's birthday a month later. Then came two major, unsuccessful, rebellions: in 1715, when James, the Old Pretender, had actually landed, and in 1719. Now the King had provided another opportunity. Too late, he tried to escape responsibility for the Bubble, by telling the Lord Mayor and aldermen of the City of London: 'I am truly concerned at the calamity brought upon you by the wicked management of affairs in the South Sea Company; I have however this comfort that the reproach of any part of this misfortune cannot with the least justice be imputed to me.' But his intervention could not stop the ugly rumours which began to swirl around the capital about the extent of his culpability as the Company's Governor-General. His mistresses, too, were variously alleged not just to have spent some of their ill-gotten gains on paying for Knight's escape, but to have secured their fortunes abroad within a Hanoverian safe-haven.

The exiled James III probably sensed that his moment had come and gone, but this did not stop him now from making his pitch for power, and in doing so he attempted to strike a far nobler note than the King: 'Some may imagine that these calamities are not displeasing to me,' he proclaimed in Rome, 'because they may in some measure turn to my advantage. I renounce all such unworthy thoughts. The love of my country is the first principle of my worldly wishes, and my heart bleeds to see so brave and honest a people distressed and misled by a few wicked men.' Left implicit was the contrast with George I, and the *two* countries he represented. Sufficiently encouraged by James's intervention and by the birth of his heir, a barrister of the Middle Temple, Christopher Layer, enlisted a group of men in east London to try to seize three key buildings, the Tower, St James's Palace and the Royal Exchange. In the resulting confusion, he aimed to capture George and restore the Stuarts to the throne. The plot was discovered, however, and Layer was later executed at Tyburn.

But if the threat could be contained, there were, nonetheless, two pressing problems for the government. First, the initial official draft of the South Sea Company's financial position showed a deficit which was almost too horrible to contemplate. The Company owed the Exchequer at least £14 million, which was nearly half the size of the national debt it had bought from the government. It had nothing in the bank, despite the promise of the fabulous wealth owed to it by its shareholders – a cold, but realistic, assessment was that its prospects of forcing the debtors to pay up was nil. So entangled were the fortunes of country and Company that the latter's demise meant the nation's financial future was at stake. If the Company, the holder of the much vaunted national debt, was declared bankrupt, then the state, too, was effectively in default.

On 16 February 1721 (ironically, the same day that a bill 'to prevent the infamous practice of stock-jobbing' was given its second reading), the Committee of Secrecy presented its initial findings to the Commons. For more than two and a half hours, MPs listened in amazement as Thomas Brodrick recounted in great detail the events of the previous year. He had, declared one parliamentary commentator, uncovered 'the deepest and largest scene of villany and fraud that ever was contrived and perpetrated'. In its report, the committee laid bare the subterfuge carried out by directors as they had scurried to hide the evidence of their wrongdoing. In some of the ledgers 'false and fictitious' entries had been made; in others, the space for the names of investors had been left blank. Some entries had been erased or scored through, and pages had been torn out. Worse still for the investigators, some of the Company's books had gone missing, including the notorious green book taken by Robert Knight, and others had been destroyed before they could lay their hands upon them. Despite all the difficulties, however, the committee members told the Commons, they had been able to reveal a 'scene of iniquity and corruption, the discovery of which your Committee conceived to be of the highest importance to the honour of Parliaments, and the security of his Majesty's government'.

The committee's first finding was that £574,000 worth of stock, which was supposed to have been sold for £1,259,000, had gone missing – or rather, as the committee remarked, it was 'very observable' that it could find no names of anyone who had bought the stock, even though the Company's own treasury committee had approved the accounts. The report, with a delicious use of understatement, pointed drily to the political event which had so quickly followed the issuing of this stock: the passing of the South Sea Act itself. 'Your Committee, upon this occasion, take the liberty to remind the House of a remarkable period in the last session of Parliament: that the House agreed . . . that the proposals made by the South Sea Company should be accepted. . . . Your Committee, surprised to see so large an account of stock disposed of by the Company, before the passing of the bill . . . proceeded to examine carefully that transaction.'

The committee members had indeed been careful. Reading their report, it is impossible not to be struck by the assiduousness with which they conducted their inquiry, and by the thoroughness of their methods. Following up the clues that they picked up from inconsistencies in the evidence of the witnesses who appeared before them, the investigators cross-checked ledger against ledger, cash book against cash book, to find the discrepancies that would point to the guilt of those in high places. It was eighteenth-century detective work of the highest order, with only pen and ink and memory to guide the investigators as they trawled through the thousands of pages of transactions recorded by Robert Knight and his team. Carefully, the inquiry team unravelled the process by which shares had been 'sold' for notional prices with no record of a date and without any money changing hands – 'so that if the price of stock had fallen, as might be expected if the scheme had miscarried, no loss could have been sustained by investors; but if the price of stock should advance [as it did in the successful early weeks of the scheme] the difference by the advanced price was to be made good to the pretended purchasers'. None of these purchasers, the committee remarked, had appeared in any of the Company's ledgers, and it noted that only five directors, including both John Blunt and Robert Knight, had the authority to carry out such deals. The noose was tightening around both the directors and the politicians in their pay.

Slowly and deliberately, piece by piece, the committee laid down the damning evidence. One of its key witnesses had been the director Robert Surman, who had told them he had assisted Knight in preparing a draft of the accounts, and that he himself had made several entries in the green book. Surman said he did not know the names of all the investors because Knight occasionally turned over pages in the book hurriedly, without showing him the entries. But he clearly remembered that the name 'John Aislabie Esq.' had been entered alongside a large shareholding. Aislabie had been well rewarded for his promotion of the Company's concerns within the highest circles of government. His final account, when it was discovered, showed a staggering profit of £794,481.

The next set of allegations, read out by Thomas Brodrick, was even more damaging, if such a thing were possible. Here he provided evidence of corruption at the very heart of government, spelling out, in detail, allegations that Sunderland himself had taken bribes. These claims stemmed from John Blunt himself, who had proved to be the inquiry's star witness – a status acknowledged by the report, which noted that he had provided 'your Committee with the first material information'. Blunt claimed that in February 1720 Knight had told him he was going to supply £50,000 worth of free stock to Sunderland, with another £30,000 for Postmaster Craggs. Later, as the Company collapsed and events began to unravel, Blunt said he had asked Knight how he would conceal Sunderland's role in the affair – to which Knight had replied, 'I would go through thick and thin rather than give Sunderland away.' And it seemed that Blunt was telling the truth. His evidence was supported independently by several of his fellow directors, who also testified to their belief in Sunderland's infamy. Edward Gibbon recalled that Knight had mentioned to him that Sunderland was to be given £50,000 worth of Company stock; Deputy Governor Charles Joye said Knight had insisted that £100,000 worth must be reserved for Sunderland's 'friends'; and Richard Houlditch said Knight had confided in him that £50,000 worth was held for 'a noble Lord in a high station', which he had taken to mean Sunderland. Crucially, in the light of Walpole's later tactics and in the absence of the vital green book, much of the evidence against Sunderland was circumstantial.

The Commons had already heard allegations of corruption on a staggering scale, but the share dealings carried out by the Treasury Secretary Charles Stanhope were even more extraordinary. John Blunt had told the inquiry that as the South Sea Bill was making its way through the Commons, Stanhope had written a letter to request 10,000 shares, which were then worth £25,000. The committee could not find any record of Stanhope paying for them, but they had certainly made him wealthy. As the price of the shares rose, the committee found, Stanhope had regularly received his profits from the Company. On 7 May he had been given more than £5,500, a week later another £600; on 18 June he had accepted more than £40,000, and on 10 September, £4,865. In all he had made more than £50,000 at no risk to himself. But, as the committee soon discovered, he had made even more money later. A second tranche, of 50,000 'shares', had been massaged through the Sword Blade Bank's accounts at the time of the South Sea Bill's passage through the Commons. By careful inspection of the books, the Committee found that these shares had been cashed in at a value of £750 each, and that on 11 June the full sum they had realised had been placed in Stanhope's account. Then on 12 December 1720, long after the Bubble had collapsed, the minister had pocketed a quarter of a million pounds, the profit he had made over and above the notional cost of the shares. It was as much as Thomas Guy, the bookseller, had made through legitimate trading.

The case against Charles Stanhope looked cast-iron. Despite his position in government, Stanhope had taken few steps to disguise his involvement. One clerk testified that he had seen Stanhope – 'a tall thin man of a black or brown complexion' – turning up to collect some of his money in the summer months. Several times, he recalled, he had seen Stanhope and Knight writing together as if settling their accounts. Belatedly, however, there seemed to have been attempts to cover the minister's tracks. While the committee could find no sign of Stanhope's name in the ledgers, they found an entry which had been altered, far too obviously, to Charles *Stangape*. The pathetic attempt at concealment seemed, in retrospect, to sum up the course of the South Sea Company's history. With the benefit of hindsight, it was easy to see it for what it was: not a sophisticated financial operation, as many fondly imagined it to be, but a relatively crude and vastly successful attempt to exploit human greed.

The Committee of Secrecy proceeded to lay bare the appallingly lax internal controls which had existed within the South Sea Company, stripping away the pretence that it was a great financial institution with a properly ordered set of accounts and financial systems, to show that it had been run like a dictatorship for the enrichment of a tight-knit group at the top. When the Sword Blade Bank director Jacob Sawbridge was asked why he had signed off the South Sea Company's accounts, complete with blank spaces where the names of shareholders should have been written, he declared he had done so simply because Robert Knight had told him that the accounts were in order. In addition, the committee revealed that Blunt had, on Chancellor Aislabie's advice, lent far more money and sold far more stock at each share launch than he had agreed with the Company's Court of Directors: a quarter of a million excess shares were sold in the First Money Subscription, and half a million extra shares in the Second. Each time there was a share launch, Blunt had taken a hidden profit, and Aislabie had received a bribe.

In all, the committee estimated that perhaps as much as £3 million was unaccounted for in the Third Money Subscription, and a quarter of a million pounds in the fourth and final share launch. It had not found any satisfactory explanation for the gap in the accounts. 'Your Committee cannot but observe that some persons made great gains, whilst the price of the said subscriptions continue high; so when the price of the subscriptions fell, many other persons were favoured, by having their subscriptions withdrawn, which was the cause of the deficiency.' The committee also discovered the share support scheme which had been operated by the directors through the Company's brokers. It found that Knight had artificially controlled the level of the shares as if the market was his own personal fiefdom, stopping the brokers from flooding the market with shares by lending too much money when prices were too low, and forcing them to intervene when prices were slipping from their peak. All this was done, the inquiry concluded, with one aim in mind: 'The said directors, in all their proceedings in the execution of their scheme, appear to have had chiefly in view the raising and supporting the imaginary value of the stock at an extravagant and high price, for the benefit of themselves, and those who were in the secret with them.'

The committee's report made clear, by implication, that in its rapid rise the South Sea Company had not just corrupted government ministers and MPs, but had gone far beyond the capacity of the politicians to control it. There were no financial checks and balances placed upon it by Parliament, despite the fact that it had taken upon itself the role of guardian of the nation's finances through its purchase of the national debt. Relieved of their onerous burden, the country's rulers had surrendered themselves either to bribes or to the power of the market, without any way of monitoring the Company's internal workings. The roaring success of the South Sea Company had bred only complacency in Parliament. In contrast, the diligence of the Committee of Secrecy had put the government to shame, and the Commons knew it. The question was – who would pay the price for this year of infamy? It was not going to be a simple matter of justice. Even James Windham, at the Salt Office, could see that withdrawal of political support would be the vital factor in determining who would be blamed. He wrote to his brother William, to reflect upon his own parlous financial state and upon the likely outcome of the inquiry into the Bubble's collapse: ''Tis said the Court have given up ye directors and in a little time they will be in ye state of bankrupts for the good of ye Company. Aislaby must suffer and some say Craggs.'

The Commons, outraged by the deceit that its inquiry had uncovered, decided to take the law into its own hands by putting on trial the Company's directors and the politicians who were allegedly in their pay. There was no clear basis in law for the step it was taking, but it decided that its own self-fulfilling declaration was enough: 'the taking in, or holding of cash, by the South Sea Company for the benefit of any member of either House of Parliament or person concerned in the Administration . . . were corrupt, infamous, and dangerous practices, highly reflecting the honour and justice of Parliaments, and destructive of the interest of His Majesty's Government'. On the last day of February 1721, therefore, Charles Stanhope became the first defendant to be brought before the Commons. It was barely a year since the Bubble Act had received its royal assent.

Stanhope was still Secretary of the Treasury, and he probably expected to be the first serving minister to be found guilty. But by the time his trial started something curious had happened. Blunt, who was the main witness for the prosecution, had watered down his story that Knight had shown him Stanhope's letter in which the minister had asked for £10,000 worth of shares. Now he simply said that he did not know whether or not the letter was genuine. So, too, Jacob Sawbridge and Elias Turner from the Sword Blade Bank insisted that the parcel of fifty thousand shares Stanhope had allegedly received had been put in his name without his knowledge or permission. Stanhope's own story was similar. For many years, he said, he had given all his spare money to Knight for investing, and he could not be held responsible for the cashier's actions.

Walpole, too, spoke in Stanhope's defence, and his intervention perhaps helps to explain the second curious event which occurred during Stanhope's trial. When a vote was held to decide his guilt or innocence, it was discovered that three members of the Committee of Secrecy, the hitherto outspoken Molesworth, Jekyll and the Pay Office official William Sloper, had all gone home. Their absence was to prove crucial. Stanhope was acquitted of the charges against him by precisely three votes – 180 to 177. Some sort of deal had clearly been done behind the scenes, either by Walpole, or the King, or both. Stanhope had been found not guilty of corruption, leaving half the chamber fuming. In its impotent fury, all the Commons could agree on was that whoever had made use of Charles Stanhope's name in order to conceal the £50,000 worth of stock had been guilty of an 'unjustifiable and unwarrantable' practice.

This was far from enough to placate the crowds outside. The news that Stanhope had been acquitted caused fierce protests in the streets and 'put the whole town in a flame', according to the aggrieved Thomas Brodrick, who had put so much effort into the exhaustive inquiry, to no good purpose. He spelled out his anxiety for the country's future in a letter to his brother: 'What consequence it may have I cannot imagine; I think it is a very bad piece of policy, for the whole kingdom are enraged against the South Sea scheme, and not less so, against those who support their abettors.' Two weeks earlier the newspaper editor Nathaniel Mist, who had poked fun at the Bubble, had been punished for criticising the King's foreign policy. He had been ordered to stand in the pillory not just once, but twice – at Charing Cross and the Royal Exchange – and had been sent to prison for three months. It seemed a fitting commentary on the way justice was dispensed that Stanhope, a key villain in the South Sea scandal, should escape punishment, while a mere journalist should be so harshly treated at the King's Bench.

Walpole could see, however, that the country was not in the mood to stand for another acquittal so soon after Stanhope's, and that there was going to have to be a political victim if the government was to survive. On 8 March it was the turn of the former Chancellor, John Aislabie, to face the Commons' hearing. Walpole knew it would not cost him anything to let Aislabie face its full wrath, and his tactics were the exact opposite of the ones he had adopted in Stanhope's case. Brodrick noted complacently that Walpole's supporters sat 'as mute as fishes' while the allegations were read out: among them, that Aislabie had made a profit of around £1 million from the South Sea scheme and that, specifically, he had collected £300,000 from Francis Hawes, who had been his Secretary to the Treasury. It was left to Aislabie, without Walpole's support, to make a long speech in his own defence. In it, he showed few signs of remorse, even declaring with a hint of arrogance which irritated MPs that he had burned all the account books Hawes had kept.

In fact there was little direct evidence against Aislabie, though he was of course deeply corrupt, and there were no witnesses who spoke incontrovertibly against him. But this was not a court of law, despite the judicial veneer that had been given to the proceedings. This time the vote was not even close: the Commons decided unanimously that the former Chancellor had accepted thousands of pounds' worth of stock from Robert Knight – which was 'a most notorious, dangerous and infamous corruption'. Aislabie was expelled from the House of Commons and, in time-honoured fashion, sent to the Tower of London, the first victim of the inquiry into the Company's rise and fall. Where before there had been street protests over Stanhope's surprise acquittal, now the bonfires were lit in celebration, just as they had been when Harley had founded the Company on the back of his dubious peace deal with France.

The next defendants to stand before the Commons were Sir George Caswall, and two other partners in the Sword Blade Bank, Elias Turner and Jacob Sawbridge. Again, Walpole calculated that there was no political advantage to be had if he were to fight for their acquittal; and, indeed, by protecting Charles Stanhope he had already, in effect, condemned them as the recipients of the profits of illicit share-dealing, rather than as the mere agents of corruption who had helped line Stanhope's pockets. Caswall had a case to argue, however, which was that he had struck a lawful deal with Robert Knight for the £50,000 worth of stock which had gone to Stanhope but that Knight had continually refused to accept any payment. He was certainly entitled to feel bitter. Caswall indicated, with some accuracy, that MPs were picking off the innocent victims of a scheme which they themselves had supported in order to help the government borrow cheap money. He was 'not conscious of any crime', he stated, 'unless it was the extraordinary zeal and affection he had shown for having assisted the government with vast sums of money at three per cent, when they could get it nowhere else'. But without Walpole's help, the vote against him was overwhelming. Caswall, too, was expelled from the House and sent to the Tower. The estates of all three banking partners were seized to recoup the missing quarter of a million pounds for which Stanhope was no longer held to be responsible.

But the trials so far were just dress-rehearsals for the key battle, over Sunderland's fate. Walpole realised it even if, perhaps, Brodrick had been lulled into a false sense of complacency by his success in securing a sudden rush of convictions. It may have seemed obvious to Brodrick, too, that Walpole would sacrifice his party leader to claim the role himself. Surprisingly, though, the reverse was true. Walpole was determined to protect Sunderland, even though a superficial reading of the political runes suggested that if he succeeded his own route to power would be blocked. Walpole's genius, however, was that he could see beyond the horizon, realising not only that Sunderland's acquittal was vital to the political stability of the Whigs and to the nation, but also that Sunderland would still be politically enfeebled even if he was acquitted and escaped being sent to the Tower. Far better for him to be damaged, but not a martyr, as Walpole himself had become during his incarceration. Walpole would fight for Sunderland.

The Commons, so boisterous earlier on, was now facing the reality that it had to judge not one of its own number, but a peer of the realm and pillar of the establishment, and it made MPs more diffident about the judicial process that they had engineered. Already, the Prince of Wales had intervened on Sunderland's behalf to try to persuade them against a conviction. MPs were under severe political pressure, and to make matters worse the evidence against Sunderland was far from conclusive. The main evidence to support the key charge against him – that he had received the bribe of £50,000 – was a note which he had allegedly written to Knight. If Walpole had not decided to support his leader, this alone might have been enough to secure Sunderland's conviction. But the Commons was in a cautious mood, despite the verve with which it had conducted itself since the Bubble burst. MPs were not prepared to be as cavalier as they had been when consigning Aislabie to the Tower. If they were to convict a peer, then they wanted hard evidence. Archibald Hutcheson, the economist and Hastings MP who had devoted himself to the detailed analysis of financial reconstruction, was among the first to recognise that the key difficulty the Commons faced was the absence of Robert Knight. The public were concerned, he said, to punish the authors of the present distress. But it was 'impracticable, on the other hand, to proceed in this important inquiry so long as the principal agent of the South Sea directors was kept out of the way'. Walpole had been one step ahead of them all along.

Knight's absence also gave Walpole a free hand to attack the evidence that the Committee of Secrecy had provided. Apart from the note, the case against Sunderland stemmed almost exclusively from Blunt's claim that two witnesses had heard Knight talking about the shares Sunderland had received. Walpole set out to undermine the credibility of the witnesses. One of them, under cross-examination, insisted that Blunt had not been present at any time during his conversations with Knight; the other suggested that Blunt had, in fact, been in the room but out of earshot. Three other witnesses backed Blunt's story, however, but a combination of the doubt that Walpole had cast upon the committee's report, the continued absence of Knight himself and the pressure that had been applied to the Commons from above, divided the House almost equally. In the end, it was a tribute to their remaining sense of independence that so many MPs voted against Sunderland, when he was acquitted by a majority of fifty-one. Watching events unfold, Edward Harley, the third Earl of Oxford, wrote to his Aunt Abigail: 'I suppose you have before this heard the majority by which Sunderland got clear, a 172 was a great number against a Prime Minister . . . it is remarkable that the Prince was in the gallery all the while, and that all his people voted against Sunderland.' Despite his apparent victory, Sunderland had been terminally damaged, which was the outcome Walpole had anticipated. A month later, Sunderland resigned from office.

But the country was restless at seeing another politician escape justice. The weighty petitions arriving at the House of Commons were testament to that. From Leicester came a suggestion that the authors of the national calamity had raised themselves above the reach of ordinary justice; from Kent, a complaint that Robert Knight should be returned to face the inquiry; from Nottingham, a demand to sequester the estates of 'some of the actors in this black tragedy'. Walpole knew that another victim was needed to assuage popular opinion, and the great political fixer himself, the elder Craggs, could tell that such a fate had been reserved for him. On 17 March, still mourning his son and due to face his trial in the Commons the next day, the Postmaster-General killed himself by taking a large overdose of opium.

Through his policy of screening the key players in the South Sea drama, Walpole had protected much of the established order. But, at the same time, he had overseen the destruction of just enough of it to clear his way to power. Of the ministers who had thrived either directly or indirectly under the South Sea Company's stewardship, the incorruptible Earl Stanhope and the venal Craggs the younger had died, Craggs the elder had killed himself, and Aislabie had been sent to the Tower. A great swathe had been cut through the government, leaving only Walpole and Townshend standing. No ambitious rival travelling to Hanover to curry favour with his monarch, nor any foreign mistress, could stand in their way. Their hold over the House of Hanover was complete.

Walpole lost no time in spreading his influence, root and branch, through the whole make-up of the government. One of his brothers took Craggs's job at the Post Office; the other, Charles Stanhope's at the Treasury. Walpole himself became First Lord of the Treasury and Chancellor of the Exchequer. The King perhaps harboured doubts about the wisdom of promoting the *arriviste* but, weakened by his own involvement in the Company and by the political decline of his favourites, he could not stand in the way.

Walpole had, as promised, taken his revenge.

CHAPTER XVI

Doubtful and Desperate Debts

How do the wealthy deal with this financial downturn? Switch
from imported to domestic caviar? Opt for a Lexus SC over the
BMW roadster? Board up that third mansion in the south of
France? None of the several representatives of the wealthy we
contacted would say exactly what a billionaire does to make ends
meet – 'That's private,' was the refrain.
But there are a few downmarket indicators. Cellular phone
mogul Craig McCaw, for one, is selling or has sold three jets,
three homes, his yacht, a 5,000-acre ranch in Carmel, and his
$50-million private island near Victoria where he entertained such
Hollywood B-listers as Pamela Anderson and Tom Arnold.
At the least, Craig McCaw's sellathon is helping other rich
guys get through the tough times. He sold his Gulfstream V,
valued at $38 million, to actor Jim Carrey six months ago and
wants to sell a custom, unfinished $54 million Boeing 737 to
anyone who can afford it. McCaw also recently peddled his
year-old 300-foot yacht, the Tatoosh, *to Paul Allen. It includes*
a speedboat, swimming pool, gold-leaf interior decorations, and a
price tag estimated at $100 million.
OK, so it's used. We all have to make concessions.
Seattle Weekly, 6 December 2001

The political events stretching back to the Bubble's birth had nearly
run their course. The Commons now turned its attention away from
trying to convict members of the corrupt administration, and by
drawing a line under the affair it allowed Walpole to make repairs
to the stability of the government and the monarchy. There would
be no more political victims, and no further threat to the King. As
if in celebration, at Leicester House in April 1721 the Princess of
Wales gave birth to her third son, William Augustus, the future Duke
of Cumberland. A happy enough event, it helped to lighten the dark
mood of depression which had settled over the nation, but it also
gave the country a fixed point of certainty that it had lacked in the
last few traumatic months. The birth, in the very place where the
Prince had once established his rival court, seemed to symbolise a
new sense of purpose within the previously divided royal family, and
a gathering sense of unity between the country and the monarchy.

Where there had been some doubt over the King's future, now there was none, and the Commons felt moved enough to express, if in somewhat cloying terms, their 'unspeakable joy' at seeing the Protestant succession more firmly established and secured. The change in mood was clear. When the MP William Shippen, in yet another debate on the South Sea Company, told the story of a 'great lady' who had been given a large quantity of stock, he drew parallels, none too subtly, with a mistress of Henry VIII – and for his pains was firmly slapped down by his colleagues.

But MPs had found a new outlet for their anger. With Walpole's blessing, they moved to seize the vast fortunes that the South Sea directors had amassed. Such wealth was far simpler to establish than the guilt of politicians who had been so successfully screened by Walpole's devious manoeuvrings. The irony, which was lost on the members themselves, was that where earlier they had rushed through the South Sea Act without seriously questioning the suspiciously generous terms that had removed the national debt from the government's hands, they were now wholeheartedly scrupulous in their attention to financial detail. Never again would the national economy be lashed to the deck of such an unseaworthy vessel as the South Sea Company.

For the next few months, MPs were occupied in reviewing the Company accounts, which were placed before them in a further half-dozen detailed reports from the Committee of Secrecy. As they did so, more petitions flooded into Parliament from every corner of the country, appealing to them to take harsh measures against the guilty parties. From the cities of Worcester, New Sarum, Rochester, Exeter and York; from the town of Maidstone; from the boroughs of Amersham, St Albans and Leicester and from the counties of Essex and Buckinghamshire, the petitions came, all of them complaining about the 'unparalleled miseries and misfortunes' visited upon the nation by the corruption and mismanagement of the South Sea directors and their political conspirators. The petitioners were anxious that the House's appetite for justice, or its courage, might flag as the summer wore on. It must, they demanded, continue to pursue justice with exactly the same spirit and zeal it had shown so far. In the end, the pressure from the petitioners, and the Committee of Secrecy's continued revelations, helped to inspire the drafting of a bill which ordered the seizure of the

Doubtful and Desperate Debts

directors' assets, to help pay for the financial damage they had done 'to the unhappy sufferers of the South Sea Company'.

The South Sea Sufferers' Bill proposed a levy on the directors' estates. They were forced to list all their assets and to detail every transaction they had carried out between June 1720 and March 1721. Their accounts show that they had spent their money widely: their financial interests ranged from the ownership of a West End square to country estates, and from businesses in Portugal to plantations in the West Indies. But the bill allowed the directors to list their liabilities, too, and this enabled them to massage downwards the calculation of their worth.

At the end of May, each case was debated in the chamber so that the bill could enshrine the individual penalties to which the directors would be subjected. As with the conviction or acquittal of the politicians at their trial before the Commons, it was a highly subjective exercise; but those who had put their money into traceable assets such as land, rather than laundering it through business enterprises, suffered the heaviest penalties. Sir John Fellowes had spent much of his money on building the splendid Carshalton House in Surrey. He was a man who liked his pleasures. He built a tower to pump spring water to his mansion and to the fountains in the garden which he had landscaped. No expense was spared: the water tower, which rose elegantly from the south-facing orangery, was the centrepiece of a small formal pleasure garden, and included a robing room and a delft-tiled bath-house. Fellowes had assets totalling close on £250,000, but was allowed to keep just £10,000; Charles Joye kept £5,000 out of his £40,000; but Theodore Janssen, a man of hitherto impeccable reputation, was dealt with more leniently than anyone else. Janssen's interests included his estate at Wimbledon valued at £22,000, a £4,000 house in Hanover Square, £2,000 worth of jewels, plate and furniture, and £85 worth of china. He also had more than £100,000 worth of South Sea stock, which he had not offloaded, but his assets had declined by £56,000 since June 1720 as the price of his shares had fallen. He told the House, 'I injured nobody and I am myself one of the greatest sufferers by that unsuccessful undertaking', and he was allowed to keep £50,000 out of his assets of £243,244, though he was still forced to sell Wimbledon Manor to the Duchess of Marlborough.

217

In contrast, the Commons punished the corrupt Hawes severely for allowing his account books to be burned, although they were able to establish that more than £1 million had passed through one account in six months, mainly money he had siphoned off from the Navy. He, too, was forced to list every single asset he owned, and to give an estimate of his outgoings. So thorough was the required inventory of his affairs that it ran to eighty-seven pages – in effect, a vast and sprawling income-tax declaration. From it, his inquisitors learned the details of his land deals – among them, £6,400 for a farm and land in Wiltshire, £4,800 for another farm and coppice in Wiltshire, and £8,140 for one at Inglefield in Berkshire. Among his stated outgoings was a payment of £250 to his brother's wife for housekeeping, £120 to Evans the plumber, £40 to Wagget the farrier, and money for a variety of domestic servants: Ned the postilion, Fuller the coach-maker, John the footman, and Jos the coachman 'for wages, corn and beans'. The highest single payment was £500 to William Prat, the carpenter at his fine residence, Purley Hall, but he even claimed a £2 allowance for 'postage of letters'. In this way, Hawes, who had spent much of the fortune he had made on art and antiques, was able to reduce the calculation of his worth from £165,000 to £40,031. It did not serve him well. He was allowed to keep just £31, and his family was forced to rent out his mansion, near Reading, for many years to come.

But despite his cooperation with their inquiry, the Commons' main target was John Blunt. Blunt was required to list everything he owned, laying bare his life on sheet after sheet of paper for his inquisitors. From the garret to the cellar, every single item had to be recorded, an exercise in acute humiliation for a man who had risen to such heights, and one which stripped away the trappings of his success as if to lay bare the business illusion he had created. Blunt's grand image was reduced to the level of the day-to-day mundanity of his most basic necessities. In his house in Birchin Lane, the public learned, his kitchen contained 'a cleaver, a chopping knife, one iron dripping pan and stand, two candle-sticks, two ladles, a scummer, a fish-kettle, a tea-kettle, two tossing pans, five saucepans, thirty-nine pewter dishes, seven dozen plates, a collander, one stool and some earthen and wooden ware'. In his grand sixteen-room house in Stratford, his possessions ranged from twenty pairs of sheets and fifteen tablecloths in the linen room, to the laundry which contained 'two chests, six chairs, a fire shovel, tongs, poker and fender, four box irons and heaters, a horse for clothes, a pair of steps and a bell'. The paperwork also revealed that Blunt had lent money to poor relations. With unintended irony, these were called 'doubtful and desperate debts'.

In total, Blunt's assets were put at £185,349 and the subsequent debate in the Commons over how much of this sum he should be allowed to keep was a stormy one. One backbench MP argued vehemently that he should be allowed only a shilling, another, £1,000, and a third MP, £5,000. But the frankness of Blunt's evidence before the Committee of Secrecy had won him some friends, among them Jekyll and Molesworth, who wanted to reward their leading witness. They may even have promised him a deal in return for his evidence. Lord Hinchinbroke appeared to give the game away when he argued that Blunt should be allowed to keep £10,000 because the Committee of Secrecy 'had promised him favour for his openness'.

Blunt, however, leaving nothing to chance, made his own application for leniency – an appeal which, by exploiting the difficulties that a severe financial penalty would cause his wife and family, was carefully crafted to play on the emotions of the MPs who sat in judgement upon him. He used his family pitifully, and pitilessly, as a lightning rod for his dishonest conduct, pointing out that he had seven children to support by his first wife, and that his second wife had eleven children and grandchildren to support from her first marriage. He had 'solemnly promised' her before their marriage, he declared, 'that he would make a considerable addition to her fortune, which he always thought himself bound, and did ever intend faithfully to fulfil; and therefore did put several sums into the South Sea stock and subscriptions which he publicly declared and fully intended should be for her use and benefit'. His wife had sunk her children's money into the South Sea Company, he said, and had lost most of it, 'wherefore he most humbly hopes for the compassion of the honourable House of Commons towards himself, his wife, and their numerous family, and that he may have an allowance out of his estate, in some proportion to what his estate is, and suitable to so large a family'.

Walpole was having none of it: for Blunt to escape lightly might risk upsetting the careful balance of the political settlement he had put in place. Blunt, he argued, was 'a projector of many years' standing and had been the author of several fallacious schemes, by which unwary people had been drawn to their utter ruin'. In the end, by 138 votes to 94, Blunt was allowed to keep just £1,000. Eventually, this was raised to £5,000, but the practical impact was the same: Blunt was forced to retire to Bath to contemplate the ashes of his career.

In total, the Commons reclaimed nearly £2 million of the directors' money, and having done so it moved its target, to try to penalise the politicians who had been found guilty at their trial. To the surprise of MPs, Walpole now changed his tactics, to argue that the politicians he had previously sacrificed should be allowed to retain their wealth. He told the House that he hoped 'it would not break its known rules, which were not to condemn anyone without first hearing them, denying this piece of justice to its own members'. He spoke first on Aislabie's behalf, declaring that the former Chancellor needed to keep his money because he had a family to support, and because much of Aislabie's estate had belonged to him before the events of 1720. The Commons should have been able to guess at Walpole's intent. His intervention was not the altruistic gesture that it appeared to be, but rested on the fact that Aislabie's family controlled two parliamentary seats in Yorkshire which might one day prove vital to his cause. The country's new leader was demonstrating again his ability to see beyond the rush of daily events. He had calculated precisely the risk of taking a course of action which went against the political grain, offsetting the initial damage to his own reputation by weighing up the greater longer-term benefits which might eventually accrue. For the same reason, Walpole helped the family of the late Postmaster Craggs. When the Commons tried to seize Craggs's estate, which he had left to his three daughters, Walpole forced a division which he knew he was going to lose. But the family controlled three seats in Cornwall and, by his stand, Walpole managed to preserve enough of their fortune and friendship to gain their support for his cause in the years of power ahead. When Caswall and Sawbridge, too, faced ruin because of the £250,000 which Charles Stanhope had pocketed, Walpole manoeuvred behind the scenes to delay the bill that would strip them of their wealth, and in doing so ensured that Caswall continued to support him in the Commons.

By now, however, Parliament had tired of the affair, and when the South Sea Sufferers' Bill reached the Lords, the peers could not raise the energy to overturn any of the Commons' proposed financial sanctions against directors or politicians. Walpole had protected King and country, preserved the Whig hegemony, and had made himself the indissoluble element that bound all three together. He had punished those whose enmity he did not fear to provoke, and protected those who had no previous cause to admire him but who could only be grateful for his patronage. There remained only the task of finally removing the country's finances from the ebb-tide of the South Seas and placing them in the government's control. It was still a difficult manoeuvre. 'It was known to everybody,' he pronounced, disingenuously, that he 'was ever against the South-Sea scheme, and had done everything to hinder its taking place.' But now the damage had been done it was his duty, he declared, to extricate the nation from its difficulties, though he 'did not pretend to work miracles'. Walpole suggested that a grand committee should be appointed to consider the state of public credit.

The grand committee's task was complicated, not least because of the tangled nature of the Company's relationship with its shareholders and with the government itself, but also because the country was scrutinising its every move. On one day alone, new petitions came in from Pembroke, Tamworth, Leicester, Lichfield, Aylesbury, Oxford, Cambridge and Reading. The reconstruction of the country's finances depended, in the end, on what was politically feasible. One of the main problems was that, because they had bought at widely differing prices, the South Sea shareholders couldn't agree on what was best. Those who had bought early, and therefore cheaply, did not want their holdings devalued by any change in the purchase terms. Because the Company had launched four different money subscriptions, at four different price levels, and had offered widely different terms of credit, there was no single solution which would placate everybody.

Under such pressure, the government decided to forgo the £7.5 million the Company had promised to pay it for the right to take over the national debt, in order to increase the funds available to shareholders. The grand committee also proposed to cut, retrospectively, the price at which shares had been launched in the Company's last three money subscriptions, a measure which reduced shareholder debts by £9 million. Another huge sum, £11 million in total, was still owed by investors who had taken out Company loans to buy their stock. The committee decided to write off this debt, so that investors did not have to pay for any more instalments, provided they paid the Company 10 per cent of the money they owed and gave up any claim to further stock. This measure alone cost the Company £7 million, but the price was probably a small one for Walpole to keep the political peace: of 462 MPs who had held South Sea stock, 138 had borrowed from the Company and so benefited from the generosity of these terms. Nothing like Walpole's rescue plan had ever been attempted before, and he managed to balance the demands of all the different shareholder interest groups with skill. In the end, investors received about £1 for every £2 they had put into the Company, which was better than they could have expected when the Bubble burst, though there were still big losers.

As the summer went on, Walpole drove his legislation through Parliament with a fixity of purpose which exceeded the stamina of his opponents. MPs and peers melted away to enjoy the summer, leaving Walpole firmly in control. Where George I had addressed a crowded chamber little more than a year ago to appeal to MPs to reduce the debts of the nation, now he addressed barely a hundred of their number, and he was asking them, in effect, to make good the damage that had been done in the intervening months. There was no point, he implied, in taking too much time about it; he asked MPs to confine their deliberations 'to what is absolutely necessary on this extraordinary occasion'. In three days flat, Walpole pushed through his plans for financial reconstruction, thwarting any objections to his measures by referring to the will of the absent members. In the end, only fifty or so MPs stayed to see the bill through all its stages. The chamber which had been so assertive of its rights after the collapse of the Company bowed its knee to a force far stronger than its own – Walpole's sheer determination. The Lords, too, were quiescent. As if washing their hands of the affair, they took only one sitting to turn the bill into law.

Walpole had put the final piece of his jigsaw in place, but still he was not satisfied. The monarchy was safe, and so were the Whigs, but the foundations of his rule had to be made as secure as possible. In his view, the Committee of Secrecy's reports, should they be made public, would stand in the way of his all-consuming desire to protect the balance of the political world he had inherited. One night, the presses which were printing the reports were mysteriously sabotaged, and the full extent of the government's culpability in the wreck of the South Seas was to remain half known, half hidden – a topic of rumour and conjecture laced with some established facts, a mixture vague enough for the established order to reassert its authority without any further challenge to its powers.

In these long and tiring summer months, few objections were raised to Walpole's tactics, but one day discontented shareholders, who had been gathering on the streets outside Parliament, crowded into the lobbies to hand out complaining leaflets to MPs. The terms of the financial settlement were unnecessarily harsh, they insisted, and were designed to penalise the poorer investors by protecting vested interests. Before long, they were threatened with prison under the terms of the Riot Act, and expelled by the half-dozen constables on duty. As they left, one protester cried out, 'First you pick our pockets and then send us to jail for complaining.'

MPs, too, though they did not know it, had had their pockets picked successfully by Walpole. What he had stolen from them was the truth.

Within a year, Walpole's ascendancy was assured. In April 1722, Sunderland died unexpectedly, removing the one senior politician who could still threaten his power and influence. Walpole was one of the first to visit the late minister's house. The door to Sunderland's study had already been sealed, to protect his private papers. But Walpole broke the seals, and spent several hours reading Sunderland's documents, some of which he removed. He would always make sure that the slightest trace of his secret dealings was removed from the private papers of any senior government politician: today only the official version can be found among his colleagues' documents. It left only the threat of disclosure by the Austrian Netherlands, and as Walpole quickly realised, the Emperor could not afford to undermine the Hanoverian monarchy for fear of something worse. He was right to be so confident. In the end, the incontrovertible evidence of

Walpole's manoeuvrings was locked away in the Austrian archives until the twentieth century. For the same reason, Walpole forced Robert Knight to stay abroad throughout the next two decades. It made him feel more secure. Knight and his son based themselves in Paris, where they ran a private bank, and where the father harboured hopes of returning to England. But Walpole refused to end Knight's exile. He knew too much to be allowed back to England in his political lifetime. Not until Walpole fell was Knight allowed to return, at which point he was able to buy a royal pardon for £10,000.

After Sunderland's death, Walpole set about destroying his rivals, promoting men who would be loyal to him in the government, the Army, the Church and the law. Relations and friends came to populate every reach of government, as he took an ever-tighter grip on power.

George I, he knew, was in his debt politically. Later, he made sure George II, too, was in his debt financially, by introducing such a generous Civil List settlement that the new King could not but remark upon its size and the fact that their destinies were hitherto inextricably linked. It seemed as if the House of Hanover, and Robert Walpole's political suzerainty, would stand or fall together. In 1726 he was knighted, and the Order of the Bath was revived in his honour.

The Bubble made rich men of some, and fools of many. But the ruling classes, though deeply corrupt, survived to tell the tale, and England was left remarkably unscathed, if more cautious, from its encounter with the stock market. Under Walpole, the country entered into an unprecedented period of parliamentary stability. There was no centre of influence that eluded his grasp. With the Tories routed and the court quiescent, Walpole controlled both the Lords and the Commons and established Whig supremacy for a century. On the foundations of a disaster of their own making, the natural party of government was ever more firmly entrenched in power, establishing the political stability which had eluded the country since the Glorious Revolution of 1688. But it was also a time of introspection. Unlike Earl Stanhope, who had negotiated a quadruple alliance against Spain and a Baltic coalition against Russian expansion, Walpole had no time for foreign affairs, which first through war and then through economic rivalry had helped create the conditions for the Bubble. He never set foot outside the country.

Under his hegemony, in contrast to the vibrancy of the year of the Bubble, political and financial life became insipid and dull. Parliament, so determined in its search for the South Sea culprits, was once more subdued, and the stock market sank back into the shadows, corralled by new legislation against bubbles and the activities of stockjobbers. The country was no longer seduced by the lure of change, by the excitement of new inventions, or by the possibility of quick money. It took a long time to forgive the speculators and businessmen.

Walpole ruled for twenty-one years, an unparalleled period of political power, but as the years went by his reputation was undermined by those who, though they had no proof, guessed at his serpentine manoeuvrings, which were even more cynical than they imagined. As an outlet for their impotence and jealousy, to cut him down to size, his enemies gave him a nickname. He became known as the 'the Skreen-Master'.

Of the other players in the drama, John Blunt did not give up his attempts to rejoin the establishment. But it had cast him out for good, and he lived the remaining years of his life in obscurity in Bath, surfacing from time to time to demonstrate his love for the trappings of aristocracy. In his twilight years, he had a disagreement with the Court of Chivalry over his unapproved use of the crest of the ancient family of Blunt of Sodington, which consisted of 'a wreath, on it a sun rising in glory, therein an eye goutte de larmes'. He died in Bath in January 1733.

Surprisingly, the South Sea Company outlived him, a shadow of its former self but more respectable than the corrupt enterprise he had run. It established a new business, whale-fishing off Greenland, but the whales were less keen to take the bait than the British public had been, and once again the Company failed to make money. It lingered on in attenuated fashion until Gladstone, as Chancellor of the Exchequer, put it out of its misery more than a century later.

Gladstone's onetime predecessor in that office, John Aislabie, spent the remaining twenty years of his life cultivating his garden. He did so on a grand scale, creating a vast water garden on a geometric pattern at his home at Studley in Yorkshire. He also commissioned a local stonemason to carve a pair of sphinxes with human faces, though they were not portrayed in marble as the elements demanded, but in Yorkshire sandstone, so that time has eroded the features of the matronly lady and the proud young girl. Appropriately, Aislabie used a waterborne metaphor to try to wash away his own role in the events of 1720: 'Let those gentlemen who opened the floodgates wonder at the deluge that ensued as much as they please: it was not in one man's power, or in the power of the whole administration to stop it, considering how the world was borne away by the torrent.' Like the Bubble, the Studley Royal Water Garden was inspired by a French design. Unlike the Bubble, it has lasted for centuries. It is owned by the National Trust, a permanent memorial to the honest labours of a corrupt politician who found more lasting solace in earth and water than in the chimera he had helped to create.

Of the investors in the Bubble, bookseller Thomas Guy died in 1724 at the age of eighty-one. His body lay in state at Mercer's Chapel, and a statue was erected in his honour. In his will, he left £240,000 to found the London hospital which still bears his name. The Bubble's legacy had a silver lining. In contrast, young James Windham of the Salt Office, who had been so keen to make his fortune, found himself ruined, and went away to sea with the Navy. In 1721 he was given command of the *Solebay*, cruising first to Sweden and then to Scotland, where he was ordered to patrol the east and north-east coasts to prevent smuggling. Two years later, he was given command of a larger ship, the *Diamond*, and sailed to the West Indies to tackle the pirates there. He proved a remarkable success, saving eight merchant ships from capture and wresting the *Bristol* back from the pirates' control. He lost his life in a battle at the Bay of Honduras in 1725, and was buried at sea. He was not quite thirty-eight years old.

John Law, unlike Knight, was finally allowed to return home by Walpole, and was granted a pardon for the murder of Edward Wilson over a quarter of a century earlier. Unlike the corrupt directors of the South Sea Company, who had been granted an allowance by the Commons, he had no money to his name. The man who had published the most brilliant economic treatise of the day was forced to write begging letters to his friend, Henrietta Hobart, the Countess of Suffolk. In one, he entreats her:

Can you not prevail on the Duke to help me . . . or is there nobody that would have good nature enough to lend me 1000 pounds? I beg that if nothing of this can be done that it may only be betwixt us two as I take you as my real friend.

Excuse this my dear madam and only put your self in my place and know that at the same time you are the only friend I have.

Eventually Law returned abroad once more, to resume the wanderings of his earlier life. He died in Venice, aged fifty-eight, and did not live to see historians recognise in him not a corrupt adventurer, but an honest economist whose theories were far ahead of the time. He had created a 'beautiful edifice', mused the contemporary commentator Du Tot; 'Its beauty even surpassed all the hopes that had been placed in it since it caused people to scorn gold and silver; it is a type of miracle that posterity will not believe.' In October 1722, the commissioners who had examined the transactions of the Mississippi Company burned all its paperwork in a cage, as if to symbolise the end of Law's dream. Not until 1793 did France again use paper money, and even then it could only be imposed by the threat of the guillotine.

As for Law's vision of a trading empire, in time Louisiana, and its capital New Orleans, came to prosper, though not under the French flag. First it was conquered by the British and the Spanish, then part of the territory was reclaimed by Napoleon. In 1803, he sold the land to the United States for $15 million.

Even in death, Law was restless. The church in which he was interred was destroyed in the Napoleonic wars, but by chance the Governor of Venice was Law's grand-nephew Alexander Law, the Comte de Lauriston, and he supervised a new burial for his forebear in the church of San Moisè, near St Mark's Square and the Grand Canal. Near the west door of the church, on the stone floor, is an inscription in Latin which tells visitors that beneath their feet lies a 'most distinguished Controller-General of finances in France'.

It is an appropriate location. Nearby are the gambling rooms, the old Ridotto, where Law first made his fortune.

CHAPTER XVII

The Architecture of Eternity

The Architecture of Eternity

When the Dow Jones industrial average first surpassed 10,000 in March 1999, Merrill Lynch took out a full-page newspaper advertisement with a headline saying 'Even those with a disciplined long-term approach like ours have to sit back and say "Wow."' In the bottom left-hand corner of the page appeared the words 'HUMAN ACHIEVEMENT.'

Robert J Shiller: *Irrational Exuberance*

For thirty years, until St Paul's Cathedral was completed in 1710, Christopher Wren drove his workers hard. At the King's Quarry in Dorset, hundreds of labourers with picks and shovels had to dig deep to remove the earth covering the best stone, the whitbed, which ran through the quarry more than a dozen feet below the surface. It was noisy, hot, gruelling work. Hour after hour they toiled, loading the spoil on to wooden carts pulled by mules. The air was thick with stone dust, a cloud which settled on to the workmen's hair and clothes. But the whitbed would last longer than ordinary stone, and it was a glistening white, of a purity to match the higher purpose for which it was intended.

From time to time, work would halt and the air would ring with explosions as the quarrymen blasted their way through to this perfect rock. But even then their task had barely started. First, straining muscle and sinew, they had to lever out single pieces of a size to match Wren's design, and then cut them into blocks, driving in steel wedges before splitting them with blow after blow of the hammer. When they had been extracted, the blocks were trimmed with pick-axes, and marked up so that the exact purpose of each could easily be established at the end of the sea journey to London. Then it could take a whole fortnight to move one of the heavier blocks from the Thames-side wharf, dragged by horses along the city streets, to the cathedral worksite.

Wren would not compromise in his search for perfection. As he laid the foundations at the west end of the cathedral, he was just a half-dozen feet from completing his task when he unearthed a pit full of broken pottery. This would not support the weight of the new building. Wren's workmen wanted a quick solution – to sink wooden piles into the ground. But he refused, convinced that they would rot. He was sure that there was solid ground under the low-water mark of the Thames. So he dug deep, shoring up the sand with timber, until he came upon water and sea-shells, forty feet down; and below this, clay. Only then did he allow his masterpiece to rise.

Three decades later, to make the huge cathedral dome more solid and to prevent it from collapsing under its own weight, Wren resorted to an architectural subterfuge which was so clever that, in the unlikely prospect that the men of business might lift their eyes from their money-making activities in the City below, they would have been quite taken in – they might even have said 'bubbled' – by the sheer brilliance of the illusion thus created. Wren gave his dome two layers, which had the added advantage that it would appear smaller, and more in proportion, from inside. A funnel of bricks and iron chains, hidden from view by the inner layer, supported the huge weight of the main dome. The dome itself was made of eighteen-inch brickwork – it was two bricks thick – with an extra layer of bricks every five feet, to bind it together. 'The rendering,' Wren would boast, 'is as hard as stone.'

On the floor of St Paul's Cathedral, under the dome, is carved the salutary inscription: *si monumentum requiris, circumspice* ('If you seek his monument, look about you'). Preoccupied with the architecture of eternity, Wren had no doubt his building would survive. His son, a year old when the project started, laid the last stone of the lantern above the dome, with his father and the stonemasons watching. 'All London poured forth for the spectacle,' wrote a cathedral historian, 'and looked up in wonder to the old man who was on that wondrous height setting the seal to his august labours.'

Of the Bubble, not a trace remains. An insubstantial structure, created for the moment, its foundations lay in nothing more enduring than shallow human nature. As Swift concluded:

> While some build castles in the air,
> Directors build them in the seas;
> Subscribers plainly see them there,
> For fools will see as wise men please.

When it burst, the Bubble left its imprint on a chastened population, but as the years went by even the memory of it faded, so that fresh generations, across the centuries, were quickly parted from their money by the next investment boom. Appropriately, even South Sea House has vanished from the landscape, consumed by fire two hundred years ago.

Perhaps there is a reason for this strange amnesia, this curious refusal to remember. Capitalism, and the cause of progress, can ill afford too stark a reminder of the depth of human folly in the pursuit of riches, lest our willingness to gamble on the future also disappear into thin air. And so the story of the Bubble was turned into a footnote and quietly filed away, reduced to an eighteenth-century eccentricity, an oddity, a curiosity recalled more and more vaguely, until finally it was worn down and polished smooth to a hollow phrase, an empty metaphor – a comfortable cliché for our times.

Postscript

I have generally avoided using 'Britain' rather than 'England', even when describing events after the Act of Union in 1707. Despite the influence of the brilliant Scot working his alchemy in Paris, the Bubble was an English phenomenon which was inflated by the corruption of the English political system (though there were, as I have pointed out, Scottish investors in South Sea stock, and also Irish ones). But the drama was played out in England, for which Scotland, scarred by the Darien venture, could at least be grateful.

Christopher Wren, it appears, regularly inspected his dome from high up in a basket. The Duchess of Marlborough complained bitterly about the cost of employing Vanbrugh, who was demanding £300 a year to build Blenheim, 'when it is well-known that Sir Christopher Wren was content to be dragged up in a basket three or four times a week to the top of St Paul's, and at great hazard, for £200 a year'. Perhaps Wren also measured the cost of building his cathedral, as I have done, against the instant fortunes which were soon to be won, and lost, in the stock market down below.

There was one further irony which may have given Wren cause for reflection. In 1710 Her Majesty's commissioners, appointed by a penny-pinching Parliament, expressed their disbelief at the cost of building the new cathedral, accusing Wren of corruption. Accordingly, half his salary was suspended to encourage him to finish the building more quickly, and he was forced, ignominiously, to petition for full payment. Within a decade, the corruption of the body politic itself would contrast sharply with the pettiness of the commissioners' stance:

Report on Frauds and Abuses at St Paul's

If the Church be not finish'd, 'tis the fault of the Persons belonging to it; that it might have been finish'd by this time, but is delay'd on purpose to spend time and waste Mony . . .

Every one that comes to the Church, or passes by it, can't but take notice that he sees no men at work: The iron-fence has been a long time in the same unfinish'd State; the Church-yard is the same heap of Rubbish it was a year ago . . .

These are some of the things that everybody wants to be done; and yet, except the Queen's Statue, everything else is at a stand. And this, I confess, I think not only a neglect, but a very inexcusable one; but whose neglect is it? Or at whose door does this Fault lie?

The Fault, in short, is in Sir *Christopher Wren.*

Such base Endeavours would make a Man's Hair stand on end, who has any Sense of Religion or Humanity.

Bibliography

General

Baynes, John: *The Jacobite Rising of 1715*, Cassell, 1970

Beattie, J. M.: *The English Court in the Reign of George I*, Cambridge University Press, 1967

Bennett, J. A.: *The Mathematical Science of Christopher Wren*, Cambridge University Press, 1982

Jean-Bernard Bossu's Travels in the Interior of North America 1751–1762, University of Oklahoma Press, 1962

Boyer, Abel: *Political State of Great Britain*, 1711

— *History of Queen Anne*, 1735

Cameron, H. C.: *Mr Guy's Hospital*, Longman, 1954

Carswell, J.: *The South Sea Bubble*, Alan Sutton, 1993

Chambers, James: *Christopher Wren*, Alan Sutton, 1998

Champigny, Chevalier de: *Memoir of the Present State of Louisiana*, New York, 1853

Chancellor, Edward: *Devil Take the Hindmost*, Pan, 1999

Clark, J. G.: *New Orleans, 1718–1812: An Economic History*, Louisiana State University Press, 1970

Collier, W. F.: *Pictures of the Period*, 1865

Cowie, L. W. *Plague and Fire*, Wayland, 1988

Cowles, Virginia: *The Great Swindle*, Collins, 1960

Coxe, Revd, William: *Memoirs of Sir Robert Walpole*, Cadell & Davies, 1800

Cunningham, P.: *Hand-Book of London*, John Murray, 1850

Defoe, Daniel: *Anatomy of Exchange Alley*, 1719

Dickinson, H. T.: *Walpole and the Whig Supremacy*, London, 1973

Dickson, P. G. M.: *The Financial Revolution in England*, Macmillan, 1967

Downes, Kerry: *Christopher Wren*, Allen Lane, 1971

— *St Paul's and Its Architecture*, Redhedge, 1998

Dufour, Charles L.: *The Flags in the Wind*, Harper & Row, 1967

Erleigh, Viscount: *South Sea Bubble*, Peter Downes, 1933

Ewen, C. L.'Estrange: *Lotteries and Sweepstakes*, Heath Cranton, 1932

Fairchild, Thomas: *The City Gardener*, 1722

Farge, Arlette: *Fragile Lives – Violence, Power and Solidarity in Eighteenth-century France*, Harvard University Press, 1993

Francis, John: *Chronicles of the Stock Exchange*, London, 1849

French, B. F.: *Historical Collections of Louisiana*, 1851

Grew, M. E.: *William Bentinck and William III*, John Murray, 1924

Heade, R. H.: *In the Sunshine of Life*, Dorrance & Co., 1874

Hill, Brian W.: *Robert Harley*, Yale University Press, 1988

Holmes, G.: *The Trial of Doctor Sacheverell*, Eyre Methuen, 1972

— *Politics, Religion and Society in England*, Hambledon Press, 1986

Hyde, H. M.: *John Law*, WH Allen, 1969

Ketton-Cremer, R. W.: *Norfolk Portraits*, Faber & Faber, 1944

Lang, Jane: *Rebuilding St Paul's*, Oxford University Press, 1956

Law, John: *Money and Trade Considered*, 1705

Bibliography

— The Present State of the French Revenues, London, 1720
Letters from Liselotte, ed. Maria Kroll Gollancz, 1970
Lillywhite, Bryant: London Coffee Houses, George Allen & Unwin, 1963
Mackay, Charles: Extraordinary Popular Delusions and the Madness of Crowds, Harrap, 1841
McInnes, Angus: Robert Harley, Speaker, Secretary of State and Premier Minister, Gollancz, 1970
Mead, R.: A Discourse on the Plague, 1721
Melville, Lewis: The South Sea Bubble, Daniel O'Connor, 1921
Miller, John: An Interesting Historical Account of the South Sea Scheme, London, 1845
Minton, R.: John Law: The Father of Paper Money, Association Press, 1975
Moore, J. R.: Daniel Defoe, Citizen of the Modern World, University of Chicago Press, 1958
Murphy, A. E.: John Law: Economic Theorist and Policy-maker, Clarendon Press, 1997
Nicholson, Colin: Writing and the Rise of Finance, Cambridge University Press, 1994
Old English Coffee Houses, Rodale Press, 1954
O'Neill, C. E.: Church and State in French Colonial Louisiana, Yale University Press, 1966
Oudard, George: John Law – A Fantastic Financier, Cape, 1928
Petrie, Charles: The Jacobite Movement, Eyre & Spottiswoode, 1959
Phillimore, Lucy: Sir Christopher Wren, Kegan Paul, 1851
Phillips, Maberly: The South Sea Bubble, 1912
Plumb, J. H.: Sir Robert Walpole, Allen Lane, 1956
— The Growth of Political Stability in England 1675–1725, Macmillan, 1967
— The First Four Georges, Fontana, 1972
Prebble, John: Darien, the Scottish Dream of Empire, Birlinn, 2000
Robinson, E. F.: Early History of Coffee Houses in England, Kegan Paul, 1893
Scott, W. R.: Joint Stock Companies to 1720, Cambridge University Press, 1911
Sedgwick, Romney, ed.: The House of Commons 1715–1754, History of Parliament Trust, 1970
Seymour, Robert: Survey of the Cities of London and Westminster, 1735
Shiller, Robert J.: Irrational Exuberance, Princeton University Press, 2001
The South Sea Bubble and the Numerous Fraudulent Projects to which It Gave Rise, 1825
Sprat, Thomas: History of the Royal Society, 1702
Steer, F. W.: History of the Worshipful Company of Scriveners, Phillimore, 1973
Swift, Jonathan: Journal to Stella, 1711
Taylor, Stephen, and Clyve Jones, eds: Edward Harley's Parliamentary Papers, Boydell Press, 1998
Timbs, John: Clubs and Club Life in London, 1872
Whinney, Margaret: Wren, Thames & Hudson, 1997
Wood, J. P.: Memoirs of the Life of John Law of Lauriston, Edinburgh, 1824
Wren, Christopher: Parentalia, 1750

Contemporary pamphlets, poems and reports:
Amhurst, N.: An Epistle to Sir John Blunt, London, 1720
Bradley, Richard: The Plague at Marseilles Consider'd, 1721
— The Virtue and Use of Coffee with regard to the Plague, 1721
Browne, Joseph: A Practical Treatise on the Plague, 1720
A Continuation of Frauds and Abuses at St Paul's, 1713
A Full and Impartial Account of the Company of Mississippi, 1720
A Journey through England, 1714
A Letter from a Gentleman in the Country to a Member of Parliament, in England, 1721
An Exact List of All the Bubbles, 1721
An Historical Account of the Plague at Marseilles, by a Physician, 1721
Articles of Impeachment, 1739
A Sermon Preach'd at the Chapel at Deal in Kent, 1720
A true state of the South-Sea-Scheme as it was first form'd, 1719
As Bob is to Robin, 1712
Census tables for the French colony of Louisiana, 1699–1723, compiled by Charles Madnell
Forms of Prayer, 1708–60

Four Letters to a Friend, 1710
Facts against Scandal, 1713
Frauds and Abuses at St Paul's, 1712
Inventories of the South Sea Directors, 1720
Loimologia sacra, a discourse showing that the Plague is sent immediately from God, 1721
The Battle of the Bubbles, By a Stander-By, 1720
The Bed-Tester Plot: A Ballad, 1718
The Bubble: A Poem, 1721
The Delights of the Bottle: Or the Compleat Vintner, 1720
The Westminster Bubble, By a Water Poet, 1722
Letter to Mr Law upon His Arrival in Great Britain, 1721

Acknowledgements

No one who writes the story of the year 1720 can fail to acknowledge the work carried out by its previous historians, and in particular John Carswell's meticulous account, *The South Sea Bubble*. The later edition of his book drew attention to the first documentary evidence for Walpole's 'screen', the letter from William Leathes which I have quoted on page 208–9. Viscount Erleigh's 1933 version of the story is scornfully amusing, while Virginia Cowles's *The Great Swindle* (1960) strikes a balance between story-telling and historical research. Several of the contemporary quotations I have used come from these books, for which I am grateful. After much reflection, I decided not to add notes, because this is not a work of scholarship. But I am in the debt of many authors.

I'm also in the debt of Peter Robinson at Curtis Brown, who saw the merit of the idea immediately, and Clive Priddle, again my editor at 4th Estate, for his keen eye and sharp observations. I'm grateful to the British Library and its staff. Karen Meager read the first draft, and put up with me while I was writing it. She is, as ever, central to the story.

Index

Page numbers in italic refer to the modern parallels in the chapter headings